# Embracing Exile

# Embracing Exile

*The Case for Jewish Diaspora*

DAVID KRAEMER

Oxford University Press is a department of the University of Oxford.
It furthers the University's objective of excellence in research, scholarship,
and education by publishing worldwide. Oxford is a registered trade mark of
Oxford University Press in the UK and in certain other countries.

Published in the United States of America by Oxford University Press
198 Madison Avenue, New York, NY 10016, United States of America.

© Oxford University Press 2025

All rights reserved. No part of this publication may be reproduced, stored in a retrieval system, transmitted, used for text and data mining, or used for training artificial intelligence, in any form or by any means, without the prior permission in writing of Oxford University Press, or as expressly permitted by law, by license or under terms agreed with the appropriate reprographics rights organization. Inquiries concerning reproduction outside the scope of the above should be sent to the Rights Department, Oxford University Press, at the address above.

You must not circulate this work in any other form
and you must impose this same condition on any acquirer

CIP data is on file at the Library of Congress.

ISBN 9780197623541

DOI: 10.1093/oso/9780197623541.001.0001

Printed by Sheridan Books, Inc., United States of America

# Contents

| | |
|---|---|
| *Preface* | vii |
| 1. The Lay of the Land | 1 |
| 2. Biblical Explanations of Exile | 20 |
| 3. Biblical Narratives of Diaspora | 31 |
| 4. Zion in Babylon | 62 |
| 5. Medieval Jewish Teachings on Exile | 87 |
| 6. Exile, the Jewish Mystical Tradition, and the Sephardi Diaspora | 109 |
| 7. The Great Theorizer of Diaspora: The Maharal of Prague | 127 |
| 8. Hasidism and the Eastern European Diaspora | 135 |
| 9. Haskalah, Reform, and Early Zionism | 146 |
| 10. Modern Jews on Diaspora | 162 |
| 11. Exiles and Their Diasporas: The Lessons of the Jews | 205 |
| *Notes* | 215 |
| *Bibliography* | 225 |
| *Index* | 229 |

# Preface

My interest in Jewish teachings and traditions concerning the Land of Israel and the people Israel's relation to it began when I was a junior in college in the mid-1970s. My experience while attending Hebrew University that year could not have been more thrilling. Unlike many of my fellow students, who lived in university housing for overseas students, I chose to live, with two new friends, in the midst of Israeli society, and we were lucky to find for rent a newly built apartment in the Jewish Quarter of the Old City of Jerusalem. There, we found ourselves in a living history—not only a new one, which included the rebuilding of the Jewish Quarter itself, but an ancient one, surrounded as we were by historical sites and important new excavations.

As we hung up our wet laundry to dry on the roof that year, we overlooked the mosque known as the Dome of the Rock, along with Al-Aqsa, both on the platform we called the "Temple Mount," the location of the ancient Jewish Temples. And I will never forget the day I heard excited yelling coming from the narrow street beneath my window, which I discovered was in reaction to the uncovering of a famous Byzantine road, the Cardo. Yes, that's right: I saw the Cardo the very day it was rediscovered. How could such experiences not leave their imprint on me forever? How could I not be drawn to the land where the historical roots of my people were to be found?

Later that year, I had a formative and, in some ways, contrary experience during the Jewish holiday of Shavuot, which commemorates the giving of the Torah at Sinai. It is a custom on Shavuot to stay up all night studying Torah = traditional Jewish texts (this ritual is called a "*tikkun*"). It is also a custom on this holiday to read the biblical book of Ruth. So I found myself late at night in the living room of a private apartment in Jerusalem with a group of American Jews who had recently "made Aliyah" (immigrated; literally "gone up") to Israel, discussing the story told in Ruth. Early in the book, Naomi, on account of a famine in the Land, leaves Bethlehem for Moab, accompanied by her husband and two sons. In the space of just a few verses, all three of the men die.

viii  PREFACE

What was the reason for their death? An early rabbinic commentary, shared by one of the circle of students at the tikkun, suggests that they died because they had left the Land of Israel. You can only imagine the enthusiasm of the assembled recent immigrants, inspired by their experience of Israel's post-1967 "miracles," for this particular explanation. If living outside the Land is sinful, then their choice to move to Israel was, from the perspective of traditional Judaism, a laudable one. But while they were nearly gleeful, I experienced a distinct sense of discomfort. I was, like most of them, a child of the American Jewish diaspora. But unlike them, I had not decided to make Aliyah, and I was soon to return to my home in the diaspora. Did the tradition I was then learning to love think such a move would be wrong? Did it think I deserved to die for going "outside the Land?" I knew from personal experience the potential of Jewish life in diaspora, and though I, like many young Jews of that time, felt the pull of Jewish life in Israel, I certainly did not feel myself a stranger or foreigner in New York (in whose suburbs I had grown up), Boston (where I attended college), southern Florida (where my family lived at the time), or elsewhere. On balance, I felt that America was more my home than Israel. Were my feelings condemnable in the eyes of Jewish tradition?

When I returned to the United States for my final year in college, I first devoted myself to exploring the Land-centered part of the tradition that excited me. That year I researched and wrote, under the guidance of distinguished professor, Marvin Fox, a senior honors thesis on "The Commandment to Settle the Land of Israel in Rabbinic Literature." In this work, extending for some 130 pages, I explored the entire canon of classical rabbinic teachings pertaining to the Land and the Jewish obligation to settle there. At the time, I heard the voice of these sources calling me, as a result of which I heard only them, failing to appreciate how they functioned in context, a context that, I would later learn, sometimes preserved contrary voices. I also failed to appreciate that a canon the examination of which could be contained in a mere 130 pages (even if those pages were written by an undergraduate and could certainly have been supplemented with other examples) was hardly massive.

Soon after this, first as a graduate student and then a professor of Jewish history and tradition, I began studying the Judaism of the diaspora, commencing with the Babylonian Talmud and then turning to communities where that Talmud held sway. In the course of my studies, I learned that Jewish history in the diaspora was not one long story of persecutions and woes. In fact, Jews in diasporas have often lived comfortably, and even flourished—creating, adapting, and simply living, often in conditions that were little different than those of their neighbors. I also grew increasingly aware of the fact that the longing to return to Zion was not the only motivating ideology of Jewish life and dreams.

Over the years, I learned more and more of the Jewish teachings and traditions that affirmed and even celebrated Jewish life in diaspora. Some of these I learned from the writings of others with interests similar to mine, but most I had to pursue, to seek out, or simply to encounter serendipitously. No work, I discovered, had been devoted to collecting them systematically. As I taught these traditions to excited students at various levels, I realized that if the job of documenting this "alternative" tradition had not yet been done (it was "alternative" only because it had been neglected, not because it stood for a counter-tradition in Judaism), I had to do it. My students encouraged me, insisting that I had an obligation to help make this part of Jewish tradition better known. The product of my long exploration of this neglected Jewish voice is this book.

There are many people to whom I owe gratitude for the book you are holding. First are the many scholars who have explored one aspect or another of the tradition I gather and document here. Without their work examining attitudes and practices of diaspora Jews regarding diaspora through the centuries, I could barely have begun my work. You will find the names of those scholars in the endnotes. Second, I am deeply grateful to my many students with whom I have engaged in dialogue concerning these diaspora teachings. Their challenges and insights have improved my understanding immeasurably, and even if I can't identify them individually, their collective wisdom informs much of what I write in following chapters. Third, I am grateful to supportive colleagues, including Ismar Schorsch, Alan Cooper, and Eitan Fishbane, who directed me to sources with which I was not familiar. Finally, multiple readers for Oxford University Press offered astute critiques and wise recommendations concerning earlier versions of this book, from the initial proposal to earlier drafts of my complete "manuscript" (when are we going to find a more correct term for what we now produce?). What you will read is also greatly improved because of their demands for high quality. I must add that what I say about the anonymous readers is doubly the case with respect to Oxford editor, Nancy Toff. Her support and guidance through this process have been invaluable.

# 1

# The Lay of the Land

There is what might be described as a "canonical" history of the Jewish diaspora, according to which Jews in exile have experienced an unending sequence of sufferings as strangers in foreign lands. This history extends as far back as the first Judean exile at the hands of Babylonian forces, with the biblical account (in the book of Esther) of Haman's threat to annihilate Jewish exiles in the Persian realm understood to represent the danger to Jewish lives in all exiles. But the bulk of the canonical narrative focuses on events and experiences that followed the destruction of the second Temple by the Romans in 70 CE. From that time onward, according to the much-repeated story, Jews wandered from one diaspora to another, suffering in each. Diaspora Jews suffered and died at the hands of the Crusaders, then suffered and fled before the Spanish inquisitors. Diaspora Jewish life followed a path that led through ghettos and pogroms, and ultimately to the Holocaust.

Although there is undoubtedly truth to this narrative of suffering, it is partial and incomplete. Equally as true is a narrative of Jewish diasporas that emphasizes the peaceful and productive qualities of Jewish diaspora experience, and the ways those qualities have enhanced Jewish life, religion, and culture. This alternative is a narrative of Jews mixing with host faiths, cultures, and traditions, adopting both the languages of their neighbors, in the literal sense, and the "languages" of their neighbors, in the broader, cultural sense. It is the story of Jews absorbing and adapting elements of the diaspora cultures in which they made their homes, enriching the Jewish culture they had inherited and permitting them to reinvent themselves, often unconsciously, thus providing new energy and strength for diaspora communities to come. This story recognizes that medieval Jewish culture in Islam would not have been the same without Arabic poetry and philosophy, that early modern Jewish culture in Christendom would have been poorer without the inspiration of Christian artists and artisans. This version of diaspora history has been increasingly excavated and heralded by historians in recent decades, and while there is room for debate over the balance of the favorable and unfavorable in any given setting, the emergent recognition that diaspora Jewish life was often rich and rewarding cannot reasonably be denied.

Undeniable, too, is the recognition that the bulk of Jewish history *is* a diaspora history. Most historians of the ancient Jewish world agree that already in the period following the Babylonian exile and even the return, most Jews lived and would continue to live outside the Land of Israel. Subsequent to the wars with Rome in the first and second centuries, though a vibrant Jewish center continued to exist in the Galilee, an increasing proportion of Jews found their homes in the diaspora. From the beginning of the Muslim period onward, somewhere upward of 90 percent of the world's Jews lived in Muslim lands outside of Palestine, until migration patterns (along with conquests and expulsions) brought more and more Jews to Christian Europe, from south to north and from west to east.

What did Jews make of their diaspora experiences? It is essential to ask this question for several reasons. First, though one might assume that the answer to this question is obvious—after all, from the Hebrew Bible onward, Jews have often explained exile as punishment for sin—the reality is more complex. The exile-as-punishment explanation is but one of many and not necessarily the most prominent one in any given period or setting. Second, if the reality of diaspora experience was more balanced than both myth and older historiography would have it—if diaspora Jews lived peacefully and even flourished as much as they suffered—then that experience could not have been configured solely as punishment.[1] All along, there must have been more positive interpretations of Jewish life in diaspora by the side of the exile-as-punishment trope. Why "must have been?" Because humans are creatures who justify their existence, both consciously and unconsciously. The stories we tell are not neutral, nor are our laws, nor are our commentaries. We tell and repeat stories to make an argument, to justify a condition, to persuade those who are listening to us of something. The stories we tell are the ground for the laws we write and enact, which will in turn reinforce the assumptions that lay beneath our stories. And the commentaries we write, the interpretations we offer, will re-cast and re-direct the traditions we inherit, assuring that the orthodoxies of the past now speak to the experiences of the present. If humans justify their existence, then diaspora Jews must have justified their lives in diaspora.

In what we might call the traditional Jewish story, Jews were invited to think of their exiles through the ages as punishments for their sins, and they were promised that if they returned to God (*teshuva*) they would be returned to the Promised Land. This story gave them reason to persevere in times of hardship, living with the hope that they would one day leave their hardship behind. But this story did not help Jews make sense of their frequent experience of comfort in their diaspora homes—and they were their homes. Diaspora Jews living in relative peace, for whom the vision of exile-as-punishment could hardly have explained the totality of their experience, must also have justified their diaspora existence. Yet we rarely hear of such justifications, and many will be dubious that they even exist. But if we are right about human habits of justification, they must exist. It is the recovery of these justifications to which this book is devoted.[2]

Even while ritually expressing, in their daily prayers and other rituals, the hope for their final deliverance, Jews through the generations also developed what we might call ideologies of diaspora, concepts and ideational constructions that would allow them patiently to await the coming of the messiah for generations, if not forever. This book will document this claim in detail, calling upon examples from all ages and lands in which diaspora Jewish life was lived. The material we examine will be diverse, representing all manner of Jewish creativity.

What we are exploring is not ideologies in the proper sense. "Ideology" is a modern term, and it is generally used to describe a totalizing system of ideas that aims to motivate populations toward action. Jewish narratives, beliefs, concepts, or teachings pertaining to diaspora generally do not cohere into a system, and pre-modern Jewish writings rarely totalize in the way that, say, Marxism does. It is fair to say that Zionism is a Jewish ideology then, but not that Talmudic teachings pertaining to Zion or Exile/diaspora are. At the same time, even if they are not ideologies, such traditional teachings or narratives do motivate populations toward action, even if that action is remaining in diaspora homes and building a life there.

Our use of the term "ideology" is closer to what Daniel Bell describes as the "popular usage" of the term, that is, "a vague term…denot[ing] a worldview or belief-system or creeds held by a social group about the social arrangements in society."[3] In Jewish writings and expression, ideology in this sense may be contained in a narrative (such as the story of Joseph) or a spirited deliberation (such as in the Talmud). It may emerge from the assemblage of isolated comments (as in the teachings of Hasidic masters) or from more systematic expositions on the meaning of Jewish life in exile (such as in the writings of the Maharal of Prague), in ways that approach modern ideological argument. It may even be found in the illustrations of Hebrew manuscripts. We will use "ideology" side by side with "teaching," "tradition," "concept," "belief," and other words in these semantic fields, all while insisting that diaspora Jewish beliefs justifying diaspora/Exile are not isolated. They do, at least, form part of a system, adjacent to and sometimes, though not necessarily, in tension with teachings aspiring to a return to Zion.

Furthermore, while Jewish diaspora-thinking is not-quite-ideological, it does share certain qualities or characteristics with ideological systems. Thus, Daniel Bell admits, "'styles of thought' are related to historic class groups and their interests…ideas emerge as a consequence of the different world-views, or perspectives, of different groups in a society…there is an 'elective affinity' between ideas and interests…all ideas serve interests."[4] To these brief formulations could be added many others, and they all add up, more or less, to the same thing: the expression of ideas, whether in declarative statements, embedded in narratives, or intimated through rules, enactments, or rituals, serve a purpose, and that purpose will relate in important ways to the people who give them expression. In our context, this means that diaspora Jews living for generations in relatively comfortable diasporas will formulate narratives affirming and justifying that reality. In addition, as Bell writes, "What people say they believe cannot always be taken at face value, and one must search for the structure of interests beneath the ideas; one looks not at the *content* of ideas, but their *function*."[5] For us, this means that even when Jewish prayers articulate a hope for a return to Zion, we must consider whether that hope is present- or future-oriented, and how it relates to other expressions and structures that solidify Jewish life in diaspora.

If, in modernity, ideology is the realm of intellectuals—a small, elite group—the traditional Jewish equivalent, including narrative and legal writings, commentaries, and so forth, is also the realm of an elite, in this case the well-educated, male, literate elite. This means that most of the materials we encounter will directly embody the voices and values of particular Jewish elites, almost all men, and not of the people more generally. But, while recognizing their source, we should not make the mistake of thinking that these expressions speak only for such elites. Canonical writings are canonical not because of what they essentially are but because of the way they were received—because they were accepted as authoritative by the community at large. This means that what they said resonated with larger numbers of (in our case) Jews, and, being authoritative, what they said continued to influence the opinions of common Jews from one generation to the next. Crucially, for Jews, canonical works include not just biblical and classical rabbinic texts, but also such works as the Zohar—originally elite but in more recent generations, popular and influential—and collected teachings of Hasidic masters, always more popular. Further, the literate elites in the Jewish world were rarely ivory tower intellectuals. Most engaged and sought to influence the Jewish populace, in direct and indirect ways, and they often succeeded. So the voices we encounter will not speak for a lettered elite alone. It is fair to say that these voices represent the opinions and beliefs of larger swathes of Jewry as well.

Having clarified what I mean by "ideologies," it is crucial that I say something about what I mean by "diaspora." Diaspora as a phenomenon, concept, and specific historical experience has been much studied in recent years, and its essential qualities (that is, its definition) much debated. Because of the length and diversity of Jewish diasporas, it is best, for our purposes, to accept an eclectic definition, avoiding overly narrow assumptions of what diasporas must be. In the 25th anniversary edition of *Global Diasporas: An Introduction*,[6] Robin Cohen offers a list of nine characteristic "strands" that qualify diasporas, each if not all of which combine (forming a metaphorical "rope") to define the diaspora phenomenon. These strands are a refinement on earlier definitions, reflecting and responding to critiques and subsequent discussions in the field since earlier versions of his publication. They are as follows: "dispersal" = "flight from an original home, often under traumatic circumstances"; "expansion" = "movement from a homeland in search of work or a better life"; "retention" = "preservation of a collective memory about an original homeland"; "idealization" = "construction of a myth of the real or imagined ancestral home"; "return" = "development of a return movement to the homeland"; "distinctiveness" = "a strong ethnic group consciousness sustained over a long time based on a sense of particularity, a common history, the transmission of a common cultural and religious heritage and the belief in a common fate"; "apprehension" = "an uneasy relationship with host societies"; "creativity" = "the prospect of an enriching life in host countries with a tolerance for pluralism involving entrepreneurship, creative imagination, scientific achievement, and professional success"; and "solidarity" = "a sense of identification, empathy with and co-responsibility for co-ethnic members in other countries."[7]

Most of these terms obviously pertain to Jewish diasporas and Jewish conceptions thereof, and I would accept all of them without hesitation. But many students of Jewish history and thought would be puzzled by creativity

## 6  EMBRACING EXILE

(and, perhaps less so, by expansion), or at least would not include it in their definition/description of Jewish diasporas, affirming and positive as it is. Indeed, even Cohen offers as his first example of the "victim diaspora" type the Jewish diaspora,[8] and while he corrects the tragic vision by emphasizing that "the Jews' considerable intellectual and spiritual achievements in the diaspora simply could not have happened in a narrow tribal society like that of ancient Judea,"[9] he admits (laments?) that "the tragic tradition was dragooned into the service of Christian and Jewish theology."[10] The word "dragoon" says much, as the tragic view leaves virtually no room for the fruitful creativity that in reality characterized Jewish as well as other diasporas. Recognition of this reality has rarely been given its due in conventional discussions of Jewish diaspora, until, in recent times, historians have begun to correct the historical record. The history of ideas that follows will correct the parallel record of Jewish beliefs and opinions.

Cohen describes, but does not sufficiently emphasize, the dual orientation of diasporas, the Jewish one above all. A diaspora is a diaspora because it recalls, and in some measure yearns for, an idealized "original" homeland. At the same time, it admits that, at least until some unknown future, its current "hostland" is indeed home. These dual poles of orientation are crucial to the diaspora's identity. This means that diaspora Jews will never (as long as they remain a Jewish diaspora) abandon their sense of a common origin in the Promised Land, nor should we expect them to reject the possibility of returning to that "Land" (which may be conceived as an idealized, non-territorial entity) in some unknown future.[11] At the same time, diaspora Jews can be expected to rationalize, justify, and even celebrate the diaspora pole of their dual orientation. Their prayer to ultimately return to Zion will not negate the possibility that "Zion" may now be found in the diaspora. Nor will residence in Zion eliminate the essential diaspora spirit of a people returned to their land.

This book is a history of "the diaspora idea in Judaism,"[12] with a particular focus on expressions that affirm or justify diaspora life. It is not a history of Jewish diasporas as such. Such histories are the substance and focus of much historical writing about Jews, and this is a field that will continue to grow, contributing ever greater nuance to our understanding of the experiences of Jews, both good and bad, in their various diasporas.[13] I have nothing to add to the important work that has already been done in this field. But the contributions of historians of Jewish diasporas are crucial to this history, for it is impossible to understand the ideas expressed without appreciation of the settings in which they were born.

As a book about affirmations of diaspora, what follows will not be a complete, balanced representation of Jewish traditions of exile and redemption through the ages. Since the beginnings of Zionism, there have been many volumes that have gathered and commented upon traditional (and post-traditional!) Jewish teachings expressing the hope for redemption (whether religious or secular), the aspiration or longing to return to Zion. Until now, there has been no equivalent volume collecting Jewish teachings that affirm, support, or justify exile/diaspora. So this book may be understood as a corrective—as the other side of the coin, the rebalancing of scales, directed at exposing a fuller picture of Jewish teachings pertaining to the question of Jewish place and home.

One potential stumbling block in our exploration will be the language of Jewish expression and its limitations. Most of the teachings we will examine are written in one or another form of traditional Hebrew, and they overwhelmingly use the term "*galut*" (exile) to refer to what we are calling diaspora. In its earliest, biblical usage, *galut* is associated with divine punishment and, as a consequence, has an unavoidably negative connotation—describing a condition from which Jews must be delivered. In fact, due to that association, it has become customary to use "exile" and "diaspora" dichotomously, with the former implying a negative experience or judgment and the latter being more neutral. But traditional Hebrews had no word for "diaspora,"[14] so Jewish expressions about diaspora had little choice but to use the term "*galut*," whatever the message or affect of the speaker. Crucially, we should not assume that the meaning of the term, along with related terms and concepts, remained static. Language changes with usage, and this is as true for Jewish language referring to exile ("*galut*" and its reversal, "*geulah*," "redemption") as it is for any other language.

For example, the early part of Midrash Leviticus Rabbah 23 offers a rabbinic exposition of the phrase from Song of Songs 2:2, "like a lily among the thorns." Among the various interpretations offered there (pars. 5–6), we find a sequence suggesting that the lily is Israel (or the righteous of Israel) and the thorns are those who oppress Israel. Israel, the flower, is in need of redemption, and all that is necessary is God's intervention to effectuate that redemption.

In one application of this metaphor, the Midrash says, "Just as when the owner wants to pick the lily from among the thorns, he will burn around it and pick it," in similar fashion will God one day "pick" Israel from among her enemies—"Halamo [which is hostile] to Naveh, and Susita [which is hostile] to Tiberius, and Kastera to Haifa, and Jericho to Neuran, and Lod to Ono." The former are all towns with gentile populations, while the latter are towns with predominantly Jewish populations. Specifying the application of the metaphor, the Midrash concludes, "In the future [literally "tomorrow"], when the time of redemption has come for Israel, what does the Holy One do to them? He brings the fire and burns outside of them [the Jewish settlements]." To redeem the Jews, God must destroy the enemies that surround them. The gentile towns will be "burned" and the Jewish ones survive for final deliverance.

Even if we are not familiar with all the locations specified in this Midrash (and even if some are difficult to identify), one thing is unmistakable: they are all towns/cities in the Land of Israel. So what this Midrash is saying is this: Jews living in the Land, who are, as the Midrash says earlier, "enslaved to the nations of the world," need redemption from the enemies who surround them in the Land itself. To which period or reality does this teaching apply? "To these generations."[15] In other words, rabbis—and presumably other Jews—who lived in the Land of Israel in the Byzantine era, subject to the domination of others and surrounded by adversaries, believed they were in need of redemption. Those who need redemption are now living—existentially, at least—in "exile" (whether or not the term in actually used). So it is possible to be in "exile" even in the Land of future redemptive realization. "Exile" need not be in exile.

Conversely, we should also not assume that use of the term "exile" implies any given set of conditions—say, suffering and oppression. As we will see in later chapters, lamenting exile became a ritual for Jews, and speaking of "bitter exile" a formula—even a verbal tic—even when Jewish writers or speakers lived in relative comfort and celebrated their Jewish lives in a particular "exile." In different settings, Jews may mean or feel something very different when they speak of exile, and we must judge meaning according to the evidence of the setting, not according to some pre-conceived notion of exile deriving from another time or context.

To lay a foundation for the history of ideas, we begin with a brief history of Jewish diasporas, as understood by the best of recent Jewish historical scholarship.

The history of Jewish diasporas begins with the Persian emperor, Cyrus, who, sometime in the 530s BCE, gave permission for exiled Judeans to return to their former homeland. Despite their freedom to do so, many did not return. Instead, they voluntarily remained in their comfortable new

Babylonian homes, the first generations of what would become the longest-lived diaspora community in Jewish history (this community effectively came to an end only after the founding of the state of Israel in the twentieth century). Probably from this time onward (and certainly not long after this), the combined populations of Jewish diasporas would always exceed the Jewish population of the Holy Land. At the same time, Jews who returned to the Land from Babylonian exile were not exactly independent. On the contrary, Jews in their Holy Land were first dominated by Persians, then Greeks, and then (with an interruption of less than a century for the Hasmoneans, the successors of the Maccabees) Romans.

There was a revolt against Rome between 66 and 73 CE, and the Jewish forces were defeated. But Rome did not first conquer Judea during this war. Rather, Rome had taken control of Jewish territories with the downfall of the last of the Hasmoneans, a full century earlier. Under Rome and before the revolt, Jews in Palestine, in their various small territorial domains, enjoyed "autonomy," but certainly not independence. So the shift to direct Roman rule after the revolt was meaningful but not world-changing. This was not a case of independence followed by defeat and subjugation.

Equally importantly, there was no new exile as a product of the Jewish war with Rome. Unlike Babylonia centuries before, Rome did not have a policy of exile for its defeated peoples.[16] Rome did take prisoners of war—such as those prisoners of the Jewish war famously depicted on the Arch of Titus in the Roman forum near the Colosseum—and there were certainly Jews who fled the violence and ravages of the war. But Palestinian Jews were not exiled as a matter of policy, and most remained in or near their former homes in Judea or greater Palestine. That there continued to be many Jews in the Land in the following centuries is evident from contemporary histories, documentary evidence, and archaeology. Rabbis in the Galilee produced the Mishnah in the late second to early third centuries, and they produced the first Talmud and many Midrashic texts sometime in the fifth century. In the late fourth through the sixth centuries Jews built significant synagogues in the Galilee and the Jordan Valley. They had recognized political leadership in the person of the Jewish Patriarch. The Jewish population in the Jewish Holy Land did not dwindle significantly until the sixth century, and this for reasons that had nothing to do with defeat and exile.

Nor did Jewish life outside the land change substantially as a result of the Roman wars (though the Jewish populations of nearby territories certainly increased with refugees from the wars). There had long been a Babylonian

## 10   EMBRACING EXILE

diaspora, and by the time of Jesus there were well-established diasporas in Egypt, throughout Asia Minor, and even in Rome. Diaspora was already a regular part of Jewish life when the Jerusalem Temple was still standing, and it would continue to be so for the next two millennia.

The post-destruction diaspora community concerning which we know the most, thanks to the rabbis and their Talmud, is that of Babylonia, the land that would come to be known as Iraq. Jews had resided in Babylon since the Babylonian exile, but we know little about the experience of those Jews before the rabbis arrived due to lack of surviving documentation. Once the rabbis arrived from Palestine in the late second century, though, they sought to join and influence the long-established community, enjoying conditions that provided little reason for complaint. Rabbis report of themselves that some were materially comfortable and some less so—just like everyone else! But nearly all, from the third to the sixth centuries, lived as they pleased, with rare exception unimpeded in their practice of Judaism. While Palestinian Jewish life was challenged and even languishing, Babylonian Jewish life was thriving, yielding eternal benefits. Babylon provided the rabbis a fertile ground for the study of Torah, and the end-product of this centuries-long experience was the great Babylonian Talmud, which would define Jewish life everywhere from the early Middle Ages until recent modernity.

In the seventh century, the Persian empire of late antiquity collapsed, making way for the Muslim conquest. The replacement of empire for empire did little to diminish the strength of Jewish life in the same lands. In the Muslim world, where the vast majority of Jews lived from the seventh until the twelfth century, Jews enjoyed protected status as a "people of the book." To be sure, sometimes Jewish protections and prerogatives were trampled by local rulers, but more often Jews lived their lives in relative peace—speaking their own dialect of Arabic, following their own customs, and participating in local trade and society.

During the first significant period of Muslim civilization, under the Abbasids, whose capital was Baghdad, Jews enjoyed ongoing peace, their leaders respected and their right to practice their religion freely undiminished. Though we know little about the old Jewish population in Iraq during this period, we know a great deal about the affairs of the rabbis and their increasingly numerous followers. Early under Abbasid rule, the Talmudic academies re-located to Baghdad, where their authority, recognized by Muslim rulers, grew to international proportions. We even have testimony of the heads of the academies being treated like royalty, a condition that persisted for centuries, when the international center of rabbinic authority moved elsewhere.

There were even so-called "golden ages" under Muslim domination, particularly in Spain, where Jews rose to significant roles in society, producing law and poetry, and mingling—even intimately—with their Muslim neighbors. One need merely think of the poetry of Judah Halevi (and others whose names are, to most, lesser known) and the philosophy and jurisprudence of Maimonides (the latter in Egypt, though he is often associated with Spain's golden age, which he did not enjoy) to appreciate the quality of Jewish life in many Muslim settings through these centuries. And it is not only the flourishing of an elite, educated Jewish culture that provides evidence of this reality. Consider the critique directed by one Jew at his compatriots, when he declared "How can you enjoy yourselves, O exiles, and find pleasure in taverns and good food?!"[17] They may have been "exiles," but they were not suffering.

Jewish life in what Jews have known as "Ashkenaz" (originally northern France and the Rhine region and later central to eastern Europe) was, during these times, but a promise, emerging gradually on soils where Jewish life had only recently arrived. Small Jewish communities grew slowly, and Jewish life was sometimes punctuated by oppressions and poverty (the latter distinguishing Jews as a people from no one). But in this region, too, the picture was far more complicated and Jewish life far richer than is sometimes recalled. Early on in Ashkenaz, the great rabbinic commentator Rashi determined the direction of Torah and Talmud study for all generations to come. While Rashi was still alive, the Jewish populations of the cities of the Rhine—Speyer, Worms, and Mainz—suffered serious losses during the first crusade, but the Jewish populations of those cities recovered within a generation, and they continued to be serious centers of Jewish life and piety. In greater Ashkenaz in the twelfth century, the great Talmudic scholars known as Tosafot learned much from the scholastic methods of neighboring Christian scholars, and their Talmudic commentaries are filled with the spirit of the enlightened "new textuality" of the contemporary French schools. And though the lives of these gentlemen overlapped chronologically with the second crusade, neither they nor other Jews suffered as a result, for both Jews and Christians learned the lessons of the abuses of the first crusade and were thereafter able to prevent violence against Jews, which was not the goal of the crusades in the first place.

12 EMBRACING EXILE

To appreciate Jewish experience in this place and period, we need to recall that Jews in Ashkenaz typically lived in small numbers in small towns or cities, where they had no choice but to live peacefully with their neighbors. Making this point clearly is various testimonies of the dependence of Jews (like everyone else!) on local resources for their survival. So Rabbenu Tam, one of the outstanding twelfth-century rabbinic scholars in France, grants permission for Jews to use mills and ovens belonging to Christian priests to prepare their own bread (Tosafot, Avodah Zarah 44b). When one recalls that medieval towns were likely to have had few ovens and that the only available oven might have been the one owned by the church, Rabbenu Tam's permission occasions no surprise. But it is worth noting nonetheless, as it bespeaks a relationship of cooperation between members of the different faiths.

We should not imagine that such relationships were only pragmatic. A colleague of Rabbenu Tam reports that "there are those who permit the purchase of warm bread from gentiles" on the Sabbath (Avodah Zarah 66b). To understand the full implication of this report, we need merely recall that, understood literally, such a transaction would be forbidden to Jews on the Sabbath, so "purchase" must mean something else, something like "acquire on credit." For this to be possible, the Jew and the gentile baker must have relatively good relations and understand one another's practices. Otherwise, the Jew would have to be satisfied with bread baked the prior day.

The evidence for such relations is not rare. Slightly later than the French case, in Vienna R. Isaac b. Moses condemned those who choose bread baked by gentiles over bread baked by Jews, suggesting that Jewish laxity in this matter is widespread. R. Isaac is very explicit in his condemnation, writing that, "everyone [= every Jew] has grown accustomed to purchase bread from his good friend the gentile, and they don't worry about [possible attraction to] his daughters" (*Or Zaru'a*, Avodah Zarah 188). Notably, the word translated here as "good friend" would literally be translated as "lover," and even if such literalness goes too far, there can be no doubt that the term implies warmth and even intimacy. To state the matter simply, the evidence shows that Jews shared both bread and wine with their neighbors, a consequence of living side by side in trust, peace, and sometimes even affection.

That Jews and gentiles lived and worked in such cooperative proximity, and even with warm relations, may come as a surprise to many, who have learned that Jews lived in ghettos and only "emerged from the ghetto" with the enlightenment and advent of emancipation. But the Jewish ghetto is an early modern invention—the first ghetto was established in Venice in 1516—and before that Jews lived in a variety of settings and configurations, none of them actual ghettos. Jewish texts from Roman and Byzantine Palestine, along with the Talmud of Babylonia, all assume that Jews and gentiles might live in homes sharing a common courtyard. Medieval towns typically had "Jewish streets" or small neighborhoods, but these were not ghettos. Jews, like all peoples, are comfortable living among their own, so such clusters of Jewish dwellings were as likely to be a consequence of choice as of anything else, and such streets or neighborhoods were not exclusive—Jews could live elsewhere in town, and Christians could live in Jewish neighborhoods. Even when the Jewish quarter was located by the side of the cathedral or church complex, as was often the case, this was informed by the fact that this was likely to be the safest place in town; uninformed crowds could sometimes act in an unruly fashion and act out against Jews, but official church policy, usually well enforced, required that Jews be protected.

When we turn our focus to the Renaissance and early modernity, we similarly have to revise the better-known version of Jewish history. The earliest actual ghettos in Italy were places where Jews were required to locate their homes, that is, to sleep at night. But the ghettos were open to two-way traffic during the day, as Jews did business elsewhere and gentiles made their way into the ghetto markets. Moreover, many Italian Jews in the fifteenth and sixteenth centuries actually lived quite well. Illustrated and illuminated Italian Hebrew manuscripts of this period are often quite lavish, written by expert scribes on fine parchment and decorated by artists working with vibrant colored inks, and often with gold leaf. These books were clearly commissioned by very wealthy families, families who often created their own coats of arms to claim their distinguished status. Jews living in northern Italy more generally dressed and adorned themselves just like their neighbors, and on the street they would have been hardly distinguishable from their neighbors to the untrained eye. We even know, from Jewish testimonies, that Jews drank the wines of their neighbors, forbidden according to Jewish law but only to be expected in a setting in which Jews felt so comfortable.

One of the greatest of the Jewish diasporas of all time was that of the greater Polish lands, beginning with the Polish "golden age" of the late sixteenth and early seventeenth centuries and continuing, even following anti-Jewish outbreaks, into the eighteenth century. This was a period of

## 14 EMBRACING EXILE

unprecedented Jewish autonomy and material success in Polish lands (this condition was interrupted in the mid-seventeenth century but resumed thereafter). Jews made their homes, by invitation and subject to official protection, in both royal and noble Polish towns and territories, and they came to be relied upon as trusted subjects who often served the king or noblemen directly. The relative comfort and security that came with these arrangements led to growth in the Jewish community, both through natural increase and by attracting Jews from elsewhere in Europe. As a result, it was increasingly common for Jews to constitute at least a significant minority— and sometimes even a majority—of the populations of towns in these regions, meaning that Jews and Christians lived in distinct neighborhoods, but side by side and mutually reliant, in one town after another.

These abundant Jewish populations were granted unprecedented judicial and communal autonomy. Regional Jewish councils, which could rightly be called "legislatures" (the term Jews used in Polish was "*sejm*," the same term used for the Polish legislature), and autonomous courts meant that, with respect to day-to-day affairs, Jews largely controlled their own lives. The judges who served in Jewish courts were rabbis, and the law that controlled their judgments was the law that originated in the Talmud. And while rabbis were secondary to wealthy Jews on the regional councils, it was commonly understood that the regulations that should control Jewish society as a whole were those accepted by the rabbinic authorities. It is not incorrect to call this state of affairs "Jewish autonomy," and it is fair to say that this constituted the most significant degree of self-government that Jews enjoyed since antiquity.

This was also a period of great Jewish productivity in these lands. Early in this period, prominent rabbis wrote important Talmudic commentaries and codes of Jewish law—writings that are influential to this day. Jews shared the fates of their neighboring populations when it came to prosperity or poverty, but even when Jews, like their neighbors, experienced the challenges of deprivation, their spiritual lives flourished; one need only look to the great creativity of Hasidic spirituality in the eighteenth and nineteenth centuries to understand how fulfilling Jewish life was, even in the face of material hardship.

Following emancipation, European Jews took their place next to their Christian neighbors as citizens of newly emerging nation-states. Many moved to expanding, increasingly vibrant cities such as Warsaw or Berlin, where some sought to join modern society by giving up distinguishing

Jewish customs. Jews emerged as leaders in finance and business, and outstanding figures joined the ranks of composers, philosophers, and writers. Academic Jewish scholarship was born, as more Jews enjoyed university educations. Even in cities in the Pale of settlement, in the Russian empire, evidence of modernity and its benefits was everywhere. And when, beginning in the late nineteenth century, Jews of the Pale fled for the New World, Jewish neighborhoods in cities like New York were the cradle for a vibrant, creative new Jewish culture, bubbling with theater and literature and politics, to name just a few of its outstanding expressions. Even while Zionism was first emerging, most of these Jews saw their homes, and those of their children and grandchildren, remaining in the diaspora. Why would they have to go elsewhere when observant Jews had their synagogues and kosher butchers, Jewish socialists their Yiddish newspapers and meeting halls, and upwardly mobile Jews their new homes in growing suburbs? Yes, there were concerning signs on the horizon, but Jews had known trouble before.

This, in brief, is our current understanding of the history of Jewish diasporas, which Jews called exiles. Not surprisingly, Jews in these many exiles produced writings that actually made sense of their not-so-exilic experiences, even configuring them as more positive than not. For example, regarding the Babylonian/Persian exile, the book of Esther told the story of the triumph of Jews in diaspora, according to which the cruel foolishness of one man, Haman, was overcome and Jews enjoyed prestige and power. Another ultimately biblical book, the book of Daniel, contains similar stories of the triumph of an exilic prophet and his companions.

In teachings that are less popularly known, Talmudic rabbis declared Babylon to be as good as Zion, Spanish mystics insisted that God's presence was with Jews wherever their home, and a sixteenth-century Bohemian rabbi argued that exile/diaspora is the natural home for Jews, at least before the arrival of the messiah. My purpose in this book is to uncover and highlight these expressions, making it clear that Jewish history and tradition are far more than a single, extended lament. For the present, suffice it to say that Jews living in diaspora often affirmed their diasporas. In this way, Jewish thinkers and theologians gave meaning and purpose to their scattered lives, reason to commit their lives and souls to the homes to which fate sent them.

Each chapter in this book will be devoted to a particular period and its outstanding expressions concerning diaspora. The chapter will begin with a

16 EMBRACING EXILE

more detailed historical foundation, focusing on the lesser-known tales of relatively comfortable Jewish life in diaspora. Indeed, the settings in which Jews found themselves often provided for peaceful and productive lives, offering an environment in which Jewish culture could be enriched in innumerable ways. Only by understanding what Jews actually experienced in their diasporas is it possible to appreciate what they said about them.

Having laid the historical foundation, each chapter will then turn to the central question of this book: what kind of sense Jews made of such realities? The answers will often be surprising. More than once, authoritative Jewish voices give expression to the notion that exile is natural to human existence, Jewish and otherwise. Biblical and other stories describe a God who protects Jews in exile, assuring that they triumph. Declarations by bold diaspora sages insist that living in diaspora is as good as living in Zion. Hasidic masters share their belief that the sacred spirit of the Holy Land can be found in the hills of eastern Europe. And so forth. For every traditional expression of the Jewish longing for Zion, another insists that Jews may be fully at home, living a full, legitimate Jewish life, abroad.

The overall thrust of this book is contrary to much writing and commentary on Jewish experience and belief. It will perhaps be instructive, then, to consider why the "lachrymose" (to use Salo Baron's descriptor) view has dominated Jewish consciousness while contrary ones are often suppressed.

The first and most obvious answer to this question is that there has been much in Jewish history to lament, and Jews have excelled in composing lamentations, which have often been incorporated into communal rituals. As a result, these expressions of suffering and lament have been well known by Jews in general and extremely influential in shaping their understanding of Jewish experience.

Second, the notion that Jews suffered frequently, a product of the punishment expressed in their exiles, is what Jews were supposed to believe. Standard explanation of exile originated (for traditional purposes) in the Torah and the biblical prophets, which warned a rebellious "Jewish" (= Israelite) population of punishment-by-exile for their sins. This exile would be filled with unbearable suffering, suffering that would both punish and atone, re-directing Israel toward obedience of God's covenantal commands and leading, in the end, to a delivery from the pains of exile. This explanatory scheme was repeated in Jewish liturgy, in which no Jew could escape the claim that "on account of our sins we were exiled from our land."[18] If exile is punishment for sin, a punishment that will one day end in redemptive restoration, then actual exile had to be read within the framework of this traditional explanation. Exile must be painful, whatever the current local reality.

The third answer is the success of Zionism and the Zionist understanding of history,[19] particularly with the establishment of the State of Israel. Zionism began in Europe in the nineteenth century, in part as a response to increasing antisemitism in the last decades of the century but mostly as a Jewish expression of the wave of new nationalisms—and new nation-states—that swept Europe in the same century. European Jews, as other Europeans, were influenced by the emergence of such states and the ideology that supported them, and they saw the creation of a secular Jewish state—not a messianic state, as Jewish tradition had long hoped—as the desired realization of Jewish dignity for Jews as citizens of the modern world. Notably, this modern manifestation would also, they imagined, solve the longstanding Jewish problem: antisemitism.

Zionists recounted Jewish history in a way that would support their ideology. In the service of this ideology, they told the story of the loss of Jewish independence two millennia ago, following which Jews suffered at the hands of the nations throughout their diasporas. Most did not ignore completely the more positive expressions of diaspora Jewish life, but all saw the suffering of diaspora as far more weighty. Given the shortness of human memory, new, virulent antisemitic irruptions in the Russian empire and later in Germany, suggested to most that disempowered Jewish diaspora existence was always like this, and increasing numbers of Jews accepted the notion that only a Jewish state could provide genuine protection for Jews. With the founding of the State of Israel, increasing numbers of Jews became Zionists, and particularly after the Six-Day War of 1967, to be a Jew meant to be a Zionist, with "Zionist" no longer meaning someone who aspires to settle in the Jewish homeland but simply a supporter of the State of Israel.

Zionist historians (Israeli academics and many of their colleagues working in the diaspora) wrote histories to support the Zionist vision (mostly unconsciously, I assume). Many focused on the tragedies of diaspora Jewish life and gave short shrift to its successes. There were exceptions to these rules, but the overall picture that emerged was the one described above. As the scholarship of these historians was learned and then repeated by teachers of Jewish history, at any level, this narrative became canonical. As described by Mordecai Kaplan in 1948, the message being conveyed by Jewish educators was "based on the acceptance of suffering and exile as our

18 EMBRACING EXILE

lot in life, from which there is only one escape, and that is migration to Eretz Israel."[20]

Whatever the reasons for the dominance of the view that Jewish life in exile has been, and is meant to be, one of unending suffering and longing for redemption, the fact of this dominance is undeniable. This book will counter this narrative, gathering and highlighting the contrary tradition, in the hope that all may now understand that the reality is more balanced.

But this is not my only purpose in this book. It seems to me that the Jewish example of making the best of diasporas, both pragmatically and ideologically, is of relevance, in our world, not only to Jews. Jewish justifications of diaspora are also an important model for other diasporas today. We live in a world full of refugees, with populations displaced by poverty, famine, war, and persecution. As I write this, millions of Ukrainians have been forced to flee Russian bombardments to Poland and other lands, nearby and farther away. They are not the first refugees in our lifetimes, nor will they be the last. Refugees and those among whom they live are daily challenged with questions of identity and relationship. They ask: must we, who have been displaced, give up our identities to find a safe new home? Can we maintain our distinctive customs and still be accepted? Can we remember our origins while planting roots in new soil? Relatedly, those who are asked to accept refugees ask: do those who join us from other lands have to give up their old identities in order to fit in? Can they maintain their distinctiveness and still become part of "us"? Must we insist that they assimilate into the general population if they do not want to remain strangers; must the stranger "disappear" to live in peace?

Jews are, arguably, the world's most experienced refugees, having wandered from one home to another for twenty-five centuries. We know that, in some of those times and places, exiled Jews were seen as strangers, and they saw themselves as such, at least to some degree. They spoke their own dialect, wore their own fashions, and kept to themselves. They kept their metaphorical bags at least open, if not already packed, being ultimately doomed to use those bags. But this story of the Jewish refugee experience is incomplete, and it fails to account for the more common one, according to which Jews spoke the same languages as their neighbors, wore the same fashions, and mixed in the same marketplace, though less often in domestic alleyways. Jews who lived this story also thought of themselves as Jews, maintaining their special practices and beliefs. But this did not require them to keep their bags ready. On the contrary, there was a reason they were where they were—or, at least, so they believed—and they could live full Jewish lives while also being at home abroad.

This model is a crucial one in our current world, for it suggests that refugees can be at home in their new homes without disappearing, that building new homes need not run the risk of violent erasure or expulsion. How did Jews manage this successful balancing act? With the wisdom of experience, they learned that exile need not be punishment and that life in exile need not entail suffering. For these many Jews, we might say, exile was not exile but merely diaspora. As the longest-lived and most successful diaspora in human history, the Jewish diaspora is one that offers a model for later diasporas, even ones whose origins are recent. Those who have admired Jewish intelligence, which emerges from this experience, and have wondered at Jewish resilience, can find, in the diaspora model, another reason to consider the example of the Jews. My hope is that those who have found instruction in the experiences of Jewish diasporas will find their understanding enhanced by the broader view this book makes possible. Indeed, my hope is that they will find it inspiring.

# 2

# Biblical Explanations of Exile

The Tanakh, the Hebrew Bible (known to Christians as the "Old Testament"), is not a book but a sacred library. Its books are of various genres, and they emerged at different times and places. Much of the first part (canonically speaking) of the Tanakh—the Torah—is devoted to law and cult. Other biblical books represent a kind of wisdom tradition, collecting maxims or teaching through narrative. Poetry plays a significant part in a book like Job or the collection known as Psalms. But as much as anything else, the Tanakh is a history of the ancient people of Israel and of their relationship with God, and though not all of the Tanakh's history books emerge from a single tradition, most of them do, and the tradition from which they emerge is the one most clearly articulated in the book of Deuteronomy. That book and the school it represents have a clear view of the arc of Israelite history and its meaning. It is that view that predominates in the Tanakh's "history" from beginning to end.

So, what is that arc, and how do most biblical histories incorporate it? Stated briefly, following its description of God's creation of the world and humanity, the early chapters of the book of Genesis focus on the descent of humankind from Adam and Eve to Abraham and Sarah. God chooses Abraham as a covenantal partner, declaring that his offspring will be blessed, and as numerous, through the ages, as the stars of heaven. From the moment that the covenant is sealed, the Tanakh gives almost exclusive attention to the offspring of Abraham and Sarah. Thus, the Tanakh's history focuses on the growth of Abraham's and Sarah's family into a people, a development that occurs while they are slaves in the land of Egypt. Then, following their Exodus from Egypt and acceptance of the covenant of Law at Sinai, we learn of this people's conquest of the Land promised by God in the covenant and of their establishment of a kingdom therein. The books of Kings preserve the stormy history of those kingdoms, a history that ends in exile, a punishment for their sins according to the conditions of the covenant. The Tanakh's last historical books (in terms of the chronology of the events they recount), the book of Ezra and the book of Nehemiah, tell the story of the return from exile, ending at a point of tension, with the Temple rebuilt but the kingdom not yet restored.

The actual history of ancient Israel was far more complex than this relatively straightforward story would suggest. To begin with, many biblical historians doubt whether the forefathers and foremothers actually existed, whether there was ever a sojourn of Israel in Egypt, whether there was ever a Moses or an exodus or a revelation at Sinai. Some still doubt the reality of the first biblical kings, Saul and David.[1] Where agreement emerges is in the histories of the two related kingdoms, Judah and Israel, and in their constant battles with their imperial neighbors. No one doubts that the northern kingdom of Israel was conquered and scattered by the Assyrians, to be lost in the fog of history, nor that the southern kingdom of Judah was defeated and exiled by the Babylonians. But many will doubt whether the reason for these defeats was the failure of the kingdoms to uphold the conditions of the covenant. They would instead suggest the obvious: that small kingdoms in the path of great empires tend to be defeated.

Also attracting widespread assent is the history of the biblical texts themselves.[2] It is clear that the ancient Israelite kingdoms developed traditions, both oral and written, and kept chronicles. Obviously, those kingdoms had an understanding of their origins. And, like any society, they had their laws and customs. But, biblical historians agree, during the period of the kingdoms, none of these traditions were yet combined into the books of history and law that ultimately constituted the Tanakh. During the reigns of Saul, David, Solomon, and the rest of the Judean and Israelite kings, there was no Torah, no books of Samuel, no books of Kings, and so forth. These works, which clearly built on and incorporated some of the traditions that emerged during the monarchies, only came to formation after them. The question is when?

Biblical historians agree that the answer is during the Babylonian exile. It was the experience of exile and the challenge it represented that inspired the consolidation of the inherited tradition. We do not know a lot about the specifics of the lives of the exiles. But there are certain things of which we can be confident: the experience of expulsion from the Land itself was traumatic; the emotions expressed in the book of Lamentations cannot have spoken only for its author, as its canonical reception attests. Once in Babylon, the exiled Judeans had to take steps to survive there. They had to build homes, protect and grow families, and find means of support. And, in some ways most importantly, if they were to survive as Jews—unlike their brothers and sisters from the northern kingdom, who, when exiled, evidently abandoned hope and disappeared (they became "the Ten Lost Tribes of Israel")—they had to make sense of their exile, seeing it not as an end but as a step along the way.

To do this, they looked to the teachings of the major prophets and the book of Deuteronomy (the only book of the Torah that existed, in something close to its present form, before the exile), where they discovered an empowering explanation for why they had been defeated and exiled by Babylon. Based upon what they found, they formulated books that both made sense of the past and offered guidance for the future. To be clear: it was exile itself that, more than anything else, gave birth to the biblical corpus. To understand the "traditional" Jewish explanation of exile, then, we must understand why it worked so well for those Judeans who were already in exile.

The phrase "Judeans…in exile," means not just a lettered elite who formulated and preserved these traditions, but large parts of the exiled population. While there can be no doubt that the documents we preserve from the exile—the Torah, the major and many of the "minor" prophets, the royal history—were produced by a small, literate class, the works that this group shaped became extremely influential in a short period of time. How can we know this?

The answer is circular, but it is a fruitful circularity. The fundamental question is why the exiles survived as a nation at all, unlike their brethren who disappeared? The answer, inescapably, is that they had a reason to survive, and that reason is the beliefs and teachings preserved in the biblical texts. Now, crucially, the covenantal vision of Deuteronomy and the special relationship between God and Israel proposed by the prophets did not originate in exile. The former was expressed with the "discovery" of Deuteronomy under King Josiah (ca. 640–609) and the latter was already inspirationally expressed by the first classical prophets, Amos and Hoshea, in the middle part of the prior century. So these ideas already had time to circulate, to "percolate," to gain momentum, before the exile. With the exile, though, they gained retroactive "proof," and just as they made sense of exile, they could also make sense of why a "Jew" (more accurately: Judean) should remain a "Jew," hoping for return from exile. This development influenced not only those who produced and recited the final books; it also persuaded many of those who listened to their recitation.

So how does the exilic shaping of the biblical account of ancient Israelite history work? Central to the entire historical arc of the Tanakh is the covenant between God and Israel. A covenant is a contract, and the contract between God and Israel required Israel's obedience to God's law. If Israel obeyed that law, they would enjoy a number of rewards, including peaceful dwelling on the Promised Land, abundant crops in their season, and other unspecified signs of divine favor. But if they failed to obey the law, they were threatened with punishment, and the specified punishments represent a complete reversal of the rewards.

One of the Tanakh's most angry and explicit threats of punishment—more powerful because of its relative conciseness—appears near the end of the book of Leviticus. Here is the portion of the threat that is most relevant to our exploration; the speaker in this section is God:

[27] And if, in spite of this, you do not listen to me but continue to be hostile toward me, [28] then I will be greatly hostile toward you, and I myself will punish you for your sins seven times over. [29] You will eat the flesh of your sons and the flesh of your daughters. [30] I will destroy your high places, cut down your incense altars and place your dead bodies on the lifeless forms of your idols, and I will abhor you. [31] I will turn your cities into ruins and lay waste your sanctuaries, and I will not smell the pleasing aroma of your offerings. [32] I will lay waste the land, so that your enemies who live there will be appalled. [33] I will scatter you among the nations and will draw out my sword toward you. Your land will be laid waste, and your cities will be ruins. [34] Then the land will enjoy its sabbath years all the time that it lies desolate and you are in the land of your enemies; then the land will rest and enjoy its sabbaths. [35] All the days of its desolation, the land will have the rest it did not have during the sabbaths you dwelled in it.

[38] You will perish among the nations; the land of your enemies will devour you. [39] Those of you who are left will waste away in the lands of their enemies because of their sins; also because of their ancestors' sins they will waste away.

[40] But if they will confess their sins and the sins of their ancestors—their unfaithfulness by which they betrayed me, and even their hostility toward me, [41] which made me hostile toward them so that I sent them into the land of their enemies—then when their uncircumcised hearts are humbled and they pay for their sin, [42] I will remember my covenant with Jacob and my covenant with Isaac and my covenant with Abraham, and I will remember the land. [43] For the land will be deserted by them and will enjoy its sabbaths while it lies desolate without them. They will pay for their sins because they rejected my laws and abhorred my decrees. (Leviticus 26:27–43)

24  EMBRACING EXILE

This brief warning encapsulates the conditions and consequences of the biblical covenant. The threatened punishment for disobedience is destruction of the Temple ("your sanctuaries") and (presumably) kingdom, and banishment to exile. In this threat, exile is not a neutral place but a place of suffering. God will draw God's sword against the people and pursue them into exile. There, they will be devoured, they will waste away—all on account of their sins.

A parallel threat in Deuteronomy offers more details of the awfulness Israel can expect in exile:

> [64] Then the LORD will scatter you among all the nations, from one end of the earth to the other. There you will worship other gods—gods which neither you nor your ancestors have known, of wood and stone. [65] Among those nations you will find no repose, no resting place for the sole of your foot. There the LORD will give you an anxious heart, weary eyes, and a despairing soul. [66] Your life will be precarious to you, and you will be afraid both night and day, never sure of your life. [67] In the morning you will say, "If only it were evening!" and in the evening, "If only it were morning!"—because of the terror of your heart that you will experience and the sights of your eyes that you will see. [68] The LORD will send you back in ships to Egypt on a journey I said you should never make again. There you will offer yourselves for sale to your enemies as male and female slaves, but no one will buy you. (Deuteronomy 28:64–68)

This vision is even more frightening than the earlier one. In exile, Israel will worship other gods—presumably because their own God will be unavailable to them. They will never rest; they will live in fear and constant anxiety. They will be so desperate that, like anyone who lives in constant terror, they will long for the passing of night, and then for the relief they hope will come when the day is over. For such sufferers, a return to slavery itself would be a relief, but they will be so despised that no one will want them even as slaves.

The importance of this latter text lies in the fact that, as we noted earlier, virtually the entirety of the historical sequence from the book of Joshua through Kings is shaped by what scholars call "the Deuteronomist"—a historian-theologian (more probably a school of historian-theologians) who suggested we understand all ancient Israelite history through the lens of the covenant just described. This historian had a lot to explain, but he also had, in the covenantal agreement, a lot to help him make sense of the exile. The history of the ancient kingdoms was filled not only with failure but also with sin, at least as far as these ancient Israelite visionaries were concerned. The united kingdom of David and Solomon (according to the biblical account, Saul, the first king of Israel, ruled for but a short time, and what he ruled over could barely be called a kingdom) divided against itself in short order, leading to competing kingdoms north (Israel) and south (Judah). From the perspective of the Tanakh's winners, the Judeans, the rebellious north was always sinful, and its conquest and exile could easily be justified as a product of that sin.

But the kingdom of Judah was hardly better, and, in the view of the Deuteronomistic historian, its sin too had to be punished. That punishment came at the hand of the powerful Babylonian empire, whose onslaught brought Judah to its knees. The story of the Babylonian conquest is told in some detail in the final chapters of II Kings, but the biblical historian's understanding of events comes down to this:

> [26] Nevertheless, the LORD did not turn away from his great, fierce anger, which burned against Judah because of all that Manasseh had done to arouse his anger. [27] So the LORD said, "I will also remove Judah from my presence as I removed Israel, and I will reject this city that I chose, Jerusalem, and this temple, about which I said, 'My Name shall be there.'"
>
> [12] …in the eighth year of the reign of the king of Babylon, he took Jehoiachin prisoner. [13] And he removed from there all the treasures from the temple of the LORD and the treasures of the royal palace, and cut up the gold articles that Solomon king of Israel had made for the temple of the LORD, as the Lord had said. [14] He exiled all Jerusalem: all the officers and fighting men, and all the skilled workers and artisans—a total of ten thousand. Only the poorest people of the land were left. (II Kings 23:26–27 and 24:12–14)

So there it is, and it is official: the Babylonian exile was a punishment for the sins of Judah. Only when the people returned to God would God return them to God, presumably erasing the exile to which the sin had led (in reality, this exile never disappeared).

The "woe" of exile is first and most heart-wrenchingly expressed in the biblical book of Lamentations. There, the reason for exile and the bitter experience of exile is expressed again and again. Consider only these few cases of many:

26 EMBRACING EXILE

³ Judah has gone into exile because of misery and much labor; when she settled among the nations she found no rest.

⁵ The Lord has afflicted her for her many transgressions; her infants have gone into captivity before the enemy.

¹⁸ The Lord is in the right, for I have disobeyed Him. Hear, all you peoples, and behold my pains: my maidens and my youths have gone into captivity. (Lamentations 1:3, 1:5, and 1.18)

These verses, and the book as a whole, are recited liturgically, year after year, on the Ninth of Av ("*Tisha be'Av*"), the day on which the destruction of both Jerusalem Temples (the one destroyed by the Babylonians and the one later destroyed by the Romans) is memorialized. The haunting tune with which these verses are chanted, along with the annual solemn recitation, assures that no Jew who attends the synagogue (probably most Jews through the centuries) will forget the message conveyed here: we find ourselves in the midst of this painful exile on account of our sins.

What was the power of the "exile as punishment" model for Jews who found themselves in exile? The answer is two-fold. To begin with, if exile was punishment for sin, this means that the defeat and exile were neither capricious nor evidence of God's abandonment of Israel. According to this explanation, God had not abandoned Israel. No, God had punished Israel because God cares so much about her and what she does. The analogy is to a parent, who does not ignore the behavior of a child she or he cares about but corrects the child, hoping that the punishment will improve the child for the future. Understood this way, exile was not an accident, it was a message, and if Israel heard the message, she had a chance of being saved.

Which leads to the second reason the model was powerful. If the exile "just happened" then there was nothing Israel could do to reverse it. But if it was the conduct of Israel that led to the exile, then the conduct of Israel could also bring restoration. In other words, the "exile as punishment" model comes with a "redemption as reward for repentance" counterpoint. If God cares, then God cares both about Israel's sin and about her return. This means that if, in exile, Israel collectively returns to the covenant and corrects her ways, then she has the power to persuade God to bring her back. People need to believe they have some degree of influence over their fate. For Israel in exile, the dynamic offered by the covenantal model provided the belief in that influence.

Remarkably, history itself supported the truth of the covenantal promise, as in the seventh decade following the Babylonian exile, the Persian king Cyrus permitted Jews to return to their ancestral land. It had worked! Repentance led to restoration. With "proof" of the truth of the system and faith in its efficacy even into the future, Jews had reason to remain Jews, knowing that they could rely on the God who so cared from them. The biblical books (with some important exceptions, to be sure) incorporated the DNA of this system into the narratives they told and the wisdoms they taught, and despite reasons for doubt—which generated a biblical counter-tradition—this vision of history became the dominant one for Jews in the subsequent centuries.

In fact, the biblical teaching concerning exile echoed through Jewish history, as no tradition was more authoritative than that of the Tanakh. Being biblical, the notion of "exile as punishment" made its way into Jewish liturgy and ritual as well. One place where the ideology is particularly prominent is in the Musaf prayer for festivals. The Musaf prayer has a very particular function. When the Temple still stood in Jerusalem, a special additional sacrifice (= *musaf*) would be offered on every special day, including the Sabbath, New Moon, and Pilgrimage Festivals (Passover, Shavuot, and Sukkot). When the Temple was destroyed and the sacrifice could no longer be offered, dedicated prayers were instituted to replace the sacrifices. But the rabbis who wrote the prayers—and those Jews who recited them—were well aware that they were weak substitutes for the actual sacrifices, and the formula of the prayer makes this awareness clear when it declares, "on account of our sins we were exiled from our Land" and we can therefore no longer actually offer the required sacrifices. Being recited on the holidays of Passover, Shavuot, and Sukkot, few Jews could have missed the ritualized declaration of the reason for their life in exile. With exile being punishment, it would have been difficult for them not to see their experiences as expressions of divine disapproval.

There are many other examples of the expression of this notion in the teachings and rituals of Judaism through the ages, from the oft-recited biblical texts that are its foundation to religious poetry and philosophical expositions. But the few examples just cited should suffice to illustrate the power and importance of this explanation of exile. It is, on account of its many expressions and their authority, the best-known interpretation of the Jewish diaspora condition, among both Jews and others.

Yet, despite the power of this explanation of exile, from the very beginning there are hints that other beliefs and emotions would compete with

## 28  EMBRACING EXILE

this one, casting exile in a very different light. Indeed, the very assertion that exile = punishment embeds a recognition that exile has a crucial purpose, one more positive than the explicit tone of these teachings would suggest. You see, punishment functions, in biblical theology, to cleanse the sinner of the stain of sin. Without such cleansing—either through animal sacrifice or through punishment = suffering—the rupture in the relationship between God and Israel caused by sin could not be repaired. If exile accomplishes this function—if the land of exile is the site of purification from sin—then the value of exile cannot be denied. And if God, through human agents, destroys the Temple, this means that God is insisting that, at some point, only exile can cleanse. Does this mean that the Land where the people of Israel sin is the place of stain and exile the place of purification? Such a conclusion would not be a distortion of the covenantal theology.

But we need not rely on such interpretations to yield the tradition's more positive valence concerning exile. Even Leviticus 26, which so well enunciated the dominant biblical explanation of exile, follows its threat of exilic punishment with a promise, one offering a very different picture:

> [44] Yet in spite of this, when they are in the land of their enemies, I will not reject them or abhor them so as to destroy them completely, breaking my covenant with them, for I am the LORD their God. [45] I will remember the covenant with their ancestors whom I brought out of Egypt in the sight of the nations to be their God. I am the LORD.

According to these verses, God cares too much about Israel—God's covenantal partners—to abandon them in exile. On the contrary, though God may be angry with Israel, casting them out of "His" house for a time, God so loves Israel that God "will not reject them nor abhor them." The covenant, like a marriage bond, will not be forgotten. Anger and expulsion will be followed by reconciliation and love. Even in the lands of their enemies, in the midst of their diaspora, God will care for them.

Still another text, modest though it may be, offers a subtle but unmistakable rejoinder to the horrific visions portrayed in the covenantal "texts of reproof" quoted earlier in this chapter. Revising the portrait of exilic agony and offering a radically different take on the exilic experience, Psalm 105, which speaks of God's covenantal servants, plays a chronological game that is of immense consequence for our discussion. The relevant verses are these:

Remember the wonders God has done, His signs and the judgments of His mouth. The seed of Abraham His servant, the children of Jacob His chosen one. He is the Lord our God, his judgments are over all the earth. He has remembered His covenant forever, the thing He commanded for a thousand generations, which he made with Abraham, and his oath to Isaac. And He upheld it to Jacob as an ordinance, to Israel as an eternal covenant. Saying: to you will I give the land of Canaan, the lot of your inheritance. When they were few in number, dwelling there. And they went from one nation to another, from a kingdom to another people, He allowed no person to oppress them, and He reproved kings on their account [saying] don't touch my anointed ones and do no wrong to my prophets. (Psalm 105:5–15)

At first blush, this seems to be a psalm about the patriarchs and the covenant that God entered with them. But a literal understanding of this reference quickly breaks down. The description declaring that "they went from one nation to another" hardly applies to the generations of the patriarchs and matriarchs; Abraham and Sarah went down only to Egypt, and Isaac remained in the land of Canaan. Moreover, the description of wandering from nation to nation suggests a far broader phenomenon—a diasporic wandering, in fact.

For this reason and others, biblical scholar Adele Berlin understands this psalm to be equating the "exiles" of the patriarchs with later exiles. In her words:

The psalm portrays the patriarchal period as one of multiple exiles. The psalm is a history of exile, the various "exiles" experienced by Israel's founding fathers, whose experiences prefigure the exilic experience of the contemporary audience....

The patriarchs are re-imagined as having experienced the Babylonian exile. The psalmist does this by applying exilic language and imagery to the patriarchal stories....

In all these examples we see that the psalm repeatedly inscribes the exile and restoration onto the patriarchal stories in a manner that identifies the patriarchs with the exiles and the exiles with the patriarchs. To put it another way, the allusions to the patriarchs are being read as double-entendres, as references to the Torah traditions and as references to the contemporary moment.[3]

30    EMBRACING EXILE

In this reading, the author of this psalm, himself probably a Jew who experienced or at least witnessed (if only from afar) the extended Babylonian exile, comments on it by equating it with the "exiles" of the patriarchs. The fates of the patriarchs were assured by the covenant—a covenant that still binds God to Jews in the Babylonian exile—as was their well-being. The same, the poet asserts, applies to the later exiles.

This means that the psalm may be taken as a testimony to the experience of those latter exiles, and what a testimony it is. Speaking, evidently, of Jews in the Babylonian exile, the Psalmist reports, "God allowed no person to oppress them, and He reproved kings on their account [saying] don't touch my anointed ones and do no wrong to my prophets." Jews are, the poet believes, God's anointed ones and prophets. God will not permit their oppression, therefore. In fact, despite the narrative of the book of Esther, there is no evidence that Jews in the Babylonian exile experienced any sort of oppression. On the contrary, the diaspora of Babylonia turned out to be one of the greatest successes of Jewish history. The Psalmist's words, then, can be understood as a sort of blessing, and as an alternative view of diaspora itself: God, for various reasons, wished Jews to find homes in diasporas as well as in the Holy Land, and God assured their protection there, whatever the odds.

These examples are but the tip of the proverbial iceberg of what we might call the Jewish "counter-tradition" regarding exile. Indeed, there are many places, whether in focused narratives or entire books, where the biblical authors themselves give expression to this counter-tradition, according to which exile is not to be equated with suffering nor necessarily with punishment.

# 3

# Biblical Narratives of Diaspora

The Bible's history of Israel, from Genesis through Kings, came to formation in the Babylonian exile. The same is true of the books of the major prophets—Isaiah, Jeremiah, and Ezekiel—whose experience of exile was rather direct. Jeremiah witnessed the Babylonian onslaught, Ezekiel went to Babylon with the exiles, and Second Isaiah (the prophet whose voice commences in chapter 40 of that book)—known as "Isaiah of the Exile"—lived in Babylon and promised return therefrom. For the authors behind these books, the "exile as punishment" explanation explored earlier was essential, helping them make sense of what Israel had experienced.

But while this scheme explained the pain of exile, it did not explain its comforts. The simple fact is that a one-sided, sorrow-laden take on exile could not have rung true, as it did not accurately mirror the experience of exile. Sure, exile began with fear and alarm, loss and sorrow. But, before long, exile also offered home, a home in which Jews could meditate on their fate and offer creative,[1] unprecedented reflections on the place of God in history. The literature had to give voice to that experience too, for without such honest expressions, the literature would have been rejected as inadequate. Even the Torah, formed in exile, expresses a keen appreciation of exile and its centrality, not only to the Israelite experience but even to the human experience.

Those who are familiar, in a general way, with the arc of the biblical narrative might readily describe it as directed toward Israelite occupation of the Promised Land. And they would not be completely wrong. From the moment of God's dramatic appearance to Abram in chapter 12 of Genesis, when God directs Abram to leave his birthplace to a land newly promised, much of the narrative seems devoted to describing the circuitous steps by which that promise is ultimately fulfilled. But exile itself is also one of the Bible's central themes, and it is a theme treated with far more complexity than is generally observed.[2] How could it be otherwise, given the fact that many of the biblical books, from the Torah onward, were the product of exile?

32   EMBRACING EXILE

The Bible lays out a more nuanced view of the meaning of exile almost literally from the very beginning. The Bible's story of humankind begins with the first humans—Adam and Eve—in the Garden of Eden, humanity's first home. But that home does not last long (according to one rabbinic midrash, the sojourn in the Garden lasted less than a day!). Eating, against God's command, from the tree of the knowledge of good and evil, Eve and Adam are exiled from the Garden, to find a home in what we might call "the real world."

This last point is crucial. While exile from the Garden is contemporaneous with the challenge of laboring for one's food, the expulsion as such is not represented as punishment; the punishment came earlier (Genesis 3:16–19), when the curses to Eve and Adam—pain in childbirth and struggle in producing food—were articulated. Rather, the expulsion was to assure that Adam and Eve not eat from the Garden's Tree of Life, which would have allowed them to live forever, effectively becoming gods (Genesis 3:22–24). At the same time, on some fundamental level, Eve and Adam in the Garden were not yet fully human. Until eating from the tree, they presumably did not know good and evil, and they thus lived without full temptation or the free-will to choose their path. They also bore little responsibility for their world, as what they needed was provided for them. Thus, it was the exile itself that ushered the first humans into the world of full humanness. Exiting the womb of the Garden, humanity, in its full sense, was born.

The next biblical exile comes at what is arguably the key transition point in Israel's history: God's calling of Abram. True, that calling brought the first hint of a land to which Abram and his offspring would be directed. But the actual words of God's call are pregnant with an alternative meaning.

God begins God's call to Abram with these words: "Go from your land, from your birthplace, and from the house of your father to the land I will show you" (Genesis 12:1). Clearly and unambiguously, God is here asking Abram to exile himself in order to begin his appointed mission. That this will be an exile is expressed emphatically in the repeated pronominal suffix of the biblical language; God declares to Abram, "leave *your* home, *your* birthplace, the house of *your* father." To undertake their mission, Abram and Sarai must leave their home. They must distance themselves from the place of their birth, the place of their personal histories, the place where they have lived their whole, already long lives (Abram is seventy-five years old when he is called; see 12:4). Only by submitting to exile may Abram effectuate the covenant that would change all of history. Jewish history, like human history, begins with an exile from home.

Astoundingly, no sooner have Abram and Sarai come to the land than they are forced to leave it. Facing famine in the land, Abram and Sarai head to Egypt, the "breadbasket" of the ancient Near East. On their way, Abram is fearful that he will be endangered when the Egyptians see how beautiful Sarai is (she is at least sixty-five years old at the time!); will they kill him in order to take her? But the story makes clear: Abram flourishes and Sarai is protected by God, who afflicts Pharoah with plagues (for all of this, see Genesis 12:10–20). This is a point that should not be rushed over—God is with the patriarch and matriarch of Israel even in exile, protecting them from harm against the powerful.

It is hard not to ask how the experience of Babylonian exile may have shaped this narrative, which presumably circulated in oral form for centuries before it came to this final, literary form. The families of Abraham and Sarah originated in what we might call "Greater Babylon." What does it mean to say that leaving that homeland, that family home, itself counts as exile? And what is the significance of the fact that the same family, once arriving in the Promised Land, immediately leaves that land to survive? Babylonian Jews early in their exile already experienced Babylon as a home, and they knew they were protected there. Is this what they express, however indirectly, in their version of the story of the origins of their people? It is impossible to know the answers to these questions, but we cannot dismiss this conjecture.

This story is not the last time in the Torah's narrative that Israel will descend into Egypt. It is to Egypt that the clan of Abraham and Sarah's grand- and great-grandchildren travel, beginning a generations-long experience of—at first—flourishing, and then slavery. It is in Egypt that Joseph rises from captive to governor, second in power only to Pharoah himself. And it is in the delivery from Egypt that God's covenantal promise (see Genesis 15:13–14) is fulfilled. Crucially, central to God's promise is the assurance of offspring, and it is the fertility of the clan in Egypt that transforms the clan into a people, into a nation. Indeed, it is in Egypt that the clan of Abraham and Sarah became the people of Israel; as Jews would later declare when bringing the first-fruits in Jerusalem: "He became there a great nation" (Deuteronomy 26:5). In fact, as many have observed, to be born as a people, Israel had to pass through the "narrow place"—this the meaning of the Semitic name for Egypt. The Egyptian "exile" was the womb

34 EMBRACING EXILE

of Israel. It was within that exile that Israel was formed and from which it was born.

If Egypt was the womb, then the Sinai Desert was the original diaspora—prefiguring future diasporas. The text of the Torah recounts Israel's journeys through the desert over the course of forty years. Wandering from place to place, from encampment to encampment, the "Jews" in the desert were history's first "wandering Jews." What is easy to miss when reading about these various travels, though, is that, aside from the first year in the desert and the last, Israel traveled relatively little during these forty years. According to the figuring of Rashi—the greatest of medieval Jewish Bible commentators—during the middle thirty-eight years of their sojourn, Israel had to uproot itself and travel to the next camp only twenty times (see Rashi's comment on Numbers 33:1). What does this teach us, Rashi asks. That God had mercy on Israel, assuring them rest and comfort in this first diaspora. If the desert is a prototype for future diasporas—and it seems to me that it must be, as sacred history always prefigures subsequent history—then the lesson of the desert must be that diaspora is not always unrest and wandering. In fact, life in the desert was not so bad.

In the Torah's account, as the tribes of Israel approached the end of their desert wanderings, a question arose that forces us to focus on the legitimacy of life outside the Land, even if the Land stands as fulfillment of the covenantal promise. To make possible Israel's entrance into the Land, the tribes, under Moses' command, had to conquer Midian and its adjacent territories (Numbers 31), on account of Midian's refusal (along with Moab) to permit Israel's peaceful passage (see Numbers 22:2–7). The conquest accomplished, the tribes camped comfortably in Trans-Jordan, as Moses and his successor, Joshua, prepared for the conquest to come. This territory being already in the possession of Israel, the tribes of Reuven and Gad realized that it was perfect for the raising and sustenance of their cattle, so they approached Moses and the other leaders of Israel with a request: "This is cattle-country, and your servants have cattle...do not force us to cross the Jordan" (Numbers 32:4–5).

Israel's settling in the Land had been the goal since her exodus from Egypt forty years earlier; indeed, it had been the apparent destination of this people since the covenant was first articulated to Abraham generations earlier. So there is no surprise when Moses responds to Reuven's and Gad's request with anger. What does surprise, however, is the ultimate focus of that anger, as well as the way it is resolved.

In the Torah's account, Moses immediately recalls the incident of the spies who misled Israel those many years before, as a consequence of which the generation that had exited Egypt was not permitted to enter the Land. He accuses the Reubenites and Gadites of likewise turning the hearts of the current generation aside, seeming to suggest that, once again, their sin is to propose that Israel—or at least part of it—need not enter the Land. As it turns out, however, this is not their offense at all. In response to Moses' accusation, they offer to build shelter for their "flocks and children" (32:16) in Trans-Jordan, while they themselves take up arms at the head of the armies of Israel that cross the Jordan. "We will not return to our homes," they promise, "until the Children of Israel settle in their portion" (32:18)— meaning the rest of the Children of Israel, whose portion will indeed be found in the Land of promise. This proposal shows the Reuvenites and Gadites as responsive to Moses' fear that their refusal to fight for the Land would weaken the resolve of the other tribes. But it maintains their resolve to make their home outside of the Land.

It is perhaps shocking, then, that Moses accepts their terms (32:20–30), agreeing that, if they fight at the forefront of the conquering Israelite troops, endangering their own lives in solidarity with their brethren from other tribes, then they will be free to return to their chosen homes in Trans-Jordan, in diaspora, if you will. Notably, nowhere in Moses' statement is there a hint of condemnation of Israelites settling outside the Land. Evidently, Moses' concern had not been settlement outside the promised Land at all, but fear of the loss of courage of the rest of Israel if the Reuvenites and Gadites broke solidarity in the face of battle. That the successful result of this agreement would be that a not insignificant portion of the Israelites would make their home outside the Land did not seem to bother Moses (who himself never entered the Land). In other words, even the authoritative leader of Israel, in the authoritative book—the Torah— often called by his name (the five books of Moses), expressed no misgivings that some of Israel, from the very beginning, would live as "diaspora" Jews.

Supporting this reading is the great medieval commentator and mystic, Nachmanides. Nachmanides notices (in his comment on Numbers 32:33) that from the initial approach to Moses through the negotiation over terms, it is only the Reuvenites and Gadites who ask for permission to settle in Trans-Jordan, but when Moses finally apportions them the Trans-Jordanian land, he includes "half of the tribe of Menasseh" in his distribution. Where did this new group come from? Nachmanides suggests that "when he

36 EMBRACING EXILE

[Moses] apportioned the land to the two tribes, he saw that the land was too big for them and he sought others who would want to settle with them, and there were people from the tribe of Menasseh who so desired." Not only does Nachmanides sense here (correctly, in my opinion) that Moses had no misgivings about a portion of the people settling outside the Land, but he even suggests that Moses supported it, to the extent that, if there was more land to be settled, it should be settled. And whether or not we go along with Nachmanides' precise reconstruction of the Torah's events, we must grant that he is right to notice the expansion of the Trans-Jordanian population in Moses' distribution. This is not a minor detail. A significant minority of the tribes of Israel—two and one-half out of twelve tribes—made their homes outside the Land. They would be the first "Jews" to do so, but certainly not the last.

Crucially, the Torah—Judaism's most sacred book—ends in the desert of Trans-Jordan, before the people pass over into the Promised Land. This did not have to be the case. As many scholars have observed, the book of Joshua, in which the people enter the land, is, historically and literarily speaking, a natural extension of the Torah, and the Pentateuch (the five-book Torah) might just as easily have been a Hexateuch (a six-book Torah). Why then, we must ask, did the Torah's sacred narrative end outside the Land?

Scholars of the biblical text believe that the Torah as we know it is a product of the Babylonian exile. There must be a connection between that exilic experience and the works produced there, including the Torah in its final shape. So our question must be what was it about the Babylonian exile that led to a five-book Torah, whose narrative ends outside the Land, as opposed to a six-book Torah, where entry into the Land represents the fulfillment of the divine plan? In the immensely insightful observations of the great twentieth-century biblical scholar, Yehezkel Kaufmann, the answer is this:

With land, temple, and king gone, only one contact with the holy was left: the divine word.... Israel's religious self-confidence having been shattered, it sought to re-establish its relationship with God upon the written word....

In crystallizing and sealing the Torah, a way was opened to overcome the ethnic-territorial limitation of the old religion. The Torah was destined to leave the land and the temple and to accompany Israel from exile to exile. The product of the mood of exile, it was well adapted for the needs of a dispersed people.[3]

A product of the exile, intended to serve the needs of a people in exile, it could only end its account of Israel's most sacred history in exile.

This is a most extraordinary claim. What we understand, through this insight, is that whatever the Torah's promise might be with respect to the Land, its whole purpose is to assure that the people of Torah will not need the Land. When Israel would ask, "Where does this all lead?" the answer, the Torah taught, was not necessarily to the Land. More than anything, it was to the Torah itself. The covenantal law of God, revealed to Israel in exile—at Mount Sinai—would serve them forever in exile. At the most fundamental level, the covenant might have promised the land, but it did not need it.

To Kaufmann's observation, we must add two others. First, the Torah is commonly known as the "five books of Moses," and it was referred to by Jews after the exile as the "Torah of Moses." This association with Moses is significant, for Moses—arguably the most important "Jew" in Jewish history—was himself a child of exile (Egypt), one who never stepped foot in the Promised Land. The liberator from Egypt, the receiver of Torah, the lawgiver, was himself a "diaspora Jew." What greater affirmation of exile could there be? Second, by ending in exile, the Torah reflects the experience of the people who gave it its final shape. The children of the Exodus, standing in Trans-Jordan, are a reflection of the Jews in Babylon, themselves on the other side of the river. As the most sacred part of Israel's sacred history, the Torah declares that exile, too, can be a stage for sacred history—an affirmation of the lives of the exiles in Babylon. Some exiles might return to the Land, and Jerusalem and its Temple might be rebuilt, but this affirmation could never be erased. What begins in exile leads back to exile. Once and forever, exile is an essential part of the Jewish story.

From the end of the Torah to the end of II Kings, the history the Bible recounts is the history of conquest, settlement, and ultimate exile from the Land. The Promised Land is undeniably central to the Bible's scheme of history. Furthermore, though biblical history ends, in the common memory, with exile, the truth is that that history actually ends with return to the Land, however tentative and insecure that return may be. Still, if there is post-exilic Jewish life in the Land, there is at the same time ongoing Jewish life in diaspora, a life in diaspora that will never end. Given the reality of exile, what are Jews in exile to make of it, at least according to biblical teachings?

The most famous biblical advice for life in exile comes from the biblical prophet Jeremiah. Living in the latter part of the seventh century and the

## 38 EMBRACING EXILE

early sixth century BCE, Jeremiah was himself witness to the destruction of the Temple and the exile of at least the educated and affluent classes of Judah to Babylon. Anticipating that the exiles of Judah would be restored to their former home in seventy years, Jeremiah communicated with them, instructing them how to conduct their affairs in exile in the meantime. He did this in a letter, which the 29th chapter of the book of Jeremiah introduces in these words:

> These are the words of the letter that Jeremiah the prophet sent from Jerusalem to the surviving elders among the exiles and to the priests, to the prophets and to all the people that Nebuchadnezzar had exiled from Jerusalem to Babylon. ² (This was after King Jehoiachin and the queen mother, the court officials, the princes of Judah and Jerusalem, the skilled workers, and the artisans had left Jerusalem.) ³ By the hand of Elasah son of Shaphan and Gemariah son of Hilkiah, whom Zedekiah king of Judah sent to Nebuchadnezzar, King of Babylon.

In the letter, Jeremiah, speaking for God, recommends to the exiles that they:

> ⁵ Build houses and settle; plant gardens and eat their fruits. ⁶ Marry women and give birth to sons and daughters; take wives for your sons and give your daughters to men, so that they may have sons and daughters. Increase in number there; do not decrease. ⁷ Also, seek the peace of the city to which I have exiled you. Pray to the LORD for it, because if it prospers, you too will prosper.

According to Jeremiah's communication of the word of God, exile is not meant to be onerous, nor is Israel supposed to treat exile as an occasion for self-affliction leading to expiation (as we might expect if the primary purpose of exile were punishment). On the contrary, exile is meant to be *home*, in which Jews settle comfortably, create a future, and maintain peace with their neighbors. As long as Jews are in exile, Jews should invest in exile. Indeed, this pragmatic (but not only pragmatic!) advice was so good that the Babylonian diaspora became the most enduring and peaceful diaspora in all of Jewish history.

Jeremiah's contemporary, Ezekiel, shares a less-pragmatically oriented vision that is no less important in its legacy for our understanding of Jewish diasporas. Ezekiel was a "prophet of exile," that is to say, he himself actually went into the Babylonian exile (Jeremiah left the Land as well, but he went to Egypt). And what he experienced in exile is beyond the true reach of the (nonprophetic) human imagination.

Ezekiel's book begins with the prophet among the exiles "by the Chebar Canal" in Babylon, where Ezekiel saw a vision of the Lord. Ezekiel reports:

> I looked, and lo, a stormy wind came out of the north—a huge cloud and flashing fire, surrounded by a radiance; and in the center of it, in the center of the fire, a gleam as of amber. In the center of it were also figures of four creatures. (Ezekiel 1:4–5)

There follows a vivid description of the divine chariot and the creatures that supported it, along with the Bible's most explicit description of God Godself.

Ezekiel's encounter with God continues in chapter 3, where God commands him, "Go to your people, the exile community." The divine spirit carries him away, at which time he hears "a great roaring sound...with the sound of the wings of the creatures beating against one another, and the sound of the wheels beside them." As his report makes clear, Ezekiel is literally "standing in the Presence of the Lord,"—notably, in a place called "Tel Aviv, by the Chebar Canal."

Readers often read these texts for their astounding, unique descriptions of God enthroned on God's chariot, and to be sure, they are well worth reading for this reason. But such a reading misses one of the most important elements of Ezekiel's reports, that is: this direct, unmediated experience of God is happening in Babylon! (And yes, it is the height of irony that the first modern Jewish city in what would become the State of Israel was named Tel Aviv, after a biblical city that was actually in Babylon.)

In the ancient world, gods were often understood to be tied to a territory. Indeed, it is fair to imagine that most ancient Israelites understood the God of Israel to have a home in the Temple in Jerusalem. At the very least, they would have believed that the Temple was the place where God could be most intimately encountered. It was not obvious that such an encounter would be possible if the Temple were destroyed, and certainly not likely that it could happen outside the Holy Land itself.

It is this background that makes Ezekiel's report so radical. Ezekiel testifies that God's immediate, full-powered presence may be found anywhere, even in exile. When Israel left the land, therefore, they did not leave God, nor did God leave them. God can be with Israel wherever she finds herself, without restriction. So the condition that might readily have been understood as an expression of God's desire to distance Godself from the betraying partner—the partner who had strayed with other gods—could no longer be understood this way, for even when one of the partners (Israel) was expelled from home, the covenantal partners could and would be together. Indeed, this is a model that would serve virtually all future diasporas. Again and again, Jews would claim that God's presence accompanied them in their wanderings. If God could be encountered anywhere, then why would Jews ever need to insist on making their home anywhere in particular? Where God could be met—that would always be home.

Jeremiah and Ezekiel were witnesses to the beginnings of the Babylonian exile. What they could not have known (except by prophecy) is that the Babylonian empire would be conquered by the Persian, and that the Persian king, Cyrus, would allow Jews to return to their Land. What they perhaps also could not have imagined is that when the offer of return came, some Jews who had followed their advice—building homes in exile and maintaining an active relationship with God there—would be so comfortable in Babylon that they would refuse to leave their new homes and return to the Land of their grandparents. Those who remained in exile would justify their choice, a justification that would leave echoes in the subsequent literature of the Jews. Jews who returned to the Land also had to know that their brothers and sisters who stayed behind continued to live good Jewish lives, and they would have been challenged to understand that reality as well.

## Grand Narratives of Exile

Exile/diaspora is not only a theme that weaves itself, often in subtle ways, through the Bible's many non-exilic narratives. It also serves as a fundamental focus of several biblical narratives, including independent books devoted to exilic life.

The first extended biblical tale of diaspora is the story of Joseph. This story, found in the last many chapters of the book of Genesis (beginning in chapter 37), had to exist in one form or another for generations before it came to its final expression in the exilic Torah of Moses. But it is preserved, in its received form, in that exilic Torah, and it has much to say about the diasporic condition. Because it is in the Torah, it has great authority, as a result of which it would influence many subsequent tales of Jewish life in the diaspora. As part of the Torah, which is read by Jews cyclically, year after year, in the synagogue, it is also the best-known "diaspora-story" in Jewish tradition.

The Joseph story is the second-longest personal narrative in the Torah, after that of Moses; it is even longer than the account of the life of Abraham, and though Moses is a central character in most of the Torah, the Torah is actually little concerned with the details of his personal life. Why is so much attention devoted to Joseph? If Joseph is the first diaspora Jew, a representative of the diaspora experience, then it makes sense that Jews of the Babylonian exile, shaping their inheritance into what we know of as the Torah, would devote considerable time to him. What did they mean to say by offering us as a model the Joseph about whom we read? To answer this question, we shall have to read the Torah's account at some length, asking how exile shapes the experience and the outcome.

According to the Torah, Joseph is first brought to Egypt as a youth, after having been sold by his jealous brothers to a passing caravan. Once in Egypt, Joseph is sold to one of Pharoah's officers, Potiphar, in whose household he then serves (chapter 39). In such a setting, Joseph might fear for his well-being. But, the text tells us, Joseph flourishes there, for, as his master, too, quickly recognizes, "the Lord is with him" (39:3). The Jew in diaspora is favored by and protected by God.

This does not mean that Joseph's life in Egypt will be without incident. On the contrary, Joseph, blessed as he is, is also beautiful, as a result of which he attracts the eye of his master's wife. She seeks to seduce him, and upon his rebuffing her, she accuses him of having attacked her. He is, as a consequence, thrust into prison. But he will not languish there. In prison, too, God is with him, and the chief jailor therefore entrusts him with oversight of the prison and all its prisoners (chapter 39, end). Under these conditions, it is fair to say, Joseph does not suffer.

In prison, Joseph's dream-interpreting skills (again a result of God's being with him) come to be known, so when, two years later, Pharoah requires someone to interpret his dreams, Joseph is called upon to perform the task. Interpreting Pharoah's dreams of seven emaciated cows consuming seven fat cows, and then seven withered stalks of grain consuming seven full stalks, as prophecies of seven years of abundance followed by (consumed by) seven years of deprivation, Joseph advises in chapter 41 that:

42  EMBRACING EXILE

³³ Pharaoh should look for a discerning and wise man and put him in charge of the land of Egypt. ³⁴ Let Pharaoh appoint commissioners over the land to take a fifth of the harvest of Egypt during the seven years of fullness. ³⁵ They should collect all the food of these good years that are coming and store up the grain under the authority of Pharaoh, food in the cities for keeping. ³⁶ This food should be held in reserve for the land, for the seven years of famine that will come upon Egypt, so that the land may not be ruined by famine.

Pharaoh approves of Joseph's advice, asking, naively, who might wisely fill such a role. He then quickly realizes that only Joseph can be the one, and he begins a restructuring of power that will raise Joseph to the highest rank in Egypt. Consider Pharaoh's precise words and actions:

³⁹ Then Pharaoh said to Joseph, "Since God has made all this known to you, there is no one as discerning and wise as you. ⁴⁰ You shall be in charge of my house, and by your word shall all my people be directed. Only with respect to the throne will I be greater than you."

⁴¹ So Pharaoh said to Joseph, "See, I have put you in charge of the whole land of Egypt." ⁴² Then Pharaoh removed his ring from his hand and put it on Joseph's hand. He dressed him in robes of fine linen and put a gold chain around his neck. ⁴³ He had him ride in the chariot of his second-in-command, and people shouted before him, "*Avrekh*!" Thus he put him in charge of the whole land of Egypt.

⁴⁴ Then Pharaoh said to Joseph, "I am Pharaoh, but without your word no one will lift his hand or his foot in all Egypt." ⁴⁵ Pharaoh called Joseph by the name Zaphenath-Paneah and gave him Asenath daughter of Potiphera, priest of On, as his wife. And Joseph went out over the land of Egypt.

These steps are filled with meaning. On top of his explicit declaration that Joseph will be in charge of the palace, and even of the "whole land of Egypt," Pharaoh cements this appointment with several ritual steps: he takes his own ring and places it on Joseph's finger, thus transferring his authority. He dresses Joseph in royal robes with matching ornament and appoints for him a royal chariot. Finally, Pharaoh gives Joseph a new name, effectively "converting" him to new status as an Egyptian, and he marries Joseph to the daughter of an Egyptian priest, thus tying him to Egyptian nobility. As the text explicitly declares, there would be no one in Egypt superior to Joseph aside from Pharaoh himself.

So what does Joseph do with his new-found power? As the effective leader of Egypt, he takes immediate steps to prepare for the years of deprivation:

> ⁴⁶ Joseph was thirty years old when he stood before Pharaoh king of Egypt. And Joseph went out from Pharaoh's presence and traveled throughout Egypt. ⁴⁷ During the seven years of plenty the land produced abundantly. ⁴⁸ And he collected all the food produced in those seven years in Egypt and stored it in the cities; the food grown in the fields surrounding it he brought within it. ⁴⁹ Joseph stored up grain, which was like the sand of the sea in abundance, until he stopped counting because it was beyond counting.

Being prepared for the lean years, Egypt—and the rest of the "world" (the world known to the narrator)—is saved from starvation. Thanks to Joseph, the world survives.

Immediately after its recounting of Joseph's elevation, the Torah interrupts its "world-history" narrative to report on important developments in Joseph's personal life. In Genesis, chapter 41, verse 50 and following, we learn that Joseph and his wife (as you will recall, the daughter of an Egyptian priest!) have two sons, one of whom Joseph names Menashe and the second Ephraim. Names are always meaningful, and Joseph makes explicit the meaning of his name choices. "Menashe" is related to forgetting, and it is meant to communicate that, in his current state, Joseph has forgotten his hardship and "all of his paternal house" (verse 51). Ephraim is related to fertility, and the name is meant to declare Joseph's feeling that "God has made me fertile in the land of my affliction" (verse 52). Experientially, Joseph has left his birth house behind. What happened in Canaan stayed in Canaan. Finding himself now at the top of the Egyptian power-structure, Joseph feels the full fruit of his own flourishing. His exile has become his home, and, near the height of his power, nothing will hold him back.

A large part of the following chapters describes the drama that transpires between Joseph and his brothers, who come to Egypt from Canaan to obtain food to survive. The brothers do not recognize Joseph, who is by appearance and language fully Egyptian, but he recognizes them. This

44   EMBRACING EXILE

allows him, for a time, to play with their fate, out of spite for what they did to him by selling him to the trade caravan long before. Finally, though, he loses his taste for the game and reveals himself to them, telling them not to fear what he might do. On the contrary, he says, "God sent me before you to preserve life…it was not you who sent me here, but God; He has made me a father to Pharaoh, and lord of all his house and ruler over all the land of Egypt" (Genesis 45:5–8). Joseph articulates an important understanding—a "revisionist history," if you will—of his presence in diaspora: God sent him there for a purpose. It would not be an exaggeration to say that Jews through the ages have understood their diaspora fate in much the same way.

For diaspora Jews through the ages, Joseph and his fate have been emblematic of what a Jew can accomplish in exile. Through a combination of smarts and charisma—and thanks, in significant part, to the fact that "God is with him"—the Jew can be called upon to play an active, even crucial role in the court. Thereby, he can serve not only the king and the king's people, but the interests of his Jewish brothers and sisters as well. He can leave his foreignness behind, even while remaining a Jew. His Jewishness need not be a liability, and his status as a "guest" in a "foreign" home need not be burdensome; indeed, he need not feel foreign at all. With Joseph, the figure of the "court-Jew" has been established, and it will be recreated many times through the centuries.

To be fair to the legacy of Joseph, though, there is one other part of his story for which we must account. According to the biblical narrative (Genesis 47), as the famine progresses, year after year, those in need of food become more and more desperate. But according to the policy instituted by Joseph, the food in storage will not be distributed for free; it must, instead, be paid for, and the payment becomes Pharaoh's property. At first, the people spend their money on food, but when their money runs out, they trade their livestock for food. When they have no more livestock, having little left to lose other than their lives, they offer to sell their land and themselves; as they say, "we with our land will become slaves to Pharaoh" (47:19).

The story continues:

So Joseph bought all the land of Egypt for Pharaoh. All the Egyptians sold their fields, because the famine was severe upon them; and the land became Pharaoh's. As for the people, he transferred them to cities, from one end of Egypt to the other.

It was Joseph, the story asserts, who made Pharaoh absolute ruler over Egypt, master of land, person, and beast. To frame this in slightly different terms: rather than offering a humane mechanism in response to famine, he cemented his own position as second to Pharaoh by increasing Pharaoh's power beyond measure. Whatever our understanding of Joseph's motivation, its result was a monarch with absolute authority over the land and its peoples.

It is hard to read this without noting the bitter irony of what Joseph did. After Joseph's death, another Pharaoh arose who took advantage of what Joseph had created to enslave and oppress the Children of Israel. Against this background, we may now recognize that, to a certain extent, Israel enslaved to the later Pharoah was little different than the enslaved people of Egypt during Joseph's lifetime. At the very least, it is fair to say that, according to the biblical account, the later Pharaoh was able to do what he did only thanks to the earlier machinations of Joseph.

This plot formulation may be read as the Torah's warning about the Jew assuming power in the foreign court. On the one hand, Israel needs the wise Jew in the court to win the ruler's favor and thus assure Jewish security. On the other hand, even "successful" advice might backfire, and what the Jewish courtier of one generation does to protect Jewish interests might later come back to bite Jews in the heel. The Jew in power had better be careful, the text warns; but is this not true for any advisor of any king?

To what extent, we must wonder, do the diaspora lessons of the Joseph story reflect the experiences and concerns of Jews of the Babylonian exile who gave the story its final form? We shall never be able to answer this question with certainty. But it is reasonable to assume that the Joseph story was, in certain ways, a mirror of their experience, expressing the recognition that diaspora could be the source both of salvation and of danger for the Jew. Jews could flourish in diaspora—this Babylonian Jews knew for sure. Diaspora could even be the cradle of their fundamental identity. But a home among others could also be fragile. One generation's comfort could yield to the next generation's oppression. Whether they realized it or not, the scribes and scholars behind the Torah's story were saying something about their own condition. But, as it turns out, not only about their own, for future generations would have similar experiences.

Whatever we make of the Joseph story as a reflection of the diaspora condition, we need not hesitate to draw such connections with a later biblical narrative of diaspora—arguably the major such narrative—that is, the book

46   EMBRACING EXILE

of Esther (also known as the scroll of Esther, or the *megillah*). This book is, from beginning to end, a story of the fate of the Jewish exiles in Persia (the imperial successor to Babylonia), and it has commonly been understood as a story of the dangers of exile. Forming the ritual focus of the Jewish holiday of Purim, it has for many centuries been recited annually before the congregation to great horror and joy. Every time the name of the story's "antisemitic" villain, Haman, is spoken, the congregation erupts in cacophonous response in their attempt to wipe out the memory of their hated enemy. By virtue of its ritualized annual repetition, the scroll of Esther has represented the dangers and vicissitudes of every exile, and Haman has stood for every Jew-hater.

But, while this is true of the book's reception, it is fundamentally not true about the book's actual plot or purpose.[4] If anything, the book is about Jewish triumph in the diaspora, even if that triumph is occasionally challenged. And we should expect nothing else, for Esther is the product of a very successful diaspora, a continuation of the original Babylonian diaspora/exile. The book exhibits a profound and even intimate knowledge of the details of the Persian court, suggesting that the author of its main narrative was a witness to that court and the local culture, even if only after the fact.[5] He was almost certainly a Jew of the Persian diaspora himself. This means that we can rely on this book for a relatively accurate account of the experience of the diaspora Jew of that time and place (Persia, fourth or third century BCE). Though we know relatively little about the specifics of the history of Jews in Persia in that period, as the documentation, outside of Esther, is sparse, the very silence of voices suggests that Jews mostly lived comfortably and at peace. Indeed, this is the picture that emerges from Esther, however much such an understanding might surprise readers who think they already know the book.

The story of Esther begins with the king, Ahasuerus, holding a celebratory banquet for his courtiers and other dignitaries. In a state of at least mild inebriation, the king decides to enhance the festivities by commanding that his queen, Vashti, appear before those assembled wearing her royal crown—meaning, apparently, only her crown. The queen refuses, at which point she is deposed and a comprehensive search for her replacement commences. It is at this point that Jews enter the picture.

The first Jew to whom we are introduced is Mordechai, who is only three generations removed from the Babylonian exile. Nevertheless, he lives in "Shushan [Susa] the fortress" (or "citadel")—not a casual claim. Mordechai is the guardian of his cousin, Esther, a beautiful Jewish orphan. As a young, beautiful virgin, Esther is conscripted into the process to identify a new queen for Ahasuerus.

The process of preparing to "meet" the king (that is, to sleep with the king) is a lengthy one: young women are brought into special palace quarters where, under the supervision of Hegai, "guardian of the women," they undergo preparations with oils and fragrances, until their turn to spend the night with the king arrives. Esther, by virtue of her great natural beauty, finds favor in Hegai's eyes, and over the course of her year of preparation, she is treated particularly well.

Crucially, before Esther entered the harem quarters, commencing her preparation for her night with the king, Mordechai advised her to keep silent about her Jewish identity, allowing for her surprise self-revelation as a Jew at a key point later in the narrative. But even with such silence, we must wonder how she is able to hide her Jewishness. Is there nothing about her conduct to give her identity away? Certainly observant Jews of other generations and places could not have gotten away with such anonymity. Evidently, Esther neither looks nor speaks any differently than her non-Jewish Persian sisters. There could also be nothing in the way she eats or in her personal practices that identifies her as a Jew. Otherwise, living in the close and intimate quarters of the harem, her identity would quickly be known, whatever she does or doesn't say. By their third generation in Babylon, the narrative suggests, Jews like Esther were fully acculturated (some would say "assimilated").

Now, Mordechai's advice to Esther to remain silent about her Jewish identity has commonly been understood to be a result of his concern for antisemitism. But this attributed motivation actually makes little sense. Mordechai himself is perfectly public about his Jewish identity, despite the fact that he "sits at the royal gate"—not a casual description of a location but a designation of an official position; only the king's advisors were said to "sit at the royal gate."[6] It is hard to support the notion, then, that Mordechai's advice is a product of fear for Esther's security. We shall never know for sure the reason Mordechai tells Esther to remain quiet about her identity, but perhaps the answer is no more complicated than that it is necessary as a plot device; only if Ahasuerus is unfamiliar with Esther's national identity can he accept Haman's proposals against the Jews and then, when he becomes familiar with Esther's identity, intervene against Haman to protect Esther and her people.

48  EMBRACING EXILE

It is Mordechai's relationship with Haman that propels the notion that antisemitism was endemic to the Persian setting, endangering the lives of Jews who lived there. But a closer look at this story shows that such a conclusion can hardly be defended.[7] Chapter 3 of Esther begins with Ahasuerus' raising of Haman above all his other officials (we are not told why). The other courtiers who "are in the royal gate" concede this shift in power and bow down to Haman, but Mordechai refuses, for an unspecified reason. To be sure, the text observes that Mordechai told the others he was a Jew, but this is unlikely to be the reason for Mordechai's refusal to bow to Haman. There is absolutely nothing in all of Jewish law that would prohibit a Jew from paying obeisance to a royal official in this way, and, as Carey Moore remarks, "Jews regularly bowed down to kings,"[8] so there is no reason to assume that Mordechai's Jewishness somehow gets in the way here. (It is probably because of this difficulty establishing a reason for Mordechai's refusal to bow down that the rabbinic Midrash imagines Haman to have worn an image of his god on his chest; bowing down to such an image would surely be forbidden.) The most likely explanation, therefore, is that Mordechai is unwilling to grant the superiority of a fellow courtier. In his insane furor over this refusal, Haman plots to destroy not only Mordechai but also Mordechai's people.

Listen to Haman's report to the king in pursuit of his designs against Mordechai and his people:

> There is a certain people, scattered and dispersed among the peoples in all the provinces of your realm, and their laws are different from those of any other people and they do not obey the King's laws; and it is not in the King's interest to tolerate them. If it please the King, let an edict be drawn up for their destruction. (3:8–9)

Haman then adds: "and I will pay ten thousand talents of silver to the stewards for deposit in the King's treasury."

This is a provocative claim, one that, if true, might provide good reason for anti-Jewish action. But as it is in the voice of an undeniably unreliable narrator, we have to analyze it with appropriate skepticism. The first part of Haman's claim—that Jews are scattered across the entire empire—may well be correct, as it serves Haman's interests not one wink. If correct, then it is rather remarkable, for two reasons: first, it indicates that only a few generations into their exile, Jews already constitute a widespread diaspora; they are already, we might say, a diaspora people. They do not cluster in one place; instead, they willingly scatter to new homes, far and wide, where they can comfortably settle with their friends and neighbors and pursue their mostly modest dreams. In fact, the notion that Jews are already a diaspora people is reinforced by the fact, introduced earlier, that Jews have been in the Babylonian and then Persian empires for 3–4 generations. Both the prophetic and the historical record make it clear that Cyrus permitted Jewish exiles to return to their homeland in "seventy years," which would have preceded the events described here (Ahasuerus, whichever Persian king he may have been, certainly came after Cyrus, the first of the Persian kings). That means that Mordechai and Esther and other Jews in the empire are not there because they have no choice. On the contrary, they could have returned to their ancestral land but did not. They have chosen to remain in diaspora.[9]

So what about Haman's next claim? Are the laws of the Jews different from the laws of other peoples? There is no reason to doubt that this is so, as the same claim could be made about the laws of any subject people in the empire relative to the laws of other peoples. Notably, empires generally tolerate such differences, so there is nothing about this characterization that would jeopardize the Jewish position. Accordingly, it must be Haman's last point, that Jews do not follow the king's law, that is the damning one. But is it true? Can we accept Haman's testimony as mirroring some reality? Given Haman's murderous hatred of Jews on account of Mordechai's disrespect, there is every reason to doubt it, as it is the self-serving linchpin of his argument. Besides, later evidence, at least, would suggest that Jewish law does not make it impossible for Jews to accommodate to local law. Jews have lived in many lands through the ages, observing their own laws while respecting the laws of the lands in which they have found themselves. It is only very few laws, such as those requiring transgression of the Sabbath, that might create trouble for Jews, and conflicts of law have generally been amenable to compromise.

Haman's hatred for Jews is a personal grudge, not evidence of a broadly held feeling. It is an example of the perverse but common human phenomenon according to which hate for a single member of a group is extended to the whole group. There is nothing in this story to suggest that anyone aside from Haman hates Jews in an active way. King Ahasuerus seems to be manipulated into agreeing to allow Haman to do as he pleases, bearing no ill will of his own.[10] And, the text reports, when citizens of the city of

50 EMBRACING EXILE

Shushan hear what has been decreed against the Jews, "the city of Shushan was dumbfounded." Not Jews in the city of Shushan, but the citizenry of Shushan as a whole. For them, the endangerment of Jews brings not joy but horror. Now, it is true that the text speaks, near the end of the story, of the "enemies" of the Jews (see 8:13, 9:1, 9:5, and 9:22), and even, if translated literally, of "those who hate them" (9:1), but it seems clear that these faceless "enemies" are merely those who are willing to blindly execute the royal decree promulgated at Haman's instigation. It is Haman, according to Esther's own identification, who is "the adversary and enemy" of the Jews (7:6). The decree against them is a product of his plotting alone (8:5).

Hearing about the murderous decree provoked by Haman, Esther approaches the king to persuade him to reverse it. At the same time, the king discovers that Mordechai had earlier been instrumental in saving him against a conspiracy to take his life. The king resolves to reward Mordechai for what he had done, and he consults with Haman to determine "what should be done for a man whom the king desires to honor" (6:6). Thinking that the king was alluding to him, Haman recommends full royal treatment: wearing the king's garments and crown, riding the king's horse, and parading through the city to the adulation of the crowds. The king then directs Haman to have all of this done...for Mordechai! After the parade, Haman returns home, forlorn. But instead of finding comfort at home, his advisers and wife respond to him with a warning: "If Mordechai, before whom you have begun to fall, is of Jewish seed, you will not overcome him; you will surely fall before him" (6:13).

What is remarkable about this little episode is that not only has the turn in the plot—Mordechai's elevation over Haman—already suggested that Jews will triumph, but somehow both Haman's wife and advisers know that Jews win. How do they know this? What is it about Jews that causes others to fall before them (and this but a few generations after Jews fell before the armies of Babylon!)? We shall never know. But for our purposes, what is essential is that we recognize that the Jewish author of this Jewish tale of the diaspora already assumes that the Jews' hosts understand that they are blessed—not defeated, not persecuted, but ultimately triumphant, even in their exile.

What remains to be accomplished, plot-wise, is some kind of reversal of the murderous decree earlier instigated by Haman. In chapter 7, Esther reveals her national identity to the king, telling him that she and her people are endangered by what the king, following Haman's advice, had ordered.

No sooner is the king's anger over Haman's scheme expressed than Haman is hung on the stake he had earlier prepared for the (hoped for) execution of Mordechai. The king immediately transfers the royal ring he had earlier given to Haman to Mordechai, and Mordechai and Esther are appointed to the head of the House of Haman. The king then allows Mordechai to compose a new decree allowing Jews to defend themselves against those who would attack them (the earlier decree, having been issued with the royal seal, cannot be actually reversed).

As chapter 8 comes to a close, the author makes it clear that Mordechai has, in the end, effectively been appointed king. Consider the wording of the text:

> Mordechai left the king's presence in royal robes of blue and white, and a great golden crown, and a mantle of fine linen and purple wool. (8:15)

As wearing a king's garb without being a king is forbidden, wearing the king's garb with the approval of the king is to be king. Mordechai and Esther have defeated Haman, Jews will defend themselves against any attackers, and Mordechai has been raised to the height of power in the Persian empire. So how does the empire respond?

> The city of Shushan rang with joyous cries. The Jews enjoyed light and gladness, happiness and honor. And in every province and in every city, when the king's command and decree arrived, there was gladness and joy among the Jews, a feast and a holiday. And many of the people of the land became Jews, for the fear of the Jews fell upon them. (8:15–17)

"The city of Shushan"—not the Jews of Shushan—"was joyous." As at the beginning of this narrative arc, when "the city of Shushan" was saddened upon learning of the fatal fate of the Jews, so here, when the Persian residents of Shushan hear of the reversal of that fate, they respond with joy. The text does not suggest that the Persians harbor hatred for the Jews. On the contrary, at least a significant number of Persians sympathize with the Jews and their condition. In fact, some number of them are willing—if only out of fear of the strength of the Jews and what they might do when the fateful day arrives—to become Jews. Imagine that: it is not the Jews, in this diaspora, who convert out on account of the fear of what might be done to them, but the local gentiles who convert to Judaism out of fear of their vulnerability at the hands of the Jews.

52 EMBRACING EXILE

At this point, all that remains is what might be described as "cleaning-up," when the Jews act against their enemies. No one is able to stand against the Jews (9:2), and even in the fortress of Shushan (9:6) they take action, killing those who would have attacked them. According to the accounting of the text, the Jews, in their "defensive" action, kill 75,000 (!) of their foes (9:16); the text knows of no Jews who lose their lives.

In the end, the narrative emphasizes power and status. First, we are informed that "Mordechai was great in the royal palace, and his reputation spread through all the provinces" (9:4). This is reinforced at the very end of the book, where we learn that "Mordechai the Jew was second only to King Ahasuerus and highly regarded by the Jews and pleasing to the multitude of his brethren, seeking good for his people and interceding for the peace of all his kindred." He has become—like Joseph before him—the classic court Jew, exercising power like a monarch and assuring the welfare of his people in the Persian diaspora.

Ahasuerus was a manipulable king and Haman a "Jew-hater." But Haman became a Jew-hater not out of any prejudice or cultural consensus; rather, having been disrespected by Mordechai "in the king's gate," he sought revenge against Mordechai and his people—an extension that we humans, in our flawed frailty, too often make. There were, evidently, some throughout the empire who, impelled by the king's decree, were willing to act out against the strangers in their midst, but this too is no more than an expression of human awfulness, an awfulness witnessed throughout human history, and which we still often see today. At the same time, according to the "reporting" of this book, there were at least as many gentiles who sympathized with their Jewish neighbors, crying out when they were endangered and rejoicing when they were freed from that danger. Moreover, even those who sympathized with Haman knew that Jews are blessed, that they would triumph in the end. And that is exactly what happened: the Jews killed their enemies, and Mordechai became the effective ruler of the Persian empire.

According to the book of Esther, then, Jews triumph in exile—an exile that is not actually an "exile," that is to say, an experience of punishment, filled with suffering—but a diaspora.[11] And indeed, this is precisely what the Babylonian diaspora continued to be—in reality and in self-image. In reality, Jews in the Babylonian-Iraqi diaspora flourished, living in relative peace for longer than Jews in any other diaspora, and they would develop understandings of that diaspora that supported their diaspora lives, with few misgivings. Esther is the first expression of a Jewish attitude toward this special diaspora—one that, with humor and wisdom, allows for occasional danger (and what people, in any place, has lived without at least occasional danger?) while insisting on fundamental security and even prosperity. It will not be the last such expression.

The other major biblical narrative of exile is the book of Daniel. Daniel is not a single narrative but an anthology of narratives built around a common hero. The narratives, while dramatic, are redundant of one another, and they are, in significant respects, derivative from the exile narratives examined above, both Joseph and Esther. Being a biblical book, Daniel had considerable influence on the development of later traditions, Jewish and Christian. But lacking a liturgical home, one in which congregations might come to know it, it is fair to say that Daniel remained a lesser-known biblical book, at least among Jews. Nevertheless, for our purposes it is an important one.

The stories of Daniel took shape at different times, the first six chapters earlier and the latter six later.[12] Scholars will argue about the precise provenance of the earlier chapters, but the latter chapters, and therefore the book as a whole, clearly took shape at a very specific time and place—that is, in the Land of Israel, whose population was subject to the oppressive regime of the Syrian-Greek king, Antiochus Epiphanes, between 168 and 164 BCE; the book came to its final form in the midst of the worst hardships of that period, before the Maccabean revolt had any success. In this setting, the author or authors behind the last six chapters of the book give voice to the notion that they must be living in the end of days, for theirs is an apocalyptic vision. At the same time, the diaspora stories gathered in the first six chapters are in full agreement with the earlier diaspora narratives in their portrayal of Jews protected by God, Jews who, along with their God, always triumph in the end. As a result, the book as a whole has a kind of "on the one hand...on the other hand" quality: on the one hand, diaspora Jews triumph, on the other hand, Jews in the Holy Land suffer so much that they need the final redemption. Given the fact that many Jews during this period were living in comfortable diasporas, with Alexandria emerging as the most prominent among them, while Palestinian Jews were suffering under the conditions just outlined, the contrast the book expresses is probably more than mere coincidence.

The book locates Daniel, chronologically speaking, from the reign of the Babylonian king Nebuchadnezzar through the reigns of the Persian kings Cyrus and Darius (a near impossibility for a single life, but never mind). He

## 54 EMBRACING EXILE

first comes to the attention of Nebuchadnezzar when the king commands that select exiles from Judah be gathered to train them for service in the royal court. Remarkably, already at the beginning of their stay, at least some Judeans are recognized for their potential worth to the kingdom. Hence, they will be called upon to live a distinguished life, close to the court, and not the life of defeated captives.

Among those called are Daniel and his companions. They are immediately given Babylonian names, a sign of acceptance and acculturation, and their training begins. Because they are guests of the court, the court must provide for their sustenance and welfare. But at least Daniel and his group (we learn nothing about other Judeans) ask not to eat the king's provisions, as the food of others would be defiling to Judeans ("Jews"). Because "God had brought Daniel into grace and compassion with the chief of the palace servants," their request is respected and quickly granted. As in the case of Joseph, God's grace brings good grace upon them, even in exile, and as in the book of Esther, there is no evidence that anyone bears enmity toward Daniel because he is a Jew.

Like Joseph, Daniel is blessed with special wisdom by God; like Joseph, he therefore has the key to dream interpretations, which he uses to his benefit. Like Mordechai, he sits in the gate of the king, and like Mordechai, other officers of similar rank are competitive with Daniel, who seek to trap Daniel into compromising himself. Out of spite and circumstance, Daniel is confronted with religious challenges in the foreign setting, but there is no suggestion that these challenges emerge from actual Jew-hatred, and—most importantly—Daniel always triumphs. In the end, thanks to the great wisdom of Daniel, the foreign king and members of the court recognize the truth of the God of Israel. As for Daniel himself, his aid to the king leads the king to appoint him ruler over other courtiers, and even over "the entire province of Babylonia" (3:48). The plot that originated with Joseph and was seconded with Mordechai now achieves the status of an irrefutable pattern: Jews in exile do not experience a degraded existence. Instead, they effectively rule the world.

One well-known story of Daniel, in particular, illustrates the overall tone of these tales. The story is "Daniel in the Lion's Den" (chapter 6), which begins with the Persian king Darius, having achieved the ripe old age of sixty-two, relieving himself of his immediate burden of governance by appointing satraps over each of the kingdoms of his realm. At the head of this imperial structure he appoints three superior ministers, one of whom is

Daniel. But due to his extraordinary spirit (he bore the "charisma" granted by God), Daniel outshines the others, and Darius decides to appoint him over them. In response, the others plot to bring Daniel down. Knowing that Daniel regularly prays to his God, they propose to the king that, for thirty days, anyone who petitions a god or person other than the king shall be thrown into a den of lions. Not knowing of any problem, the king quickly assents to this proposal, issuing a royal decree. The king had not imagined that such an enactment would affect his favored Daniel, so when he heard that Daniel was to be punished according to his decree, "he was much distressed, and set his heart on Daniel to rescue him" (6:15).

Unfortunately, as we (and probably the author of this story) know from Esther, once the Persian king issues a decree, it cannot be rescinded, so Darius' hands are tied. But Darius expresses to Daniel his confidence that his God will rescue him, and with Daniel cast into the lion's den, Darius retires to his palace to spend the night fasting, a means of beseeching God to save Daniel. In the morning, discovering that Daniel has been protected, Darius is "exceedingly glad." The king now throws Daniel's opponents, along with their families, into the lion's den (needless to say, they do not survive), and then sends missives to the far reaches of his dominion encouraging his subjects to fear the God of Daniel, the "living God."

Daniel, the exiled Judean/Jew, is without exception triumphant. And putting aside those few who, in competitive spite, seek to take him down, he finds favor in the eyes of all who meet him. Though he is known as an exiled Judean, there is no hint anywhere that this identity works to his disadvantage. The overall impression one gets, even with the claustrophobic gaze of the narrator, is that Jews are, if anything, privileged in this diaspora. In all of these details, these stories reiterate the motifs established earlier in the stories of Joseph and Esther, while taking them one step further, for Jews—as opposed to Daniel and his companions—are never collectively threatened in these stories.

The latter half of the book of Daniel, beginning with chapter 7, is a very different document. These latter chapters record dreams/prophecies of Daniel pertaining to the end of history. To the knowing reader, who is familiar with the recent history of Judea in the imperial context of the Near East, it is clear that Daniel's "prophecies" are largely masked descriptions of military and political events in the region—the defeat of Persia by Alexander and his armies, the disintegration of Alexander's empire into separate Hellenistic kingdoms, the wars of those kingdoms in the territory of (what

56   EMBRACING EXILE

would later be known as) Palestine, the persecutions of Antiochus Epiphanes, and possibly the beginning of the rise of the Maccabees.[13] Notably, these prophecies are apocalyptic, describing, as they do, bitter events that would lead to the end of history. They focus on the calamity of recent history and insist that the sufferings of Israel will soon come to end in a final salvation.

The cultural-historical circumstances assumed in Daniel as a whole are all exilic, that is, they all take place in Babylon/Persia. In addition, large parts of the book are in Aramaic—the imperial language of Babylon—thus enhancing the books exilic quality. But the references of the book's apocalyptic prophecies, expressed in Hebrew, are focused on the Land of Israel, from the perspective of someone residing in that land. The eyewitness who speaks through the "prophecies" is an eyewitness who resides in the Land of Israel. The references contained in the "prophecies" (which are, until the end, actually retrospective) are to events of the Hellenistic kingdoms and their competition for control of the Land of Israel, and the last events hinted at in the final "prophecy" are the persecutions of Jews at the time of Antiochus Epiphanes and the beginning of the Maccabean uprising against him. These latter events took place in 164 BCE, so this is reasonably assumed to be the year when the book as a whole was completed. The place of its completion, given the references of the prophecies, must be the Land of Israel.

But if the latter half of Daniel reflects the experience of a Jew or Jews living in the Land, then why is its narrative cast in exile? What does the author gain or wish to express by setting this exilic scene if what he wishes to comment upon is the current fate of Jews in their own Promised Land? Given the differing tone of the two halves of the book, one must answer these questions at least twice. In the apocalyptic prophecies, it seems that the author wishes to comment on the hardship of Jewish life in the land during the reign of the Hellenistic kingdoms. At this time, while many Jews live in their own Land, they certainly do not control their own affairs. In fact, they have by this point experienced generations of challenges and hardships on the Land, and matters have recently only grown worse. They live in their "own" land but under foreign rulers, experiencing persecutions to which they have never before been subjected.

Such a life is not, for the Jew (at least not for the Jew for whom the author speaks) a redeemed life, a life in "Zion." On the contrary, the life of the Jew in the early half of the second century BCE in the Promised Land is nevertheless a life in exile. The Jewish king was long in the past, his place taken by a foreign king. The Temple stood, but for the last author of Daniel, it had been desecrated and now stood silent, without service and without joyous ritual. For this author, life in the Land was life in exile, for "exile" and "Zion" were, to him and to others, not geographic descriptions but existential conditions.

But why did the final author of Daniel append his alarming apocalypse of life in the Land to a series of stories about Jewish life (or at least about the lives of a few Jews) in exile—an exile that was certainly not alarming and from which deliverance was certainly not urgent? This part I-part II composition, the first part offering a benign exile and the second envisioning an alarming "homecoming," means to challenge—to "deconstruct"—conventional notions of exile. The "exile" of part I is, from the traditional perspective, the real exile, the exile of Babylon and Persia, which nevertheless allows Jews to thrive and recognition of their God to proliferate. This exile represents exile not quite as Zion, but certainly as not distinctly inferior to it. At the same time, the "exile" of part II is exile in the Land, where foreign domination can turn Zion into disgrace and danger, an exile from which deliverance is greatly needed. If this interpretation is correct, then we may state Daniel's message rather simply: it is possible to be in exile in the Land, and it is possible to be in Zion outside of it.

This latter notion resonated for centuries. As far as many later Jews were concerned, it *was* possible to be in Zion outside the Land. Or, to put it another way, Zion and exile are only notionally opposed to one another, they are not in reality so. One can be in exile in Zion or in Zion in exile, or in both at the same time. Moreover, considering oneself in Zion in exile doesn't necessarily mean that one doesn't want to return to Zion, which may or may not be conceived in strict geographic terms; "Zion" can also mean the state of redemption, which may have little to do with the Land at all, at least in this world.

It is not only canonical Jewish books that provide us with insight into Jewish experiences of exile during this period. Other texts, written by Jews but not ultimately included in the Hebrew Bible, also offer testimony relevant to our exploration.

The Greek version of the book of Daniel includes an extra chapter, the story of Susannah, a work of Jewish origin, probably from the second century BCE, that is included in the Catholic Apocrypha. In this story, Susannah is a young woman of extreme beauty who attracts the eyes of two judges. Afflicted by unbearable lust for her, they conspire to take her in the garden of her wealthy husband, Joakim. They approach her and give her an ultimatum: she can either yield to their sexual demands or they will falsely accuse her of having a liaison with a lover in the garden. When she refuses, they cry out, falsely accusing her of infidelity. She is subsequently brought to court to answer her accusers.

The false testimony of the judges, who are honored men, is believed by the assembly before which she is tried, and she is sentenced to death. But as she is being led to execution, Daniel intervenes, re-opening the deliberations and cross-examining the witnesses. Through clever, pointed questioning, Daniel demonstrates the falsity of the witnesses' prior testimony, and, following the law of "conspiring witnesses" outlined in the Torah (Deuteronomy 19:16–20), they are put to death. Susanna is saved and Daniel's reputation is enhanced.

This story, taking place in diaspora like all the other Daniel stories, says nothing directly about the condition of diaspora. But it does shed light on Jewish imaginations of the diaspora in a very direct way. In this story, a Jewess is falsely accused by Jewish judges of misdeeds. Her case is brought before a Jewish tribunal ("assembly"), which tries her, convicts her, and sends her to her execution. But then the intervention of another Jew, Daniel, saves her, and the Jewish tribunal exonerates Susanna and executes the conspiring judges. Not a single non-Jew appears in the entire story.

The Jews in this story have complete jurisdiction over their own affairs. They have the authority to try the accused and the power to execute. They are comfortable in their legal standing and free in their actions. Some are wealthy and none is oppressed or otherwise disadvantaged. As a chapter of Daniel, the story must be read as a diaspora story describing the lives of Jews in Babylon in the few generations after the initial exile. With no self-consciousness or fear of contradiction, the author imagines this setting as one of security and comfort for the exiled Jews.

A much longer story, different in tone but not in effect from what we just saw, is the apocryphal book, Tobit. Composed also, probably, in the second century BCE (like Daniel in its final form, with or without Susannah),[14] Tobit has been characterized by some as a "romance of Diaspora Judaism." The book tells a long and complex story about a diaspora Jew, Tobit, his son, Tobias, Tobias's new wife, Sarah, and various others. Though admitting the flaws and challenges of exilic life, Tobit, through its narrative, also promises at least personal redemption.[15]

As the book begins, Tobit describes himself as a righteous Israelite of the tribe of Naftali who was exiled to Nineveh by the hands of the Assyrians. According to his own testimony, Tobit performed many acts of charity, buried the dead who had no one to bury them (they thus become the "grateful dead"), and offered sacrifices at the one true sanctuary in Jerusalem (as opposed to the illegitimate one in Samaria). In addition—so he claims—while his kindred ate the food of the Gentiles, Tobit refused to do so.

Tobit's life took a dramatic turn when he risked his personal security by secretly burying Israelites whom the Assyrian king had put to death and then, later, one who had been murdered. Forced to sleep outside to escape capture, his eyes were covered by bird droppings, the treatment for which left him blind, with white films over his eyes. At the same time, Sarah, the daughter of a kinsman of Tobit in Media, was afflicted by a demon, who killed seven of her husbands. Both of these afflicted characters cry out to God, and the prayers of both are answered. The angel Raphael—"God heals"—is sent to heal them both.

Early in the book, we are told that Tobit left a sum of money with one Gabael elsewhere in Media. Later, remembering this money, Tobit asks his son, Tobias, to go and fetch it. Afraid of the journey and afraid that Gabael, not knowing him, will not give him the money, Tobias resists, but Raphael appears, offering to lead the way and assuring his safety. The journey begins, one plot twist follows another, and in the end, Sarah and Tobit are both healed, Sarah and Tobias are married, and all is well in the world.

Some details of the narrative seem to reflect a negative attitude toward exile. For example, Tobit reports that King Sennacherib, fleeing Judea (after conquering Israel!), killed many Israelites in anger (though this may be more a consequence of the residual heat of battle than of exile as such). He confiscated Tobit's property when Tobit buried the dead against the king's wishes. In his prayers, Tobit repeats common pieties about exile and its sufferings being the result of sin. He longs, with confidence, for the restoration of Jerusalem.

Reflecting a very different attitude, though, are many other details. Sennacherib's son, Esar-haddon, appoints Tobit's nephew, Ahikar, "over all the accounts of the kingdom, and had authority over the entire administration." In the next breath, we learn that this is actually a reappointment, as Ahikar had enjoyed the same status under Sennacherib. God hears and responds to the prayers of Jews in exile, sending "divine healing" to heal and protect them. True, Israelites do not have, in exile, the Temple, where they might offer sacrifices to God, but, as Tobit repeats more than once, "Almsgiving, for all who practice it, is an excellent offering in the presence of the Most High" (4:11). If there are substitutes for animal sacrifice, then who needs the altar on Zion hill?

Tobit's final, pre-death blessing (chapter 13) offers this book's most explicit statements on exile. In this blessing, Tobit calls upon Israel to acknowledge God before all the nations, "for he has scattered you among them." There is a clear suggestion that the dispersion has a purpose, and that purpose is to bring God's name to the tongues of other peoples. Tobit continues (verse 4), "He has shown you his greatness even there. Exalt him in the presence of every living being." In the narrative context of the book, this statement cannot but be personalized: God has shown God's greatness through the healing and triumph of Tobit and his loved ones. One who enjoys God's gifts should sing out in praiseful recognition of those gifts, as Tobit surely does ("In the land of my exile I acknowledge him, and show his power and majesty to a nation of sinners"; verse 6). Following his own model, Tobit encourages other Israelites in exile to similarly thank and praise God for what they enjoy in exile. There are reasons in exile to be grateful.

Later in the blessing, Tobit turns his attention to Jerusalem. Jerusalem, he says, is afflicted on account of the sins of Israel. But Jerusalem will also be gloriously rebuilt and its people restored to it. Crucially, though, it is not only Israel that will return to Jerusalem. As Tobit emphasizes, "A bright light will shine to all the ends of the earth; many nations will come to you from far away, the inhabitants of the remotest parts of the earth to your holy name, bearing gifts in their hands for the King of heaven" (13:11). In the immediate context, these words declare that the nations, too, will come to Jerusalem to make offerings to the one true God. But what Tobit declares is that the nations will come "to you," that is, to God, who is not necessarily in Jerusalem. In the context of Tobit's larger blessing, in fact, the location of Jerusalem is secondary to the fact that the nations turn from their false gods to the God of heaven and earth—thanks to the fact that the dispersion of Israel brings knowledge of God to all ends of the earth. The inhabitants of those distant parts, whoever they are and wherever they may reside, are awakened to that knowledge thanks to their Jewish neighbors, through whose model they are moved to turn their hearts to God. As Tobit says in the next, final chapter, "The nations of the whole world will all be converted and worship God in truth" (14:6).

One final detail: in his deathbed testament to his son, Tobit cautions Tobias to heed the prophecies of Nahum concerning Nineveh, where they live. According to the prophecies, Assyria will be destroyed. So, too, will the Land of Israel (remember: this book locates Tobit in the Assyrian exile, the one that led to the "Ten Lost Tribes" more than a century before the Babylonian exile). Safety will only be found, he advises, in Media, to the east. Now, in light of the chronological conceit, this is correct: safety will be found even farther from the Land of Israel. But since, in fact, this fiction was composed sometime in the late third or early second century BCE, it is hard not to read this as a comment on the conditions of that setting. As far as the Jewish writer of this text is concerned, it would be a mistake to seek refuge in the Land of Israel. Some diasporas, at least, are safer.

Beyond the details, what is perhaps most notable about the narrative of Tobit is the "taken-for-grantedness" of Jewish diaspora life. After the initial sufferings of Jews at the hands of Assyria, a product of the war and its aftermath, Jews in diaspora, whether it be Assyria or Nineveh, simply live their lives. They live and die, marry, become ill, are healed, travel, do business, and so forth, with no evident obstacles on account of their Jewishness. They may be pious or not, but their piety wins God's approval. Their prayers are as likely to be answered in exile as in the Land, and God protects and heals them. Jewish life in exile may one day come to an end—and Tobit, as a pious Jew, certainly hopes for that day. But in the meantime, Jewish life in these scattered lands is as natural as the lives of others residing beside them.[16]

All these stories—Daniel, Susannah, Tobit—are reflections of Jewish life in exile in the latter centuries BCE. This was a period when Jewish diasporas were well established, and as expressions of the experiences of these diasporas, these writings make good sense. Neither diaspora Jews, nor even their contemporaries living in the Land, saw diaspora life as "exile" in the onerous sense. Diaspora was not regularly experienced as punishment. On the contrary, diaspora Jewish life, already a taken-for-granted part of Jewish existence, was like all human life—sometimes challenging, often good. Because Jews were, they believed, God's chosen people, Jews, wherever they were, were blessed with God's presence and held close with God's covenant. As a result, Jews believed, they were more likely to flourish than to suffer, more likely to triumph than to fall. The reality of diaspora life supported this belief. This is the legacy with which later generations of Jews were left, wherever they lived: exile was not to be hated, it was to be lived.

# 4

# Zion in Babylon

One of the most important chapters of the Jewish diaspora experience began with an event that was, for Jews everywhere, world-changing: the destruction of the Jerusalem Temple by the Romans in 70 CE. This event had most significant impact on Jews residing in the Land of Israel, and particularly in the environs of Jerusalem. But it also affected Jews living in distant lands, as their Judaism assumed that their sins, too, would be cleansed by the offering of sacrifices at the Temple, and distant communities sent both funds and substance for the support of the cult in Jerusalem. Without the Temple, how could Jews, wherever they lived, repair their relationships with God after sin?

The full meaning of the new circumstances became evident only when the "messianic" revolt led by Bar Kokhba was quashed by the Romans in 135. Before the Bar Kokhba uprising, most Jews probably looked to the Hebrew Bible to understand what would come next, and according to the Bible, repentance would lead to restoration; the period without the Temple would be a short-lived "seventy years" according to the biblical prophecy. Jews who rose against the Romans at the time of Bar Kokhba undoubtedly hoped that their triumph would lead to the Temple's restoration. But things did not work out that way; the biblical prophecy did not work a second time. Instead, the Romans who defeated the rebellious Jewish forces left no doubt that anything that represented or inspired Jewish independence would not be tolerated. As a result, no Jew could reasonably have imagined that the Temple would soon be rebuilt, and so Jews far and wide had to ask what it meant to be a Jew without God's "home" on earth, the Temple in Jerusalem. How would their relationship with God be maintained? How would the national holidays be observed? The questions were numerous and weighty and answers were difficult to imagine. The future of Jews and Judaism was far from assured.

Crucially, neither of the Roman wars led to a new exile or diaspora. Rome took prisoners-of-war, and some Palestinian Jews fled on account of the violence of war or the conditions that came in its wake. But Rome had no policy of exiling defeated peoples and Jewish diasporas already existed throughout the Near East. None of this should be taken to mean that Jewish life was easy after these wars. On the contrary, these questions reflected genuinely bitter circumstances, and they had to be answered before Jewish life could move on.[1]

Into this fraught setting stepped a small, elite group of scholars in Palestine—the rabbis—who had no particular authority in the Jewish community beyond their own circles. Reacting to the catastrophe that was the destruction, they began to formulate a system of Jewish practice for a world without the Temple, even if they at first hoped that this condition would last for only a brief period. And when, in the second century, it became clear that the Temple would not quickly be rebuilt, they pushed forward with a program that would elaborate inherited traditions to adapt them for the new world, while creating new practices—and formulating new beliefs—that would ultimately be accepted as the mainstream practices and beliefs of virtually all Jews.

The rabbinic movement began in Palestine, in response to Palestinian-centered events. At first, there were no rabbis in any of the numerous Jewish diaspora communities, and the rabbis would, to begin with, have had essentially no contact with those communities. It should occasion no surprise, then, that early rabbinic expressions emphasize the value and sacredness of the Land for all Jews. But, at the same time, they do recognize the fact of diaspora Jewish life, and they understand that difficult conditions in the war-torn landscape of Palestine might lead some Jews to leave the Land for more peaceful lives elsewhere. An early rabbinic midrash, for example, elaborates Deuteronomy 11:31 in this way:

> "And you shall inherit it and dwell in it and observe to do all of these laws"—It happened that R. Judah b. Beteira and R. Mattia b. Heresh...were leaving the Land of Israel and they arrived at Paltom, and they remembered the Land of Israel. They raised their eyes and tears poured forth, and they tore their garments and they recited this scripture: (Deuteronomy 11:31, quoted earlier)....They said, "the settlement of the Land of Israel is equal in weight to all of the other commandments of the Torah." Midrash Sifri, Re'eh 80

The Midrash here describes a historical reality—rabbis in the mid-second century leaving the Land for abroad. Someone who knows the recent history (as early readers of this text would have) will imagine that they are leaving the land to escape the devastation that had been wrought by Rome's savage suppression of the Bar Kokhba revolt. And though anyone might sympathize with those who seek more secure conditions, the Midrash plays against those sympathies and declares that settling the Land of Israel is more important than any other single commandment. Still, the implication of what is recounted here mirrors the reality: if some rabbis reconsidered their journey and returned to the Land, others followed through with their self-preserving instinct and found their way to Babylonia or elsewhere.

Those rabbis who, beginning in the late second century, made their home in Babylonia joined the ancient Jewish community that had resided there since the time of the first destruction and exile of the early sixth century BCE. At first, rabbis, who originated in Palestine, were a kind of foreign implant on Babylonian soil, and local, Babylonian Jews are likely to have looked at them with considerable suspicion. "Why," they would have asked, "should we listen to you and adopt your strange Palestinian customs? We have our traditional Judaism, thank you very much, and we see no good reason to change it." But rabbis made themselves at home in Babylonia, and the evidence suggests that they gained more and more supporters. Before long, Babylonian rabbis were as much Babylonian as the more ancient community of Babylonian Jews, and they had much to say about their residence in this "foreign" but long-established Jewish setting.

From the third to the sixth centuries of the common era, Jews in Babylon—rabbinic or not—lived mostly comfortable, peaceful lives. Outside of the Talmud, there is almost no documentation of those lives, but the broad contours of Persian history during these centuries suggest an amenable home for those who adhered to non-Persian religions, including Jews, and the few chapters of intolerance referenced in surviving sources find almost no echo in at least the rabbis' reporting. Jews in Babylon lived as good Babylonians, experiencing little discernable difficulty—let alone outright persecution—and accommodating comfortably to Babylonian culture and its ways. Affirming that "the law of the land is the law," Babylonian Jews continued to feel at home in their by now ancient, biblical home, and the one significant record they did produce—the Talmud—reflects this in spades. The fact that conditions supported the production of this complex, magnificent work is itself testimony to the benefits of Babylonian Jewish life.[2]

The Talmud's magnificence is contained, in part, in its remarkable openness of spirit and encouragement of critical inquiry. It is filled with differences of opinion—differences that are celebrated, not avoided, arguments that remain open and necessitate no resolution. But at the same time, the Talmud is undeniably a work by and for a limited audience, an audience of advanced rabbinic scholars who devoted their lives to the study of rabbinic teachings. As an elite work, it cannot generally be taken to reflect the opinions and experiences of Babylonian Jews as a whole. But we should also not make the mistake of seeing the rabbis and their Talmud as being cut off from their surroundings. The Talmud is a work that often shows the extent of Persian influence in Babylonian Jewish circles, an influence the rabbis clearly had no need to hide.[3] A work like the Talmud is not the product of pressure or persecution. It is a work that could only have taken shape under conditions of comfort and security, one that was shared by all Babylonian Jews, not just rabbis. Even if the Talmud speaks directly only for a small proportion of the Babylonian Jewish population, in matters that concern us, there can be no doubt that it reflects the experiences and even some of the attitudes of Jews well beyond the rabbis. Indeed, the Babylonian Talmud is a celebration of the Babylonian Jewish experience, the experience of all of Babylonian Jewry. Babylonia was a good home for virtually all Jews who made it their home, even if the Talmud speaks in a particularly rabbinic voice.

Among its several relevant deliberations, the Talmud preserves a long and complex consideration of the meaning of diaspora/exile, one that has been mined fruitfully by several recent scholars but has still more to yield. This deliberation surely reflects the specifics of the Babylonian experience, but it carries implications that allow for generalization to other diasporas. The discussion begins, like most Talmudic discussions, with consideration of a Mishnah—that is, a *Palestinian* Rabbinic teaching, probably from the second century—that gives priority to the desire of a spouse who wishes to make Aliyah to the Land of Israel. The teaching of the Mishnah is this:

> All may coerce their spouses to go up to the Land of Israel, but not all may coerce them to leave. All may coerce their spouses to go up to Jerusalem, but not all may coerce them to leave—both men and women. (Ketubbot 13:11)

Practically speaking, what this means is that each spouse may coerce the other to go up to the Land of Israel or to Jerusalem, and if the spouse refuses, the one who wants to "go up" has the advantage when it comes to

## 66 EMBRACING EXILE

marriage settlements. So if a woman wants to go up and her husband refuses, she may demand a divorce and he will need to pay her the settlement. If he wants to go up and she refuses, he may divorce her without paying the settlement. The law is obviously designed to support the value of settling the Land. As a teaching from the generation or two after the Bar Kokhba defeat, it is sensitive to the difficulties of that period. War had depleted the Land, and current Roman decrees made settlement in Jerusalem—Roman Jerusalem—but a dream for Jews. Its privileging of the Land comes as no surprise, particularly in light of the fact that some Jews, more interested in comfort than in piety, certainly had other priorities.

The Talmud knows of other Palestinian rabbinic teachings that support the same value, several of which it quotes. Together, these teachings make clear how highly the Palestinian rabbis, at least, prized settlement in the biblical Promised Land. But what is most interesting about the Talmud's discussion is not that it quotes these teachings but how it does so: it quotes them only to undermine their message by reinterpreting or relativizing them. To help perceive this dynamic, in the translation below, I also emphasize, with italics, some of the most radical of the Babylonian teachings.[4]

Our rabbis have taught:

I.   Someone should always live in the Land of Israel, even in a town the majority of which is gentile, and should not reside outside the Land, even in a town the majority of which is Jewish. For whoever lives in the Land of Israel as though has a [true] God, but whoever lives outside the Land as though has no God, for scripture says: "To give you the land of Canaan, to be your God" (Leviticus 25:38). And is it true that anyone who does not live in the Land of Israel has no God? Rather, it is to tell you that anyone who lives outside the Land is as though he worships idols.

II.  R. Zeira was avoiding R. Judah, for [the former] wanted to go up to the Land of Israel, while R. Judah said, "*Anyone who goes up from Babylonia to the Land of Israel violates a positive commandment*, for it is said, [111a] 'They shall be brought to Babylonia and there they shall be until the day that I remember them, says the Lord' (Jeremiah 27:22)."

     And R. Zeira? That [verse] is written in reference to the utensils for the Temple service.

And R. Judah, [doesn't he recognize that the verse is speaking about the Temple vessels]?

There is yet another verse written: "I adjure you, daughters of Jerusalem, by the gazelles and by the hinds of the field, that you not awaken or stir up love until it please" (Song of Songs 22:7).

And R. Zeira, [what does he do with the verse from the Song of Songs]?

That verse means that Jews should not go up as a wall [meaning *en masse*, but it doesn't mean that Jews shouldn't go up at all].

And R. Judah, [how does he now learn that Jews should not go up from Babylonia to the Land]?

Another "I adjure you" (Song 3:5) is written [which should be understood to forbid leaving Babylonia for the Land of Israel].

And R. Zeira [what does he do with this additional "adjure"]?

He needs it for the teaching of R. Yosé b. R. Hanina [with which he agrees], for he said, "What are these three oaths for? One is that Jews should not go up like a wall, one is that the Holy One, blessed be He, has imposed an oath on Israel that they not rebel against the nations of the world, and one is that the Holy One, blessed be He, has imposed an oath on the gentiles that they not oppress Israel too much. "

III. Said R. Eleazar, "Whoever lives in the Land of Israel dwells without sin, for it is said, 'And the inhabitant shall not say, I am sick, the people that dwell therein shall be forgiven their iniquity' (Isaiah 38:24)."

Said Raba to R. Ashi, "We repeat this verse with reference to those who bear disease" [in other words, the verse refers *not* to the atoning power of the Land but to the atoning power of illness].

IV. Said R. Anan, "Whoever is buried in the Land of Israel is as though buried under the altar. Here it is written, 'An altar of earth you shall make to me' (Exodus 20:21), and elsewhere, 'And his land does make expiation for his people' (Deuteronomy 32:42)."

Ulla would regularly go up to the Land of Israel. He died outside the Land. They came and told R. Eleazar. He said, "You, Ulla—'should you die in an unclean field' (Amos 7:17)?"

They told him, "His bier is coming."

He said to them, "Being gathered in [to the Land] when alive is not the same thing as being gathered into the Land after death."

V. Said R. Judah said Samuel, "*Just as it is forbidden to go forth from the Land of Israel to Babylonia, so it is forbidden to go forth from Babylonia to other lands.*"

68    EMBRACING EXILE

> Rabbah and R. Joseph both said, "Even from [the city of] Pumbeditha to Be Cube."
>
> There was a certain person who left from Pumbeditha to Be Cube, and R. Joseph banned him.
>
> VI.   Rabbah and R. Joseph both said "The truly suitable persons in Babylonia—the Land of Israel receives them. The truly fit persons in other countries—Babylonia receives them."
>
> For what purpose [are the lands said to be in this relationship]? Should one say, this is as to genealogical purity? But did not a master state, "*All other countries are like gross dough in comparison to the Land of Israel, and the Land of Israel is like gross dough by comparison to Babylonia*"? So it must have to do with burial.
>
> VII.   Said R. Judah, "*Whoever dwells in Babylonia is as though he dwelt in the Land of Israel*: 'Ho, Zion, escape, you who dwells with the daughter of Babylonia' (Zechariah 2:11). " (Talmud Ketubbot 110b–111a)

This is a rather remarkable sequence, one that pays homage to the Land of Israel while at the same time undermining its priority.

Section I is an early Palestinian rabbinic text,[5] one that praises the superiority of the Land of Israel without compromise and pulls no punches in condemning those Jews who live outside the Land. It shares a spirit with the Mishnah that lays at the foundation of this deliberation but is even more extreme. Section II, which stands in "dialogue" with section I, offers a very different perspective. This section begins by informing us of a conflict of opinions between two prominent third-century rabbis, R. Judah and R. Zeira. Judah is by far the more prominent of the two, and he is unambiguously represented, here and elsewhere, as a great champion of Babylonian Jewry. In this section, we see that, with a confidence we would imagine to be grounded in generations of recognized rabbinic authority—even though his is only the second rabbinic generation to reside in Babylonia—he forbids Jews to leave Babylonia for the Land of Israel. Zeira, Judah's disciple who is therefore obligated to relate to him with particular honor, disagrees.

Most of this section is a typical Talmudic exercise in which each side (or the Talmud speaking for each side) cites scriptural support for their position. To avoid the confusion that trying to make sense of this exchange would cause, let us go directly to the conclusion of this section. In the end, R. Zeira—that is, the sage who supports Jews' moving to the Land of Israel and undertakes the journey himself—nevertheless agrees with R. Yosé b. R. Hanina in his declaration that "Jews should not go up like a wall," that "Jews should not rebel against the nations of the world," and "that gentiles should not oppress Israel too much." In other words, even R. Zeira agrees that mass Aliyah of Jews to the Land of Israel is not permitted, and he clearly assumes (in the second and third rules) that many Jews will continue to live in foreign lands. This is far from a rejection of the diaspora, then. Contrary to what we saw in section I, Jews are meant to live in the Babylonian diaspora, at least, and only small numbers should leave for the Holy Land. According to R. Judah, by contrast, even individual Jews are forbidden to do so.

Sections III and VI begin with teachings highlighting the greatness of the Land—the first declaring that the Land has the power to atone for sin and the latter reporting that "truly suitable" (= "Kosher") Jews in other lands are gathered into the Land of Israel. But each of these teachings is immediately undermined by the Talmud. In III Raba remarks that he does not understand the allegedly supporting verse in the same way as Eleazar; for him, the verse declares not that the Land has atoning power, but that illness has this power. In VI, we learn that the Land's unique suitability for "Kosher" Jews must apply to burial and not to the greater genealogical purity (recall that section IV had earlier spoken of the superiority of the Land for burial, granting that while it might be better to come to the Land before one dies, arriving for burial after death is also efficacious). With respect to genealogical purity, though, Babylonia is superior. This is an absolutely stupendous claim—a claim with which, the Talmud insists, all would agree. Modern Jews, and even historians of the Jewish experience, have typically assumed that Jewish-gentile intermarriage (or, before such marriage was legal, intimate relations) is more common in diaspora communities, where Jewish-gentile relations are far more common than in Palestine, where the concentration of Jews is greater. To claim that a diaspora community is superior with respect to genealogical purity is to declare that common wisdom potentially wrong.

Section V is tremendously important as a bridge to the Talmud's climax in VII. In V, prominent Babylonian rabbis (the same R. Judah, now quoting his teacher Samuel of the earlier to mid-third century) say that Babylonia is in the same status with respect to other lands as the Land of Israel is with respect to Babylonia. That is: just as the holiness of the Land of Israel makes it forbidden for a Jew to leave it for Babylonia, the holiness of Babylonia

70   EMBRACING EXILE

makes it forbidden to leave its territories for foreign lands. I say here "the holiness of Babylonia" without hesitation because the very act of respecting the barrier of its boundaries creates—because it enacts—its holiness. This is further emphasized by the teaching of Rabbah and R. Joseph, who construct a hierarchy to limit movement between different locales in Babylonia itself. This is reminiscent of what the Mishnah had done by making the Land superior to other lands for making a marital home and then making Jerusalem superior to the rest of the Land. Structuring Babylonia in a way that is directly parallel to the earlier rabbinic structuring of the Holy Land goes a long way toward making Babylonia almost as holy. Only one more step is necessary to erase any distinction at all.

This erasure is accomplished, quickly and simply, in R. Judah's final teaching, in section VII. Declaring that "whoever dwells in Babylonia is as though he dwelt in the Land of Israel," R. Judah insists that there is no reason for the Jew to make Aliyah from Babylonia to the Land of Israel, because the former is just like the latter.[6] Notably, he does not say that Babylonia is as holy as Israel, though this may be implied; he simply asserts that living in Babylonia is just like living in the Land of Israel. The once-upon-a-time exile now turned diaspora land is just like the Promised Land, the Holy Land, the Land of the Ancestors. How can this be so? How can R. Judah make such an "outrageous" claim? We could surmise an answer now. But reference to several other Babylonian teachings will help us offer a more confident interpretation of the teachings of the Babylonian rabbis concerning their diaspora residence.

The Talmud's major discussion of synagogues is found in tractate Megillah, page 29a. By way of introduction to the central part of its discussion, the Talmud expounds on the relationship of the divine presence (the *Shekhinah*—God's immanent quality) and the people Israel. The teaching is this:

R. Shimon ben Yohai says: Come and see how dear [the nation of] Israel is before The Holy One, Blessed be He, for wherever they were exiled, the divine presence was with them. [When] they were exiled to Egypt, the divine presence was with them, as is said, "was I not exiled to your father's house when they were in Egypt" (1 Samuel 2:27). [When] they were exiled to Babylonia, the divine presence was with them, as is said, "for your sake I sent to Babylonia" (Isaiah 43:14).[7] And even when they will be redeemed in the future, the divine presence will be with them, as is said, "and the Lord your God will return your return" (Deuteronomy 30:3).

It does not say "and He will cause to return" (*ve-heshiv*) but "and He will return" (*ve-shav*). This teaches that The Holy One, Blessed Be He, will return with them from among the places of exile.

This teaching attributed to R. Shimon b. Yohai—himself, notably, a second-century Palestinian rabbi—declares that when Israel is exiled, they never go into exile alone. Rather, when Israel is exiled, God (or at least God's presence) is exiled with them. This was true when Israel was "exiled" to Egypt (from the time of the descent of Jacob's sons and their families until the Exodus). It was true when they were exiled to Babylonia. And they will even be accompanied by the divine presence when they return from their exile at the time of their redemption.

This is reminiscent of the claim of the prophet Ezekiel, whose vision suggested the presence of God in Babylon following that exile. Ezekiel did not, however, translate his vision of God in exile into a general rule, as does R. Shimon; Shimon's rule suggests, in fact, that God will accompany Israel through all her exiles. Thus, all future exiled Jews may be comforted by the notion that wherever they are, God is with them. Furthermore, R. Shimon seems also to go beyond Ezekiel in claiming that God Godself—or at least God's presence—is actually exiled and will necessitate return from exile when Israel is redeemed. "If God experiences what we experience," Israel may say to herself, "then what we experience cannot be too bad."

The Talmud now proceeds to literalize our understanding of God's presence in exile. It asks, "Where in Babylonia [is the divine presence]?" offering this answer:

Said Abbaye: In the synagogue of Hotzal, and in the synagogue of Shaf VeYativ in Nehardea.

If you want to meet God in Babylon, Abbaye suggests, you need not wander to and fro. The Talmud actually provides us with a map. If we want to meet God, go the specified synagogues.

To buttress its claim for at least the latter synagogue, the Talmud here shares a couple of stories:

Samuel's father and Levi were sitting in the synagogue of Shaf VeYativ in Nehardea. The divine presence came, [and] they heard the sound of the disturbance. They got up and left.

72  EMBRACING EXILE

> Rav Sheshet was sitting in the synagogue of Shaf VeYativ in Nehardea. The divine presence came, and he did not leave. The ministering angels came and scared him [to make way for the divine presence]. He [Rav Sheshet, who was blind] said before Him: Master of the World, one who is unfortunate and one who is not unfortunate, who takes precedence over whom? He [God] said to them: Leave him alone.

Do not think that we are speaking in metaphors, the Talmud says here. The divine presence is literally present in the designated synagogue. If God may be met in at least these synagogues in exile, then what is the meaning of exile at all?

There is more to these brief teachings than meets the eye. The name of the specified synagogue—*Shaf VeYativ*—is an unusual but meaningful one. The Aramaic words of the name mean something like "slipped and settled"[8] (for present purposes, perhaps "floated and settled" would be better)—a very suggestive partial sentence. The Talmud itself does not elaborate on the name. But the great medieval Talmud commentator Rashi, repeats a tradition reporting that the synagogue was built using stones and dirt brought to Babylonia by the ancient exiles directly from the recently destroyed Temple in Jerusalem. Hence, it was the stones and dirt of the Temple that slipped from Jerusalem and settled in Babylon. So, we may surmise, it is the magic of the stones of the Temple that attracts the divine presence, all no longer in Jerusalem but in Babylon. Zion—the holy hill of Jerusalem—is effectively in Babylon.

The Talmud now goes further in making its argument for Babylon as Zion. Referencing Ezekiel's famous declaration that even in exile "I [= God] will be for them as a small sanctuary" (Ezekiel 11:16), R. Isaac adds: "These are the synagogues and the academies that are in Babylonia." His claim is that, in the absence of the Temple, God's "little Temple" is the synagogues and the study halls. But synagogues and study halls are potentially ubiquitous, as they can be built everywhere—or convened, even without new building, virtually anywhere. But this extension, as important as it is, misses what R. Isaac is truly saying, for he is building upon an equation already suggested by Ezekiel in the voice of God. God says here "I will be their sanctuary." So God = Sanctuary. R. Isaac adds that Sanctuary = synagogue/study hall. If A = B and B = C, then A = C, meaning that R. Isaac is claiming that God is promising that God will be in the synagogues and study halls. Synagogues and study halls are not restricted to one land. They may be any place. Like the Torah, which became Israel's portable homeland, synagogues and study halls may also become Israel's homeland. In this Babylonian Talmudic conversation, the importance of Zion as a Jewish destination is greatly reduced, for a Jew in exile has every bit as much access to what truly matters as he would in Zion, even a rebuilt one.

The importance of Torah, and Babylonia's place in Israel's tradition of Torah, is of great interest to the Babylonian rabbis. They know of the power of their own "Torah," and they are not quick to grant superiority, in matters of Torah, to their Palestinian counterparts. In fact, in one remarkably honest teaching, R. Shimon ben Laqish, a famous Palestinian rabbi of the same period as R. Judah, is reported to have taught:

> When the Torah was forgotten from Israel, Ezra came up from Babylonia and re-founded it. When it was once again forgotten, Hillel the Babylonian came up and re-founded it. When it was forgotten yet again, R. Hiyya and his sons came up and re-founded it. (Talmud Sukkah 20a)

We often hear echo of the prophet Isaiah's "messianic" promise that "out of Zion will come Torah" (2:3), the truth of which has often been assumed even for pre-messianic times. But according to the "history" recounted here, Zion (or the Land of Israel) is, in this world, the place of *forgetting* Torah and Babylonia the source of its recovery. Reading the Bible's history quite well, and arriving shockingly close to the conclusion of modern biblical scholars, R. Shimon observes that the Torah was observed mostly in the breach ("forgotten") during pre-exilic times, and it was Ezra, emerging from the exile, who founded (or re-founded) Israel on the foundation of Torah, effectively (at least) for the first time. But this would not be the last time Torah would come forth from Babylon. In this narrative, the great "founding father" of rabbinic Judaism, Hillel himself, was a Babylonian who brought Torah—now rabbinic Torah—from Babylon at the beginning of the rabbinic era, generations before the Mishnah would be recorded. And then again, in the period of transition from Mishnah to Talmud, the Torah of Palestine would again weaken, making it necessary for the Torah of Babylon to again save the day.

It is impossible to exaggerate how important this overall claim is. For the rabbis, Judaism was not a system focused on Temple and cult, as had been the case, thanks to the biblical legacy, in pre-rabbinic times. For the rabbis, Judaism is and would forever be a system focused on Torah—both its study

74 EMBRACING EXILE

and its performance, but particularly its study. If Torah owed its health to the Jews of Babylon, then Judaism itself was fundamentally Babylonian. What defines them as Jews, the Babylonian rabbis claim, is their own Torah, a Torah that would not exist without them. If Judaism was a product of diaspora, uniquely fit for diaspora, then it would be viable—a source of strength and reinvigoration—in all diasporas. The portable homeland that is the Torah, strengthened and expanded by the rabbinic Torah, would make it difficult to argue that Judaism relies on a foothold in Zion, itself merely a place.

The claim for the reliance of Jews of the Land of Israel on Babylonia for Torah was repeated in the name of a Palestinian rabbi. We cannot be sure that R. Shimon b. Laqish actually said the words here attributed to him, or whether the Babylonian sages simply attributed this opinion to him to their own advantage. But we need have no doubt that Palestinian rabbis actually recognized the Torah-prowess of their Babylonian counterparts, for the fifth-century Palestinian Midrash, Genesis Rabbah (11), actually teaches the same thing:

> R. Ishmael the son of R. Yose asked Rebbe, saying to him: By what merit do the Jews of Babylonia survive? He said to him: by the merit of Torah study; and those in the Land of Israel, by the merit of tithes; and those from the diaspora (literally: "from outside the land"), on account of the fact that they honor the Sabbaths and Holy Days.

Palestinian Jews, say the Palestinian rabbis—either in the late second century (the time of the rabbis cited here) or in the fifth (the period of the composition of this midrash)—are distinguished by their observance of the tithing laws, which, as agricultural laws, are practiced only in the Land of Israel. Babylonian Jews, by contrast, gain merit through their superior study of Torah.

As this Midrash reflects, Judaism is not only, nor even primarily, a religion of ideas and beliefs. Judaism in its various forms through the ages has almost always put emphasis on a combination of Torah study and action, that is, on the performance of the God's commandments. The rabbis were fully supportive of these two priorities, and while they themselves were particularly devoted to the former, they never neglected the latter. It is therefore worth considering how the rabbis adjudicated questions of Jewish law (*halakha*) when the law distinguished between the Land of Israel and Babylonia and/or other diasporas.

The first instance we shall consider pertains to the court's consideration of cases involving damages or loss in Babylonia, given that such cases require "expert judges" (this being the rabbis' understanding of the biblical term "*elohim*"—literally, "god" or "gods"—in certain biblical contexts). In the view of the Talmudic rabbis, "expert judges" require formal ordination, and according to rabbinic tradition, rabbinic ordination could be granted only in the Land of Israel. This means that in theory many cases could not be judged in Babylonia or other diasporas. How did the Babylonian rabbis deal with this restriction?

The Talmud (tractate Baba Qamma 84a–b) first sets up the problem:

> Raba said, "[Compensation for] damages done to an ox by an ox or to an ox by a human, we collect it in Babylonia, [but compensation for] damage done to a human by a human or to a human by an ox, we do not collect it in Babylonia."
>
> [The *gemara* challenges the opinion of Raba:] What distinguishes damages done to a human by a human or damages done to a human by an ox, that may not [be compensated]? [It is because to collect such compensation] "expert judges…" are needed, but they aren't [found in Babylonia]. Injuries done to an ox by an ox or to an ox by a human also [84b] require "expert judges" but they are not [found in Babylonia]!

If the Talmud sustains this challenge, this would mean that Jewish/rabbinic courts may not adjudicate any cases of damages in Babylonia, contrary to what Raba teaches. But the rabbis will not tolerate such an outcome, so they proceed to propose several distinctions or criteria that could allow for Raba's position, that is to say, for his insistence that certain kinds of cases, at least, may indeed be adjudicated by Jewish courts in Babylon. In typical Talmudic fashion, each proposal is followed by an objection, necessitating an additional proposed solution. In the end, it is the evident insistence on allowing Jewish courts to operate in Babylonia that makes the biggest impact.

Among the proposed reasons to ignore the restriction of judging to "expert judges" in cases of damages done to one's ox are the following:

1. In cases of injuries done to an ox, "we [the rabbis of Babylonia] are acting here as their [= the rabbis of the Land of Israel] agents, just as we do with the matters of admissions and loans."

2. "We act as their agents in matters of payments that are clear to us [which would include damage to oxen]. But as to matters in which the payments are not clear to us, we do not act as their agents."
3. "We act as their agents in matters of monetary compensation, but with respect to fines, we do not act as their agents."
4. "We act as their agents in a matter that is common, but with regard to humans injuring other humans, which is uncommon, we do not act as their agents."
5. "We act as their agents in a matter that is common and involves an out-of-pocket loss, but in a matter that is common but does not involve an out-of-pocket loss, or a matter that is not common but does involve an out-of-pocket loss, we do not act as their agents."

Additional deliberation narrows matters further, restricting damage cases that may be adjudicated in Babylonia to those caused by oxen under the categories of "tooth" (= damage caused by the mouth or analogous to it) and "leg" (= trampling and analogous causes).

There is no doubt that this deliberation, considered on its own, leaves sages/judges in Babylonia in a diminished position in comparison with their colleagues in Palestine, at least in theory. At the same time, even with these limitations, it is important to observe that in the cases of everyday life that probably mattered most—common cases involving monetary loss— the Babylonian sages asserted their authority, whatever their colleagues in Palestine might have told them.

Perhaps more important than the actual extent of their claimed power is the Babylonian justification of that power. The Talmud's justification of Babylonian rabbinic courts hearing certain cases is that "we act as their agents." Who authorized them to serve in this capacity? Ordinarily, a legal agent is appointed by the primary party. Did Palestinian sages appoint Babylonian colleagues to serve as their agents? Did Babylonian rabbis ask their colleagues in Palestine if they could serve in such a capacity? There is certainly no record of such a request, nor is there record of a Palestinian rabbinic request for such representation, either in this text or elsewhere. We need have little doubt, therefore, that this is a legal fiction—an arrogation of power on the part of Babylonian rabbis who claim to serve as agents of the Palestinians in matters of their choosing. Since "a person's agent is like himself," their assertion of agency is tantamount to insisting that, in certain crucial categories at least, "we are just like them." Forget the fact that they have formal ordination and we do not. Our Torah—the Babylonians insist—is all we need to justify our authority.

As it turns out, this discussion of rabbinic authority in Babylonia, important though it is, is only the beginning of the Talmud's deliberation on this question. Two related deliberations in the first chapter of tractate Sanhedrin take the relatively reserved assertion of power found in the text we just considered and leave it in the proverbial rear-view mirror, pushing ahead with a far bolder claim for rabbinic judicial prerogative in the Babylonian diaspora.

In a longer discussion of rabbinic ordination at Sanhedrin 13b–14a, R. Joshua b. Levi is recorded as saying, "There is no ordination outside of the Land" (= the view we referenced above). Despite the apparently simple meaning of this statement, the Talmud proceeds to ask whether this means that cases carrying possible fines cannot be adjudicated outside the Land at all, going on to reject this possibility because the Mishnah teaches explicitly that the Sanhedrin functions both inside and outside of the Land (m. Makkot 1:10). What is the meaning of Joshua b. Levi's teaching then? Precisely what we would assume: rabbis (= judges) may not be ordained outside the Land. (Why the Talmud sometimes engages in such seemingly pointless give-and-take, arriving at the obvious conclusion, is for another discussion.)

But a deliberation recorded earlier in the same chapter makes it clear that this restriction—despite what might appear to be so from the discussion in Baba Qamma—is ultimately of little consequence. The discussion, found at Sanhedrin 5a, rests on an important technicality: if a properly constituted court errs in judgment, it is not liable to make restitution for its error, but an informal court—such as one constituted by an individual judge, no matter how expert he may be—must make restitution if it errs. The great third-century Babylonian sage Rav (then joined by his colleague Samuel) advises that if the individual judge wants to avoid this possible consequence, he should obtain permission from the Exilarch—the recognized head of the Jewish community in Babylonia—to adjudicate cases individually. This will transform him from an informal into a formal court.

Having highlighted the authority of the Exilarch to empower judges, the Talmud asks about this authority as it might be exercised both in Babylonia and in the Land of Israel. It begins by outlining the positions it considers "simple": "It is obvious that from here to here [= the Exilarch exercising this power in Babylonia] and from there to there [= the patriarch exercising equivalent power in Palestine], and even from here to there [= the Exilarch empowering a judge to sit in Palestine] it is effective." The Babylonian

## 78    EMBRACING EXILE

Exilarch, the Talmud claims, has the authority to empower a judge to adjudicate cases in the Land of Israel! But reciprocal authority does not rest with the Palestinian Patriarch, the Talmud goes on to conclude. How can this be so? The Talmud offers a justification for this distinction:

> It is taught: "The scepter shall not depart from Judah" (Genesis 49:10)—this refers to the Exilarchs in Babylonia, who subjugate Israel with a scepter, "nor the ruler's staff from between his legs"—these are the grandchildren of Hillel, who teach Torah in public.

The Exilarch is understood to have coercive power, but the Palestinian teacher (Hillel, deemed by the rabbis the patriarch of his generation) merely the persuasive power of his Torah. This, as the Talmud understands it, means that the Exilarch may exercise authority in the Land of Israel, whereas the Patriarch does not enjoy equivalent authority in Babylon.

The great medieval philosopher and master codifier Maimonides, re-formulates these assertions into a clear system, while offering new characterizations that draw out the full implications of what the Talmud suggests. Consider his articulation of the law, which may be understood as his interpretation of the Talmud's discussions:

> The Exilarchs in Babylonia are in the place of kings, and they have the power to rule over Israel in all places and to judge them, whether they agree or not, as it says, "The scepter shall not depart from Judah" (Genesis 49:10)—this refers to the Exilarchs in Babylonia.
>
> And every judge who is fit to judge whom the Exilarch gave permission to judge, he has permission to judge in the entire world, even though the litigants don't agree, both in the Land and outside the Land, even though he may not adjudicate cases involving fines. And every judge who is fit to judge whom the court in the Land of Israel gave permission to judge, he has the authority to judge in all the Land of Israel and in the cities by its borders, even though the litigants don't agree. But outside of the Land, his authority doesn't extend to forcing the litigants, and even though he has the authority to adjudicate cases involving fines outside the Land, he may judge only those who agree to be judged by him. (Maimonides, *Mishneh Torah*, Laws of the Sanhedrin 4:13–14)

Maimonides understands the Talmud to be attributing to the Exilarch a royal power, one which allows him, as "king" of Israel, to appoint judges who may exercise authority in all lands where Jews might be found. This association of the Exilarch with the line of the Judean king emerges from a genuine historical seed, as the final king of Judah, Jehoiachin, lived out his life in the Babylonian exile (see 2 Kings 25:27–29); where else would his descendants be? By contrast, the Patriarch in the Land of Israel is not a descendant of ancient Israelite royalty, so he—and, by extension, the Palestinian court—may not empower his agent to serve beyond territories that are adjacent to the Land. What this means is that, while the judges of the Land of Israel are ascendant as far as formal ordination and judging cases involving fines are concerned, the head of the Babylonian Jewish community, along with his appointed agents, are superior in their general authority over the people of Israel. The Exilarch is the king, they are his authorized servants. The throne of Israel is in diaspora, the throne in the Land is empty. It is difficult to imagine a more forceful rabbinic response to claims of Palestinian ascendency than this.

A second relevant category of law is at least as much about geography as it is about authority. The category is divorce law. Because precision in matters of personal status is so important, the rabbis were very demanding in their requirements for a valid bill of divorce (a "*get*"). The Mishnah that begins the tractate discussing divorce declares that someone who brings a *get* to the Land of Israel from a foreign territory must declare "it was written and signed [by witnesses] in my presence." To follow this directive, one must know what counts as Israel and what a foreign land. In fact, the Mishnah itself already speculates on boundaries—R. Meir, for example, declares that "Acre (next to modern day Haifa) counts as the Land of Israel for [purposes of the law of] divorce."

What about Babylonia? The Talmud's discussion (Gittin 6a) begins by recording the contradictory opinions of two prominent Talmudic rabbis: Rab said, "It is, as to writs of divorce, like the Land of Israel." And Samuel said, "It is like overseas provinces." Their rationales are quickly explored, at which point a decision is tentatively proposed: "In Babylonia we regarded ourselves, so far as writs of divorce are concerned, as equivalent to the Land of Israel from the time that Rab came to Babylonia."[9] This, in turn, is challenged based upon the map outlined in the Mishnah, at which point the discussion ends by declaring that the stringency in the law of divorce applies to all foreign lands "except for Babylonia."

This conclusion is an argument not only for status, but also effectively for geography. What it declares is that Babylonia is not, for the Jew, a

80  EMBRACING EXILE

foreign land. Having reviewed the other Babylonian Talmudic texts above, we may now see this as part of a pattern. Simply put, the rabbis of Babylonia barely grant the primacy of the Land of Israel, or the exilic status of Babylonia. They are, they insist, at home, not only in fact but also as a matter of ideology.

Against this background, there is one other significant Talmudic "statement" we may cite, one that has generally been underappreciated: the fact that the Babylonian Talmud does not systematically comment on Mishnaic tractates that discuss laws pertaining to the Land of Israel; by contrast, the Talmud of the Land of Israel (known as the Yerushalmi, or Jerusalem Talmud) has full tractates deliberating on those laws. What explains this difference?

The most commonly offered explanation for the Bavli's omission has been that "laws dependent on the Land [of Israel]" for their performance do not apply in Babylonia, and the rabbis who created that Talmud therefore had no reason to comment on those laws. Now, this explanation is deceptively attractive, but it is almost certainly wrong. The fact is that the Babylonian Talmud comments on many matters that have no practical application, and it has complete tractates of deliberation and commentary on Mishnaic laws pertaining to sacrifice and the Jerusalem Temple—laws that had no application, in the rabbis' days, anywhere, even in Palestine! So "it wasn't practiced" simply will not suffice as an explanation for why the Bavli does or doesn't comment on something. The Babylonian rabbis' lack of attention to laws pertaining to the Land must, therefore, be a product of their lack of interest in the Land, at the very least, and perhaps even of a choice (conscious or not) to suppress interest in the Land, denying its centrality and asserting the centrality of laws and practices that could be enacted anywhere. If this is correct, then even the shape of the Talmud is a claim for Babylonian independence, an assertion of a home that needs no other.

What makes it possible for Babylonian rabbis of late antiquity to make so bold a statement about their status in their diaspora? Given what we have seen, the answer is not difficult to identify. Not only in their own view but in the view of all believing Jews, informed by biblical teachings, Jews originally came to Babylonia by divine command, at the hands of an empire that served as God's agent. In Babylon they "built homes, planted gardens, and prayed for the welfare of the government" (to paraphrase Jeremiah's letter). In Babylon, they could enjoy God's presence and live by God's ways. What had been threatened as exile became home.

This "foreign" home lasted not a few generations but many, and by the time of the rabbis who formulated the Talmud, Jews had been in Babylonia for more than a millennium. There they lived by the law of the Torah—a Torah that, in its final form, originated in Babylon—and conducted themselves fully as Jewish "citizens" of Babylonian lands. Most of the centuries of this residence left no record, but no news is almost certainly good news, and we have every reason to believe that Jews in Babylonia lived in peace, their welfare assured, during the vast majority of this period. By the time of the rabbis, Jews in Babylonia had synagogues, where they could meet their God. They had study halls, in which they could study God's words. They did not have a Temple, but neither did Jews in the Land of Israel. All in all, they were, at least in their own common opinion, in no significant way at a disadvantage in comparison to Jews in the Land of Israel.

Reflecting their condition and their experience of it, they declared boldly their "at-homeness," even despite the fact that there was a viable Jewish community in the Land of Israel during most of this same period. They asserted their prerogative and yielded greater legitimacy to no one, even to their brethren in the Holy Land. Jewish life in Babylon, they said out loud, is as good as Jewish life in Palestine. This diaspora was not an exile, the rabbis of Babylon insisted. It was as fully a home as any home could be, at least until the messiah would finally come and the world change irreversibly. Life fully lived is self-justifying. According to rabbinic testimony, at least, Jewish life in Babylon was fully justified—as would other diasporas be in the future.

Even when the Babylonian sages do not justify their diaspora by equating it—fully or nearly—with the biblical Promised Land, they *do* justify it, along with other diasporas, using another strategy. The Talmud insists, in a teaching recorded at Pesachim 87b, that "even at a time of God's anger, [God] recalls"—and implements—"the quality of mercy." As exile is biblically understood to be a consequence of divine anger, this statement leads to a brief deliberation on the ways God's mercy is expressed in God's exiling the people of Israel from the Land.

Among the several teachings on exile, one defends the latter Babylonian "exile" in particular. "God knows," the text says, "that Israel cannot withstand the cruel decrees of Edom [= Rome],[10] and therefore exiled them to Babylonia"—a place from which redemption will be easy, a place where the common language (Aramaic) is close to the language of Torah, the place where Jews originated (think: Abraham and Sarah) and is therefore their "maternal home."

82    EMBRACING EXILE

But the present defense of diaspora doesn't end with its Babylonian manifestation. The Talmud here defends exile in general. R. Oshaya defends the mercy of exile by declaring God "righteous" in scattering Israel. How so? Because, through their wide dispersion, their destruction is made impossible. No matter how much a particular tyrant may hate the Jews, there are many more beyond his reach whom he cannot destroy, and even his destruction of the Jews in his realm would destroy his reputation. (Yes, we today will think, in this connection, of the Holocaust, but the sages of old did not imagine such destructive technological capacity. Besides, even the Holocaust left many of the world's Jews alive.) Going even further is R. Eleazar's statement that God exiled Israel among the nations in order to attract converts. The attraction of more individuals to true belief being, obviously, a good thing—and something that cannot adequately be done in the less diverse Land of Israel—the "mercy" of this exile is one that allows Israel to serve God's purpose while extending God's truth to others.

## The Rabbis in a Popular Voice

If the rabbis of Babylonia were so confidently assertive in their "diasporism," then why have many, and perhaps even most, Jews believed that the Judaism supported by the rabbis was focused on the Land and return thereto? The answer lies in the fact that most Jews were not scholars, and most, therefore, had little awareness of the teachings and discussions cited above. The rabbis understood that their enterprise was an elite one, and they understood that, if they wanted to communicate with Jews at large, it could not be via texts such as the Talmud, which required a degree of education and dedication unavailable to most people. The rabbis therefore formulated a series of liturgies—prayers, blessings, and the like—that they hoped would be adopted by common Jews. Their hope was realized, and rabbinic prayers became the rabbinic words that most Jews knew best, even if they knew little else about rabbinic teachings.

In formulating their prayers and blessings, the rabbis understood that they would have to account for popular Jewish sensibilities; they could not fill their prayers with the bolder assertions of their scholarly compositions and hope for the masses to accept them. Even the Hebrew of the prayers they wrote is more "biblical" in its character than their Hebrew, for they had to formulate in the idiom that was better known. The same is true of the ideologies of their prayers for the masses.

The most significant rabbinic prayer, for purposes of this discussion, is the weekday "Amidah," the prescribed prayer, recited silently in standing position (*Amidah* = standing), three times daily. The shank of this prayer is unmistakably a prayer for redemption. In the course of reciting the prayer, the pray-er asks God that the exiles of Israel be gathered, judgment be executed against the wicked, sectarians be eliminated, the righteous (including converts) be raised, that God return to a rebuilt Jerusalem, that the scion of David be returned to the throne, and that sacrificial worship be restored in the rebuilt Temple. This is none other than a description of messianic fulfillment, at which time all of Israel will be gathered back to the holy city of Jerusalem.[11] With this as the central Jewish prayer, recited two to three times daily (originally two, when the evening prayer was considered not obligatory but voluntary), no wonder Jews thought of Judaism as a Holy Land-centered religion.

To make sense of the popular rabbinic message contained in this prayer, we must begin by locating it in time and space. The Amidah is a composition (with the themes of each blessing specified, if not the exact words) of the Mishnaic rabbis—rabbis who lived in Palestine in the decades following the destruction of the Temple and the failure of the Bar Kokhba revolt. This was a period of defeat and desperation for Palestinian Jews and, to a lesser extent, their brethren abroad. A Jew living in Palestine during these years could not have helped but wonder whether God had abandoned the Jewish people. Indeed, some Jews during these decades despaired of the biblical God and covenant and turned to Roman ways. To help fight such desperation, the rabbis had to offer the Jewish populace the seeds of hope for restoration. The daily Amidah does so by laying out the steps toward redemption, one by one. God who has redeemed Israel in the past (in the Exodus from Egypt, repeatedly referenced in rabbinic liturgy) would one day do so again. In light of this promise and expectation, Jews had no reason to abandon hope.

Such a focus made immense sense in the years after the destruction and failure of the Jewish revolts. But how did common experience of this prayer change as the years passed, as it inevitably would? How did Jews who learned of the collapse of the emperor Julian's authorization to rebuild the Jerusalem Temple in the mid-fourth century, who knew that its rebuilding could only be far off, adjust their understanding of the rabbinic prayer?

84  EMBRACING EXILE

Serendipitously, the original rabbinic formulation demanded little rein-terpretation to account for such new realities. It was the ultimate hope for Jews, the prayer taught, to be returned to the Land sometime in the unspec-ified future. In its vision, the return would require divine intervention and would therefore be miraculous, not mundane. Indeed, by emphasizing that redemption would be brought about by God, the prayer communicated that there was little people could do to hasten the return. According to the prayer's program, they could repent and return to God's ways, hoping that God would forgive them their trespasses. But beyond that, all they could do is wait. As it became clear, with the passing of the years, that God's plan did not include a speedy redemption, waiting became the characteristic posture of those reciting the prayer.

Reinforcing this posture was the routinization of the prayer, which was recited by the pious three times each weekday. What does such a routin-ized, repetitive ritual of recitation do emotionally to the reciter? Each gen-eration of Jews who recited this prayer knew that it had been recited by their parents and grandparents to no immediate avail. At the same time, they knew that those before them did not give up recitation, still hoping that its vision would one day be realized. Over time, the routinized expres-sion of the hope suppressed its urgency. The Jew could hope for return to the Land, where the Temple will be rebuilt and the Davidic monarchy restored, but he knew he would express that hope again tomorrow and again the next day, all while remaining in his diaspora home. Whatever the prayer meant to early generations of post-Destruction rabbinic Jews, it meant something different as this practice was perpetuated in the diaspora, hundreds and then thousands of years later.

Ironically, understood this way, the Amidah may even be seen as a kind of diaspora-affirming ritual. What it says on behalf of generations of dias-pora Jews is, "we hope one day, in an unspecified, miraculous future, to return to the Land from which we were once exiled. But for the present, we can live where we are." The expression of a hope to return is not meaning-less, but the emphasis is on the hope, not on the return.

As rabbinic prayer liturgy developed and grew, first in Babylonia and then elsewhere, the redemptive hope expressed in the Amidah came to be enveloped in a textual frame that balances the hope for redemption with a very different theological message. Early in the daily service, a collection of texts to be recited in preparation for the prayers that follow includes a selec-tion from I Chronicles 16, which is none other than a quotation from Psalm

105, discussed in an earlier chapter. The key words, speaking of the forefathers and hence their descendants, are these (verses 5–15):

> And they went from one nation to another, from a kingdom to another people, He allowed no person to oppress them, and He reproved kings on their account [saying] don't touch my anointed ones and do no wrong to my prophets.

This text offers a clear and uncompromising picture of the diaspora: it is a world where God protects Israel, allowing no hand to molest them. It is a world in which the force of God's covenant with Israel continues unabated. The quotation, now in the version from Chronicles, continues: "Recount His glory among the nations, His wonders among the nations." Arguably—and surely in the experience of the vast number of Jews who recited these words through the ages, who lived in diasporas—such recounting could effectively happen only "among the nations." Hinting at a justification of exile that Jews will often repeat in later generations, the writer of Chronicles affirms the purpose of diaspora—to spread awareness of the true God—along with his favorable evaluation of the diaspora experience. By reciting these words early in the service, the pray-er is left with the idea that Israel has a special purpose in exile and that she need not return to the Land before she can enjoy the special care of God. When the hope for redemption is later voiced in the daily prayers, it must be understood in light of this foundation. Without irony or sense of contradiction, the message is that Jews can hope for redemption while living unaccosted in their diaspora home. The characteristic dual orientation of the Jewish diaspora is present here in full force.

A related point is made later in the service, after the recitation of the Amidah, in the liturgy known as the *kedushah*—the sacred recitation. A *kedushah* is recited three times during the service, and in each of the recitations part of a verse is pronounced (Ezekiel 3:12b) declaring "blessed is the Honor of the Lord in His place" (or "from his place"). But in the last *kedushah* each morning, a fuller version of the verse is recited: "A spirit carried me away, and behind me I heard a great roaring sound: blessed is…." This fuller quotation places the reader in the larger biblical context, in which the spirit—of God—carries Ezekiel away to Babylon. In other words, the fuller quotation reminds the reader that God's spirit is not restricted to the Holy Land. It extends to the exile of Babylon as well.

So the daily prayer service, at the center of which is the prayer for redemption, reminds the reader, at the beginning and at the end, that being in exile does not mean being removed from God. On the contrary, as the Talmud also enunciated, God's spirit is in exile too, and God protects Israel from their enemies in exile as well as in the Land (that in reality God may not do so in either place is for a separate discussion). At the very least, this framing embodies the dual orientation that makes a diaspora. Now living in diaspora homes, now protected by God's living spirit, Jews simultaneously pray for return to the Land, at the time of their redemption, which will be enacted by God in some unknown future.

# 5

# Medieval Jewish Teachings on Exile

Between the sages who created the Talmud and their successors at the heads of the Babylonian academies, the world experienced a world-changing transition. The Talmudic rabbis had lived in a period known by historians as late antiquity, when Rome and then Byzantium in the west and the Persian empire in the east controlled the territories in which Jews lived. But Byzantium weakened and Persia collapsed, and into the power vacuum they left exploded a new force and religious civilization. In the seventh century, Muhammad and his armies conquered first the Arabian Peninsula and then vast territories east and west, beginning a process that would unify the world from Spain to India under the banner of the one God, known in Arabic by Muslims, Jews, and others as "Allah" ("the God"). This new world, the medieval world, differed in significant respects from the one it replaced for all populations outside of the far east, including Jews. In Islamic lands, the language of the Quran—Arabic—and the culture of Islam shaped the lives of millions, Muslim and non-Muslim alike. During these centuries, upwards of 90 percent of all Jews lived in the realm of Islam.

Crucially, in the middle of the eighth century, the capital of most of the Muslim world was relocated to Baghdad, right in the middle of the home that Jews had long called Babylonia. When the Talmudic academies relocated to Baghdad from short distances away, the Babylonian-Rabbinic center gained considerable force and prestige, which its leaders exercised vigorously. For the next couple of centuries, the capital of the Jewish world, the birthplace of the Talmud itself, was Baghdad and its environs.

During this period there was also a Jewish community in Palestine, one whose sages defended the primacy of their authority and practices, with some success in the nearby Mediterranean world. But the Palestinian Jewish community was a much diminished one. Small and insecure, in a land that by this point had come on hard times, the argument of Palestinian Jewish leadership relied more on the historical-religious claims of the Holy Land than on anything else. Any outsider would quickly have understood that the

88   EMBRACING EXILE

Babylonian Jewish center was the more powerful one, one that did not hesitate to push its ascendancy.

Jewish life in Islamic territories was mostly secure during the early Islamic centuries. Though the Quran preserves record of Muhammad's resentment of Jews for their failure to accept his revelation, the status of Jews in Islam was protected, from the earliest generations, as "people of the book." Muhammad accepted Jewish prophets as genuine prophets and recognized God's special relationship with Israel.[1] The precise status of Jews was defined, from the early eighth century onward, by the Pact of Umar, a set of rules that protected but limited the rights of Jews, Christians, and Zoroastrians. But while Christians and Zoroastrians would have experienced the limitations of the Pact as degrading relative to their prior statuses, Jews actually viewed it as providing relief, as it afforded them protections they had not earlier had in a Christian empire.[2]

The language of the Quran—Arabic—and Muslim religious concepts dominated the lands of Islam in which Jews found themselves, and these were often identical—or nearly so—to Jewish beliefs and terms. The sacred vocabulary of the Quran is often cognate to the Hebrew with which Jews were familiar in their holy writings, and the monotheism of Islam, its emphasis on law, its notion of holiness, its vision of final reward, and many other details of its system, were thoroughly familiar to Jews from Jewish sources. The Arabic spoken by Jews even used Islamic terms that they experienced as natural, not foreign.[3] As a consequence, Jews could feel very comfortable in the cultural milieu defined by Islamic canons and institutions.

If Jews could feel relatively "at home" in Islamic territories, this was especially the case in Iraq-Babylon. To begin with, Jews had actually been at home in this land for centuries, and nothing Islam brought changed their attachment to this ancient home. In addition, though we know relatively little about common Jewish life in Babylon during this period (it is always the case that common folk leave little tangible or literary record), we know that the heads of the academies were accorded considerable honor by Muslim authorities, and they wielded their authority like local royalty. Furthermore, the authority they accrued in the Jewish world was not only local. Jews from the far ends of the Muslim empire and beyond granted priority to the authority of the Babylonian yeshivas, seeking their opinions on the full range of Jewish religious questions.

Some of what we know about Jewish life and status in Babylon, and particularly in Baghdad, comes from the admittedly later (roughly 1170),

MEDIEVAL JEWISH TEACHINGS ON EXILE   89

effusive reports of Benjamin of Tudela. Even correcting for the distortions of hyperbole, Benjamin's account is very impressive. Consider the following excerpts, in the order in which Benjamin offers them:

> Bagdad, the great city and the royal residence.... There the great king, Al Abbasi the Caliph (Hafiz) holds his court, and he is kind unto Israel, and many belonging to the people of Israel are his attendants; he knows all languages, and is well versed in the law of Israel. He reads and writes the holy language [Hebrew].
>
> In Bagdad there are about 40,000 Jews, and they dwell in security, prosperity and honour under the great Caliph, and amongst them are great sages, the heads of Academies engaged in the study of the law. In this city there are ten Academies. At the head of the great Academy is the chief rabbi R. Samuel, the son of Eli. He is the head of the Academy Gaon Jacob. He is a Levite, and traces his pedigree back to Moses our teacher.... R. Elazar the scholar is the head of the fourth Academy; and R. Elazar, the son of Zemach, is the head of the order, and his pedigree reaches to Samuel the prophet, the Korahite. He and his brethren know how to chant the melodies as did the singers at the time when the Temple was standing.
>
> At the head of them all is Daniel the son of Hisdai, who is styled "Our Lord the Head of the Captivity of all Israel." He possesses a book of pedigrees going back as far as David, King of Israel. The Jews call him "Our Lord, Head of the Captivity," and the Mohammedans call him "Saidna ben Daoud," and he has been invested with authority over all the congregations of Israel at the hands of the Emir al Muminin, the Lord of Islam. And every fifth day when he goes to pay a visit to the great Caliph, horsemen, Gentiles as well as Jews, escort him, and heralds proclaim in advance, "Make way before our Lord, the son of David, as is due unto him...." He is mounted on a horse and is attired in robes of silk and embroidery with a large turban on his head...and all the Mohammedan princes who attend the court of the Caliph rise up before him.
>
> The authority of the Head of the Captivity extends over all the communities of Shinar, Persia, Khurasan and Sheba which is El-Yemen, and Diyar Kalach (Bekr) and the land of Aram Naharaim (Mesopotamia).... His authority extends also over the land of Siberia.... Further it extends to the gates of Samarkand, the land of Tibet, and the land of India.
>
> The Head of the Captivity gives the communities power to appoint (p. 63) Rabbis and Ministers who come unto him to be consecrated and to

90   EMBRACING EXILE

receive his authority. They bring him offerings and gifts from the ends of the earth. He owns hospices, gardens and plantations in Babylon, and much land inherited from his fathers, and no one can take his possessions from him by force. He has a fixed weekly revenue arising from the hospices of the Jews, the markets and the merchants, apart from that which is brought to him from far-off lands. The man is very rich, and wise in the Scriptures as well as in the Talmud, and many Israelites dine at his table every day. The Jews of the city are learned men and very rich.

In Bagdad there are twenty-eight Jewish Synagogues, situated either in the city itself or in Al-Karkh on the other side of the Tigris; for the river divides the metropolis into two parts. The great synagogue of the Head of the Captivity has columns of marble of various colours overlaid with silver and gold, and on these columns are sentences of the Psalms in golden letters. And in front of the ark are about ten steps of marble; on the topmost step are the seats of the Head of the Captivity and of the Princes of the House of David.[4]

In Benjamin's record, the Muslim rulers in Baghdad are favorably inclined to the Jews, who are numerous. Jewish life is comfortable. Jewish leaders, who trace their origins back to biblical royalty and nobility, are much honored, and they wield their authority throughout the known world. The Jewish community supports scholarship and piety, and its members are comfortable with public expressions of their Jewishness without any fear of oppression or disadvantage. If this was the case in the twelfth century, conditions and perceptions (if not precise details) cannot have been much different in the eighth and ninth centuries, when life in Baghdad was at its zenith.[5]

Part of the evidence for the international ascendency of the Baghdadi academies was the growing authority of their Talmud—*the* Talmud (as opposed to the Talmud that had been produced in Palestine, the Yerushalmi). It was the yeshivas in Baghdad that canonized and sponsored the Babylonian Talmud, and the success of the Talmud went hand in hand with the success of those academies. Moreover, the claimed continuity of the academies with the pre-Islamic Talmudic academies was itself a source of their authority, and few challenged either the claim or the authority.[6]

All of this meant that Babylonian Jewish leadership had little need to justify their diaspora, for the justifications had already been provided, in the Talmudic texts they had inherited. As the Talmud said, and they knew very well, Babylonia was no longer exile; a Jew who lived in Babylonia lived as though in the Land of Israel.

But the fact that they did not need justifications for their diaspora life does not mean that they did offer them anyway. On occasion, Babylonian authorities saw fit to justify their own "Zion." This was occasional because justifications tend to be offered when one's position is subject to challenge. When stopped by a guard in an "employees only" area of a store, a customer must justify his presence there because the door through which he passed to gain access said "employees only." On the main retail floor, no justification is necessary. By the same token, during these centuries, Jews living in Iraq took for granted the legitimacy of their Babylonian home. Few, therefore, saw any reason to say anything about it.

Still, there were exceptions. One of the leaders of the Babylonian community in the eighth and ninth centuries, Pirqoi ben Baboi, wrote a polemical tract defending the superiority of the Babylonian Talmud and its law over the Palestinian equivalents. In this tract, his *Iggeret* (epistle), Pirqoi comments as follows:

> Even in the days of the Messiah, they (the Babylonian academies) will not experience the travail of the Messiah, for it is written, "O Zion, escape, you who dwell in Babylonia…(Zechariah 2:11)" and "Zion" is none other than the academy, which is distinguished in Torah and precepts…. And redemption will come first to the academy of Babylonia, for, as Israel is redeemed through their virtue (= of the academies), redemption comes first to them.[7]

Building on teachings contained in the Talmud (Ketubbot 111a), Pirqoi begins by echoing Abbaye's opinion that, with regard to the final redemption, Babylonia (or at least its academies) is in no way secondary to the Land of Israel. Just as those living (or buried?) in the Land of Israel will be restored without travails, so too will those in Babylonia be redeemed without pain. Pirqoi then goes further, insisting that redemption will actually come first to Babylonia. Why? Because redemption will only come by merit of the academies, and the academies—the superior academies, that is—are found in Babylonia.

In the ninth century, the superior academies were indeed in Baghdad. But the implications of Pirqoi's argument are broader than its specifics. If the "center" of Judaism is located in its premier academies, and if those

92 EMBRACING EXILE

living in the land(s) of such academies will be the first in the march toward redemption, then what is to stop the Jewish center from being anywhere outstanding academies are located? As the Talmud already recognized, synagogues and study halls are not restricted geographically. They are infinitely portable. So if God is to be found in these homes (the *beit* knesset = "house of gathering" = synagogue; the *beit* midrash = "house of study" = study hall or academy), and if these homes are themselves what define the land where redemption commences (a kind of deferred Zion), then what is to stop Zion from going anywhere? The answer is "not much."

In the eleventh and twelfth centuries, the yeshivas of Baghdad experienced a significant decline, along with the city as a whole. This was the product of multiple factors. To begin with, Muslim authorities, defensive of their power, had become more conservative and rigid; Jewish authorities followed suit. Yeshiva hierarchies became more formal and the rituals of the court more monarchic. Advanced Jewish education, like nearby Muslim education, left behind the vibrant critical inquiry modeled by the Talmud, preferring memorization and repetition. To the heads of the academy, public honor and authority became more important than deliberation and debate.[8]

None of this should be taken as evidence of a decline in the quality of local Jewish life as such. Ironically, all these developments are more evidence of the comfortable embeddedness of the Jewish sages in Muslim-Iraqi society than anything else. There is no evidence that common Jews fared any worse, relatively speaking, than their leaders. Nevertheless, all of this did herald a turning point, for the absence of a vibrant Jewish study culture in Iraq, combined with the fact that the Talmud, now edited and finalized, could provide fertile soil for new Jewish discoveries anywhere, allowed for the emergence of confident Jewish life in multiple new centers. Such new centers sprung up around the Mediterranean. From North Africa to Spain, new or newly confident communities, with new, recognized authorities, quickly emerged, and these centers unhesitatingly asserted their prerogative vis-à-vis the soon-to-be former Babylonian center.

The emergence of new centers demanded the development of new stories of exile/diaspora, for unlike the Babylonian diaspora, these new Jewish homes could not claim biblical roots. This did not stop them, though, from formulating origin stories that made sense of their new place in the Jewish world. The most audacious such story—deservedly much commented upon in recent scholarship—will provide us with the map of where our attentions must turn next.

MEDIEVAL JEWISH TEACHINGS ON EXILE 93

The origin story for the newly confident diasporas is preserved in a composition written by Abraham ibn Daud, born in Cordoba, Spain, in around 1110 (meaning that his life and experience overlapped with that of Maimonides). Ibn Daud's major writing is his *Sefer Hakabbalah* (Book of Tradition), a book that defends the legitimacy of the rabbis and their tradition against their scripturalist opponents, the Karaites.

The story has come to be known as the "Story of the Four Captives." It begins by asking how the income that once supported the Babylonian academies dried up. The answer offered by the narrative is that other academies took their place, and there was no reason, therefore, for scholars to continue to gather in Baghdad to study Talmud, or for far-flung communities to support those academies to assure that Torah study would be upheld. The story details the circumstances of this shift.

According to the narrative, a ship was sent from Cordoba to farther east in the Mediterranean, having been directed by the Muslim king to capture the contents of Christian ships. In the course of its sailings, the ship encountered another ship on which were travelling four Jewish scholars, on their way from Bari, Italy, to a Talmudic convention (Kallah) in Iraq. Rather than letting the ship and its passengers proceed, the Muslim pirates took the rabbis captive and sold them for ransom at various ports of call. What is important at this stage of the narrative—and what any knowledgeable reader of the text would have recognized—is that the scholars and/or the communities to which they were sold are founders of what had become, by the time of Ibn Daud's writing, outstanding centers of Jewish learning. There were no more significant rabbinic authorities during this period than the ones mentioned in the story, and no more prominent centers in the eleventh century than those "founded" as a result of this piracy: Qairwan, Cordoba, and Fostat. (Cordoba was associated, in greater Jewish memory, with Maimonides' youth and Fostat, Egypt, with his mature life.) Ibn Daud is intimating the question: where did these centers and their authority come from? He (or his story) answers that they began with scholars who once paid obeisance to the authority of the Babylonian academies, but who now, thanks to historical circumstances, were cast their own ways, taking the authority of Babylonia with them.

The story of events in Cordoba, Ibn Daud's home, is particularly revealing:

Then the commander arrived at Cordoba where he sold R. Moses along with R. Hanokh. He was redeemed by the people of Cordoba, who were under the impression that he was a man of no education.

94   EMBRACING EXILE

Now there was in Cordoba a synagogue that was called the College Synagogue, where a judge by the name of R. Nathan the Pious, who was a man of distinction, used to preside. However, the people of Spain were not thoroughly versed in the words of our Rabbis, of blessed memory. Nevertheless, with the little knowledge they did possess, they conducted a school and interpreted [the traditions] more or less [accurately]. [Once] R. Nathan explained [the Yom Kippur ritual requiring] "immersion [of the finger] for each sprinkling," which is found in the tractate Yoma, but he was unable to explain it correctly. Thereupon, R. Moses, who was seated in the corner like an attendant, arose before R. Nathan and said to him: "Rabbi, this would result in an excess of immersions!" When he and the students heard his words, they marveled to each other and asked him to explain the law to them. This he did quite properly. Then each of them asked him all the difficulties which they had, and he replied to them out of the abundance of his wisdom. Outside the College there were litigants who were not permitted to enter until the students had completed their lesson. On that day, R. Nathan the judge walked out, and the litigants went after him. However, he said to them: "I shall no longer be judge. This man who is garbed in rags and is a stranger is my master, and I shall be his disciple from this day on. You ought to appoint him judge of the community of Cordoba." And that is exactly what they did. The community then assigned him a large stipend and honored him with costly garments and a carriage. [At that point] the commander wished to retract his sale. However, the king would not permit him to do so, for he was delighted by the fact that the Jews of his domain no longer had need of the people of Babylonia. "The report [of all this] spread throughout all of Spain and the Maghreb, and students came to study under him. Moreover, all questions which had formerly been addressed to the academies were now directed to him.[9]

Cordoba, in Al-Andalus, Spain, had become, before Ibn Daud's lifetime, the capital of the Western Muslim empire (which included Spain and North Africa). In 929 the Caliph Abd al-Rahman III declared Cordoba, his capital, to be independent of the authority of the Abbasid Caliphate in the east, undertaking to create a city worthy of its rank in the Muslim world. Cordoba was already, in this period, a large city with a sizable and diverse population, the proportions and glory of which only grew under al-Rahman and his successors. The grandeur of the city can easily be seen in the community's Grand Mosque, which can still be visited today—a magnificent, massive structure, capable of accommodating thousands of worshippers at a single time. Until the city's conquest by the Almohads in 1146, the Cordoba caliphate was generally enlightened, supporting all branches of medieval learning, with an open mind to the wisdoms of past civilizations; it is reputed to have had the largest library in the world in its day, by legend containing a million volumes. What is beyond dispute is that Cordoba was a great center of scholarship and learning, home to philosophers, grammarians, mathematicians, and poets. Jews enjoyed the fruits of these pursuits and participated in the gifts of the culture.

Representing the privilege of at least some Jews in Cordoba is Hasdai ibn Shaprut. Ibn Shaprut was a scholar, a physician to the caliph, and a trusted diplomat who represented the caliph in sensitive negotiations. Expressing his own experience of the land in which he lived, Ibn Shaprut wrote:

> It is a land of grains, wines and purist oils, rich in plants, a paradise of every sort of sweet.... Our land also has its own sources of silver and gold and in her mountains we mine copper and iron, tin and lead, kohl and marble and crystal.... The king ruling over us has amassed silver, gold and other treasures, along with an army the likes of which has never been amassed before.... When other kings hear of the power and glory of our king they bring gifts to him.[10]

It is difficult to think of another Jewish writer writing such a panegyric in praise of a land that is not the Holy Land. Though Ibn Shaprut speaks from a special position—being an insider to the court—it would be a mistake to imagine he was the only Cordoban Jew who felt as he did.

It is in this context that Ibn Daud's story can be most fully appreciated. The story suggests, to begin with, that there was a time—a "before" time— when Jews in Cordoba could not yet be proud of their accomplishments, at least not in Torah. But then things changed, and, according to this story, the change was momentous. Notably, the story told by Ibn Daud is reminiscent, in several of its details, of Talmudic stories told about the "founding father" of Rabbinic Judaism, Hillel, or other early giants of the movement. R. Moses' enlightening intervention in the halakhic discussions of local authorities— the unknown scholar whose brilliance moves those who hear him to appoint him head of the community—parallels the story of Hillel coming in the early first century from Babylonia to Palestine to answer questions asked by Bnai Beteira about the Passover offering (Talmud Pesachim 66a).

## 96 EMBRACING EXILE

The redirection of the loyalties of the Cordoban community from past authorities to future ones as they emerge from the study halls recalls the account of the High Priest and Shamaya and Avtalion emerging from the Temple on Yom Kippur, when the masses turned from the High Priest to the sages (Yoma 71b). All these stories are about the transmission of sacred authority, and by hearkening back to the Talmudic tales, the medieval story uses their model to strengthen its claim. To put the claim in other terms, while Torah might once have gone forth from Zion, and more recently from Babylonia, Torah now goes forth from cities around the Mediterranean. These diasporas have been established as new Zions.[11]

So the torch of Torah, once residing in Babylon, was passed to authorities farther to the west. Emerging from these communities were some of the most brilliant and influential figures ever to grace the stage of Jewish scholarship and culture. On account of what they created, this period is sometimes called a "golden age" for Jews in this diaspora, and, whatever the ups and downs of Jewish experience in this time and place, there can be no doubt of the attractions and comforts this world offered.[12]

A poem by one of the poets of this age reveals something about the experience of Jews in this diaspora. Dunash ben Labrat was born probably in Fez in the mid-tenth century, studied in Baghdad, and finally settled in Cordoba. While in Cordoba, he penned the following lines, which reveal something of the conflict a comfortable diaspora Jew may have experienced, feeling so at home in his "exile" from Zion:

> There came a voice: "Awake!
> Drink wine at morning's break.
> 'Mid rose and camphor make
> A feast of all your hours,
>
> 'Mid pomegranate trees…
> Where vines extend their leaves…
>
> Where lilting singers hum
> To the throbbing of the drum…
>
> The cooing of a dove
> Sounds like a song of love…
>
> We'll drink on garden beds
> With roses round our heads.

MEDIEVAL JEWISH TEACHINGS ON EXILE    97

> To banish woes and dreads
> We'll frolic and carouse.
>
> Dainty food we'll eat.
> We'll drink our liquor neat,
> Like giants at their meat,
> With appetite aroused...
>
> Scented with rich perfumes,
> Amid thick incense plumes...
> Spending in joy our hours."

It is hard to imagine a more luxurious, more sensuous poem. The picture is nothing less than one of life in paradise. Nothing could be further from exile! But such a picture may make the pious Jew a bit anxious, and the poet gives voice to this sentiment as well:

> I chided him: "Be still!
> How can you drink your fill
> When lost is Zion hill
> To the uncircumcised."[13]

But if the notion of paradise in exile is a source of discomfort, then what are we to make of the resplendent picture painted by the words in the first, major part of the poem? Translator Raymond Scheindlin, in his comment on the poem, reports that "some believe that Dunash put his heart into the descriptive part of the poem...and that the retraction...is a mere nod toward traditionalists."[14] Given the abundance and poetic richness of the first part of the poem, compared with the spare quality of the latter part, this is the understanding that makes most sense to me. But even if Scheindlin is correct when he says, "My feeling is that Dunash really believed in both parts of the poem," this changes little, because it admits that one side of the poet, at least, feels completely at home in his Andalusian paradise. This diaspora is little inferior to Eden, so even if one hopes to return to Zion, the justification of life in (to be honest: non-) exile is fully articulated.

One of the most outstanding of the figures of the Spanish "golden age" was Judah Halevi. Conventional opinion holds that Halevi was born in Toledo in 1075, but scholars dispute both the year and place of his birth.[15]

98    EMBRACING EXILE

What is clear, though, is that Halevi did spend some time in Toledo, which, though a Christian city, retained Arabic language and culture among its learned class.[16] In any case, Halevi spent his life in both the Christian north and the Muslim south, and the latter had the most profound influence on his culture and creativity. Halevi was a rabbi, poet, and philosopher, writing his philosophy in Arabic and his poetry in the Arabic-influenced Hebrew of Muslim Spain. Yet, despite his rootedness in Spain, Halevi's heart inspired him to go to the Holy Land, where his life suddenly ended, in the realm of the Crusader Kingdom of Jerusalem, in 1141.

Halevi's longing for the Holy Land is perhaps best expressed in the poem for which he is best known, "My heart is in the East, but I am in the far reaches of the West." Living in Spain, Halevi's "east" was the Holy Land, while his west was his own home, al-Andalus. He expresses here, as in some other writings, his deep longing to make pilgrimage to the land of his ancestors. For this reason, this poem is often seen as an expression of a kind of medieval "Zionism," while Halevi himself is often identified, anachronistically, as a medieval "Zionist."

But when one looks into Halevi's elaboration of his own ideas, one discovers that Halevi's thinking about Zion and exile was, in fact, far more complex than can be expressed in a few lines of poetry. It is in his great work of philosophy (or, as some would characterize it, "anti-philosophy"), the Kuzari, that one may find these ideas worked out in detail.

The Kuzari is written as a kind of Platonic dialogue, primarily between the king of the Khazars (the Khazari) and an unnamed rabbi, whose voice may be taken to speak for Halevi himself. Halevi's discussion of Jews and their Land begins with a "scientific" theory proposing that "one country may have higher qualifications than others. There are places in which particular plants, metals, or animals are found, or where the inhabitants are distinguished by their form and character, since perfection or deficiency of the soul are produced by the mingling of the elements" (*Kuzari*, book II, 10). The Khazar king accepts the theory but challenges the rabbi in connection to Palestine and what the rabbis deems its proper inhabitants, the Jews. The rabbi responds by asserting the superiority of the Land in connection to prophecy, saying that "whosoever prophesied did so either in the [Holy] Land, or concerning it,"[17] then continuing by praising the superiority of the Land in general. Citing many biblical passages, the rabbi establishes the special connection of Jews and the Land. Admitting the connection but noting the dilemma of Jews resident in exile, the Khazari remarks: "So you are to-day a body without either head or heart." The rabbi then responds:

> Thou sayest rightly, but we are not even a body, only scattered limbs, like the "dry bones" which Ezekiel saw [in his vision] (Ezekiel 37). These bones, however, O king of the Khazars, which have retained a trace of vital power, having once been the seat of a heart, brain, breath, soul, and intellect, are better than certain bodies formed of marble and plaster, endowed with heads, eyes, ears, and all limbs, in which never dwelt the spirit of life, nor ever can dwell in them, since they are but imitations of man, not man in reality.[18]

It does not take much to fathom Halevi's meaning, which we may paraphrase in these words: the people of Israel, though compromised, are at least genuinely alive. By contrast, the nations who worship marble and plaster are themselves, though possibly beautiful, of marble and plaster. Consequently, they have no genuine life at all.

The rabbi goes on to assert that exile is a place—a condition—where Israel retains life, "For [it] is our master the living God, our King, who keeps us in this our present condition in dispersion and exile." If exile is a condition perpetuated by God, then God must retain a vital connection to God's people in exile. "Certainly!" the Khazari responds, "a similar dispersion is not imaginable in any other people, unless it became absorbed by another, especially after so long a period." He goes on: "Many nations which arose after you have perished without leaving a memory, as Edōm, Mōāb, Ammōn, Aran, the Philistines, Chaldaeans, Medians, Persians, and Javān, the Brahmans, Sabaeans, and many others." If Israel survives in exile while others disappear, there must be a reason, and that reason must be God.

As the rabbi says:

> We still hold connection with that Divine Influence through the laws which He has placed as a link between us and Him. There is circumcision, of which it is said: 'My covenant shall be in your flesh for an everlasting covenant' (Genesis 17:13). There is further the Sabbath, 'It is a sign between me and you throughout your generations' (Exodus 31:13). Besides this there is 'the covenant of the Fathers,' and the covenant of the law, first granted on Hōreb, and then in the plains of Moab in connection with the promises and warnings laid down in the section: When thou shalt beget children and grandchildren (Deuteronomy 4:25)."[19]

100 EMBRACING EXILE

This is an extremely important statement. The Rabbi—Halevi—is effectively answering the question: What is our [= Israel's] connection with the divine? His answer is "the laws He has placed as a link between us and Him." The laws/commandments he enumerates specifically are those with which the covenantal relationship is particularly associated, as enunciated by scripture: circumcision and the Sabbath. But he also then expands his view to "the covenant of the Fathers" and "the covenant of the Law." The specific commandments enumerated first (the Sabbath, circumcision) may be observed anywhere; they are in no way tied to a specific territory. But the same is largely true, Halevi now suggests, for the more global covenants of the ancestors and the law. The covenant of the ancestors may offer the promise of the Land, but it is in effect anywhere, and the covenant of the law—of the commandments given at Sinai—is also in effect everywhere. And the majority of the commandments subsumed in the covenant of the law may be performed anywhere. The Land is not central to a Jew's covenantal fulfillment, as Halevi here admits explicitly.

Halevi is arguing that Jews in exile nevertheless have a relationship with God that other nations cannot hope to recreate. But is not this the same Halevi who was, in the end, willing to risk his life to travel to the Land of his ancestors? How does he square these two views with one another? He continues:

> We are not like dead, but rather like a sick and attenuated person who has been given up by the physicians, and yet hopes for a miracle or an extraordinary recovery, as it is said: 'Can these bones live?' (Ezekiel 37:3)....Israel amidst the nations is like the heart amidst the organs of the body; it is at one and the same time the most sick and the most healthy of them....The heart is exposed to all sorts of diseases, and frequently visited by them, such as sadness, anxiety, wrath, envy, enmity, love, hate, and fear. Its temperament changes continually, undulating between excess and deficiency, and moreover influenced by inferior nourishment, by movement, exertion, sleep, or wakefulness. They all affect the heart whilst the limbs rest.[20]

Halevi's argument is built on a metaphor of the heart, as the heart was understood in the Middle Ages. The heart, he observes, is the most sensitive of the body's organs. It is therefore rendered "sick" by sadness, envy, hate, fear, and other emotions. But its sensitivity is evidence of its "health"—its centrality and particular importance—as well. Without one's heart, one could not hope to survive.

Halevi now makes what is implied in the metaphor explicit:

> Our relation to the Divine Influence is the same as that of the soul to the heart.... Just as the heart is pure in substance and matter, and of even temperament, in order to be accessible to the intellectual soul, so also is Israel in its component parts. In the same way as the heart may be affected by disease of the other organs, viz. the lusts of the liver, stomach and genitals, caused through contact with malignant elements; thus also is Israel exposed to ills originating in its inclinings towards the Gentiles.... The trials which meet us are meant to prove our faith, to cleanse us completely, and to remove all taint from us. If we are good, the Divine Influence is with us in this world.[21]

Jews—the heart—are sensitive to illness, illness that originates with gentiles and is contracted by overly close approaches of Jews to gentiles. Through such contact, Jews become "ill." But the trials of illness have their beneficial consequence, as they prove the Jew's faith and remove the impurity that causes illness. Through this process, health may be restored. Crucially, this "health" is not represented as redemption = return to the Holy Land (though we can assume Halevi would see that as the ultimate goal). The simple avoidance of gentile pollution—the performance of God's will = good conduct—will draw the divine back into relationship with Israel in this world. Relationship with the divine is maintained and restored through goodness; it does not demand return to the Land where that relationship was once performed and maintained.

It is crucial to be attentive to the dynamic being played out here. Halevi was, as evidenced by both his writings and his life, an uncompromising "Zion-ist," by which I mean a Jew whose longing for Zion was unmistakable, one who put his life on the line to fulfill his dream to return to Zion. Yet even such a medieval Jew, for whom the Holy Land is so obviously important, has a well-developed conception of diaspora. Even for such a Jew, Jewish life in diaspora may be infused with holiness and divinity. To be sure, diaspora carries the risk of attraction to foreign ways (in truth, in his day, as through most of history, so did the Holy Land, though during his lifetime the attractions of Spain were certainly much greater). But the commandments required by the covenant of law can be performed in diaspora, and they can protect the Jew from the temptations of foreign ways (ironically, Halevi, who certainly considered himself a good Jew, did not

## 102  EMBRACING EXILE

overcome such influences). The Jew can therefore be a good Jew, living a fully fulfilled Jewish life, in diaspora. Bound by and performing the covenant of the ancestors, such a Jew is assured of the presence of God in their life. But recognition of this reality leads to a complicating question, one that Halevi surely must have considered. If, in exile, the covenant can be fulfilled and relationship with God maintained, then what is the meaning of "exile?" How is such "exile" fundamentally inferior to life in the Promised Land, and why would one need redemption from it at all?

Halevi would answer these questions by saying that not all of the commandments can be fulfilled in diaspora, and many are unperformable in the absence of a Temple. Jewish life in a redeemed Holy Land, therefore, would be a more complete Jewish life. And we might in theory assent and say, "All this is true." But in the real world, the one without a Temple, with foreigners controlling the Land of Israel, Jewish life in that Land can be only marginally more complete, and Jewish life in diaspora only marginally less so. To say this another way: even Halevi, the medieval "Zionist," would have to admit that Jewish life in diaspora is sacred life—a more complete life, he says, than that of the Gentiles among whom Jews live.

In his poetry, Halevi expresses his love of Zion more than once. But he also, here and there, admits the attractions of diasporic existence, even admitting that some diasporas have a sacred purpose of their own. Consider, as an example, these lines from one of his poems:

> Praise to Egypt!
> Great above all other lands,
> For there God first addressed His people;
> Where He planted His most treasured vine,
> A vine that yielded clusters with the finest fruit;
> Birthplace of the messengers of God,
> Emissaries as between a bride and groom;
> Where the Glory of God descended,
> Walked in fire, upright like a pillar,
> In a cloud enveloping;
> Where sacrifice to the Lord was made, covenantal blood
>     sprinkled—
> Bringing redemption;
> Where Moses stood in prayer, beseeching—
> And what a prayer it was!

Israel, Egypt, Babylonia—
Three equal nations,
Connected by a highway!
In its midst, an altar built for God,
To elevate His Name above all praise.
Miracles were there, and wonders, and the Name
Whose glory fills the earth.
Its river one of four Edenic rivers
Flowing from God's own garden;
Bountiful as paradise.[22]

We know more about Egypt of this period, and Jewish Fostat (Cairo) in particular, than perhaps any other medieval city, thanks to the nineteenth-century discovery of its immense "archive" of discarded Jewish writings known as the Geniza. The Geniza contains a range of letters, lists, and documents testifying to Jewish and related life in Fostat/Cairo from the ninth century to the nineteenth, and it is particularly rich in materials from the period of the lives of Halevi and Maimonides (the latter of whom was a child when Halevi was in his later years). In fact, personal writings in Halevi's own hand were discovered in the Geniza, probably from the time he stopped in Egypt on his way to Palestine, and they provide us with some insight into Halevi's aspirations and practical concerns.

From the material surviving in the Geniza we learn that Jewish life in Egypt during his lifetime was vibrant and complex. Jews were merchants, traders, shopkeepers, and many other professions, including—occasionally—scholars. They married and divorced, had children and attended funerals, made fortunes and lost them. They had their choice of multiple synagogues, which followed various regional rites. They lived in primarily Jewish neighborhoods, though not exclusively, as many of their neighbors were Muslims or even Christians. They spoke Arabic and shared considerable religious vocabulary with the Muslims among whom they lived.[23] Stated simply: they lived in their Egyptian home as home, brazenly ignoring the scriptural prohibition—one that Maimonides repeated in his Jewish legal code (*Mishneh Torah*, Laws of Kings and their Wars 5:7)—of a Jew returning to Egypt.

The first part of Halevi's poem, a paean to the land of Egypt, would occasion no surprise, then, if not for the fact that it came from the pen of Judah Halevi, who never lived in Egypt and visited it only on a relatively brief layover on his way to realizing his dream of settling in the Holy Land.

104    EMBRACING EXILE

Sensitive to this problem, Scheindlin understands the poem as a whole as Halevi's response to friends in Egypt who, upon his arrival there, seek to dissuade him from taking the next step to the Holy Land. In the latter part of the poem, Halevi rejects their attempt, arguing that "God may have turned aside there, the way a traveler stops to rest...but His real roots are in Jerusalem."[24] But if this is intended as an outright rejection of the invitation to remain in Egypt, then the first part of the poem is that much more surprising, for its argument for the nearly co-equal status of Egypt is rather strong. Egypt is, Halevi admits, the place where the people Israel was effectively born, where they were first addressed by God, where God's superior prophet, Moses, was born, where God's glory made its presence felt on earth, and more. It is hard to imagine a stronger defense of the sacred status of Egypt! At the same time, the poem's defense of the Holy Land feels pallid, almost an afterthought. At the very least, the truth to which this poem testifies is that certain diasporas—Egypt (not just of biblical times but of Halevi's time as well) and Babylon—are closer to paradise than they are to exile. Zion may be preferred, but by virtue of their place in Israel's sacred history, lands outside of Zion may not be far behind.

Though the majority of the world's Jews during these centuries lived in Islamic lands, the seeds of Jewish life in Christian Europe were planted during this era as well. Jewish communities in what Jews have known as "Ashkenaz" were, at this time, extremely small, but even at this early stage, the promise of Ashkenaz could not have been denied, as some of Jewish history's greatest scholars were already making their contributions felt in the territories that lay between northern France and the Rhineland. Jewish life in these lands was sometimes punctuated by oppressions and poverty, but the latter condition distinguished Jews as a people from no one, and even the former were occasional, not constant.[25]

Consider, for example, early Ashkenaz's most notable Jewish scholar, the great rabbinic commentator Rashi, who, in the latter years of the eleventh century, witnessed the first crusade. During his lifetime, the Jewish populations of the cities of the Rhine—Speyer, Worms, and Mainz—suffered serious losses at the hands of crusaders.[26] At time of these events, Rashi was living in Troyes, France, but he maintained close ties to the cities of his younger years (Rashi studied and taught in Worms until he was 25), which were in any case part of the same Christian cultural milieu; anti-Jewish fervent was not stopped by rivers or plains. Still, anti-Jewish sentiments did not prevent Rashi from composing incomparable commentaries on the Torah and the Talmud, suggesting that he was free and secure enough to pursue the loftiest of Jewish goals. And the Jewish populations of the Rhineland, which suffered the brunt of the crusader violence, recovered within a generation, continuing to be serious centers of Jewish life and piety. In the next generation, Rashi's first scholarly successors, known as the Tosafot, experienced the second crusade. But neither they nor other Jews suffered as a result, as both Jews and Christians had learned the lessons of the abuses of the first crusade and were thereafter able to prevent violence against Jews, which was not the goal of the crusades in any case.[27] Jewish life was not without its painful interruptions, in other words, but it also did not lack in richness or creativity.

Jews in medieval Christian Europe lived, with rare exception, in small communities of their brethren—often numbering no more than a few dozen—in small towns or "cities." To survive in such conditions, they had to live peacefully with their neighbors. This fact is made evident in various contemporary testimonies in which the writers describe the dependence of Jews on local resources for their basic needs. To bake their breads or roast their meats, Jews had to use communal ovens, sharing them with their Christian neighbors. To ease the burdens of everyday sustenance, they purchased goods from local Christian merchants, sometimes developing close relations with the shopkeepers. And living side by side in the same communities, they would sometimes become intimate.[28]

Though Jews in greater Ashkenaz were less culturally integrated than their sisters and brothers in the realm of Islam, their condition was not one of cultural isolation. On the contrary, there is clear evidence that Jews learned the wisdom of their neighbors and emulated some of their ways. For example, in the twelfth century, the Talmudic scholars, Tosafot, created a method of textual analysis that derived much from the scholastic methods of neighboring Christian scholars. Though we cannot map the precise path by which the enlightened "new textuality" of French scholastics made its way into the yeshiva, the influence of the latter is undeniable. Clearly, French Jewish scholars were French scholars, however different their textual focus.

More evidence of the participation of Jews in their local societies comes from the books they created, some of which have been preserved. There are multiple cases of "Christian" styles and themes in the decoration of Jewish books—the interweaving of dragons' necks and Hebrew letters in a High Holiday prayer-book from Esslingen, Germany, is just one stunning

106    EMBRACING EXILE

example. Even more stunning, in its way, are the sketches in the wide margins of a book of Ashkenazi customs created in France in the generation after the Tosafot: one page shows a valiant hunting-scene, another preserves an early fleur de lis. And one of the final pages of the manuscript preserves a wedding poem that alternates lines of Hebrew with lines of French. The Hebrew lines are, through their very-much-intended double entendre, nearly pornographic, while the French lines are "merely" romantic. Scholars believe that the former were intended as bawdy joking for the men while the latter, expressed in the common language, was directed at the women attending the wedding.[29] Yes, Jews spoke French, not Hebrew, and the culture in which they participated was French as well.

Against this background, it is perhaps surprising that these and other Ashkenazi authorities of this period have little to say about their "exile." Is this silence an expression of the "taken-for-grantedness" of their condition? This interpretation makes good sense, though we will never know for sure. But there is one notable brief comment found in a discussion of the Tosafot that suggests a favorable, if complex, view on the condition of exile.

The comment is offered in elaboration of a Talmudic teaching declaring that "converts are as difficult to Jews as a sore" (Qiddushin 70b). This obviously disturbing (to us, at least) statement attracts a number of interpretive comments, some doubling down on its obvious insult of converts to Judaism and others reinterpreting it to suggest that "difficult" need not be equated with "bad." One of the latter sort touches on the question of exile:

> There are those who say that converts are considered difficult for Israel because it is on account of converts that Jews are in exile, as it says (in the Talmud, Pesachim 87b), "why are Israel scattered throughout the nations more than are idolaters? In order that they may be joined by converts."

In this approach, converts are good and attracting them is a *mitzvah* (an obligation and good act), so Israel must be put in a position to do so. Where will possible converts be found? Obviously, in lands scattered throughout the world, that is, lands where Jews would be in exile. But exile brings difficulties for Jews. If it is converts on whose account Jews must live in exile, then the difficulties of exile can be indirectly blamed on converts. "Converts are difficult to Jews."

But we may construct the logic of this equation another way, that is, if winning converts is good, and potential converts can overwhelmingly be

MEDIEVAL JEWISH TEACHINGS ON EXILE    107

found in exile, then exile must be good. That doesn't mean that exilic life comes without difficulties, or that it might not be easier to live in one's own "home"—in the case of Jews, the restored Land of Israel. Still, "difficult" does not mean "bad" (childbirth is difficult but obviously not bad). If the world will be improved through conversion of more people to belief in the one true God, and if this can be accomplished only if Jews are in exile, then exile *must* be good. By living in exile, Jews are serving God's plan in a way they could not if they remained restricted to the confines of a small land in the eastern Mediterranean.

Another comment, also by one of the Tosafot, reflects indirectly on the condition of diaspora, at least as this sage understood it. The comment pertains to the law of the Mishnah upon which the classic Talmudic deliberation on diaspora, examined in an earlier chapter, is based. That law, you will recall, allows a spouse to compel their partner to move with them to the Land of Israel, or else suffer financial consequences. In the opinion of Tosafot:

> This [*halakha*] is not practiced in this time, for there is danger on the roads. And Rabbenu Hayim [a student of Rabbenu Tam] said that it is not now a mitzvah to live in the Land of Israel, because there are several commandments that rely on the Land [for their fulfillment], and several punishments [for transgressions] concerning which we cannot be careful nor uphold [them]. (Tos. Ketubbot 110b, "*Hu 'omer la'alot*")

The first of the explanations recorded here suggests that the law should not be practiced in the face of danger to life—a pragmatic and, in view of rabbinic Judaism's prioritizing of the saving of life at almost any cost, cogent analysis. But Rabbenu Hayim, living in medieval Paris, goes further, saying that the law is not practiced because there is not, in our world, a religious obligation (mitzvah) for a Jew to settle in the Land. Why not? In an ironic reversal of the oft-stated argument in favor of settling in the Land, which observes that the Torah's commandments can be more fully observed in the Land—even in the absence of the Temple—than outside it, Rabbenu Hayyim submits that a Jew's living in the Land in our day is problematic precisely because of the commandments that apply there. Some of those commandments cannot, at this time, be properly observed, so Jewish life in the Land is fuller of unavoidable transgressions than Jewish life outside it.

To state this notion in more positive terms, Jewish life in diaspora is less plagued by unavoidable sin than Jewish life in the Land. In this reality, since sin is to be avoided, the Land is better avoided, at least for extended residence. Unwittingly echoing Paul's approach many centuries earlier, the medieval sage admits that fewer obligations means fewer transgressions. Life in diaspora is less necessarily sinful and therefore to be preferred.

There is no question that medieval circumstances often brought difficulties, to Jews as to others. Famine, poverty, and even plague were a part of life. And yes, Jews sometimes suffered additional difficulties as a consequence of their refusal to identify with the dominant religious culture. But certainly under Islam, and even in the realm of Christendom, mundane life came with its mundane pleasures, and sparks of Jewish glory emerged from even dark corners. These places, which Jews may ideologically have referred to as "exile," were nevertheless their homes, where they could flourish in small and large ways. They could study and live their Torah, expounding its wisdoms while adding their own insights.

# 6

# Exile, the Jewish Mystical Tradition, and the Sephardi Diaspora

The history of the Iberian Peninsula and its Jewish residents in the Middle Ages was far more complex than the sometimes romantic and rosy picture of that experience suggests. To begin with, the so-called "golden age" of Spain met its demise far earlier than many realize. With the incursion of the Almohads from North Africa into Iberia (beginning in 1145, taking Cordoba in 1148), when Maimonides was still a youth, earlier policies of enlightened toleration yielded to intolerance. Jews found themselves suddenly under extreme pressure, finding their status under the new Muslim rulers much diminished. To escape danger, the young Maimonides fled with his family to Morocco—the very source of the religious-cultural "storm" that then battered al-Andalus.[1] There they may have adopted Muslim ways, at least publicly, in order to survive. Maimonides found peace as a Jew once again only when he moved to Egypt a decade later.

Meanwhile, the Christian reconquest of Iberia continued, and more and more Spanish Jews found themselves under Christian rule. This shift had profound consequences for Jews. To Muslims, Jews had been a "people of the book," a protected minority according to Muslim law (at least until the Almoravids, who, for a brief period even before the Almohad conquest, ignored this protection). To Christians, by contrast, Jews were "Christ killers," blind adherents to a superseded covenant. Complicating matters still further was the fact that, to Spanish Christians, Jews were seen to be (at least) former allies of the Muslim infidels who had ruled the reconquered territories, doubling the reasons to be suspicious of Jews. Christians and Jews may have lived side by side, sometimes in relative harmony. But there was always a fear that the Jew hatred that resided in Christian "DNA" would, for one reason or another, emerge and boil over, as it did in the extensive anti-Jewish riots in Aragon in 1391.[2] These transitions, both south and north, had undeniable impact on the lives of Spanish Jews, and Jews in Spain, from the mid-twelfth century onward, had good reason to feel they were living in exile.

110  EMBRACING EXILE

At the same time, Spanish Jews could not forget that Iberia had long been their home, and even though conditions had worsened, it continued to be. The legacy of the golden age did not disappear, and Jews who prided themselves on the tradition of Spanish Jewry continued to experience that pride. Though they increasingly lived in Christian-dominated Iberia, they continued to embrace the culture they had learned under Muslim control, the elite often pursuing the same fields of study (grammar, mathematics, philosophy, etc.) and the broader population enjoying the "Moorish" styles of newly built synagogues, which resembled the mosques of earlier centuries far more than European churches farther to the north. Surviving remnants of Hispano-Jewish culture from these centuries illustrate clearly that Jewish life was not merely a series of oppressions and setbacks. In fact, it is to this day possible to be inspired by the glory of illuminated Hebrew Bibles or *haggadot* produced in Christian Catalunya or Toledo in the fourteenth and fifteenth centuries. It is stunning to witness, even on the pages of Hebrew manuscripts, the ongoing influence of Spain's Muslim past. Sephardi (= Spanish-Jewish) life had a strength of persistence that continues to surprise, finding resilience even in the face of persecution. Home remains home, we might say, even when its security is compromised.

Reflecting the longing and complexity of Spanish-Jewish lives during these centuries is arguably the most significant and ultimately influential of new developments in Jewish life in many generations, the Kabbalah, and its new Jewish classic, the Zohar. An important part of medieval Jewish reflection on the condition of diaspora is found in this tradition. The Zohar, the major product of Spanish Kabbalah, preserves both hints and explicit teachings of the response of kabbalists to their diaspora position.

Modern scholarship had associated the Zohar with the great Spanish mystic of the thirteenth century, Moses de Leon. In recent years, though, the complexity of the development of the Zohar—not a single but a composite text—has become apparent, and it is now thought that the Zohar originated in circles of Spanish-Jewish kabbalists ("Zoharic circles") from the late thirteenth through the fourteenth centuries and possibly beyond. (According to one scenario, the canonical Zohar is actually the creation of Italian printers in the mid-sixteenth century.)[3]

Considerable effort was required by the Spanish mystics to make sense of their exilic condition. We might expect them, for example, to have looked to the Holy Land as a source of renewed hope. But the actual Land of Israel, too, was, in their day, in a fallen state. The Zohar, therefore, creates an *idealized* space.[4] The Zohar's narrative portrays an imagined second-century Galilee, populated by sacred sages of old, speaking an invented form of rabbinic Aramaic. But the issues they address are the issues of a people in exile—of Jews in Iberia in a later century.[5] The Zohar is an exilic text pretending to describe life before exile. As such, it is a profound reflection on the condition of exile, though certainly not that alone.

To accomplish its task, the Zohar builds on an earlier trope—the notion that the divine presence (the Shekhinah) accompanies Israel into exile. In the Zohar's construction, this notion assumes a configuration that Jews of late antiquity could not have anticipated. The Kabbalistic system, positing 10 divine "emanations" ("*sefirot*"), regards the Shekhinah as the tenth such emanation—and, as the feminine aspect of God, the lowest. In fulfillment of the traditional teaching, this divine aspect joined the Jews in exile. But in the Kabbalistic formulation, the Shekhinah's exile went even further. As a part of God, the Shekhinah was separated from other parts of God—exiled, if you will, to accompany Israel in her exiles. Exiled like Israel, God would only be redeemed—the Shekhinah reunited with other emanations of God—when Israel is redeemed.

A simple formulation of this notion is the Zohar's interpretive elaboration of Psalms 3:9 (Emor 3:90b):

> He began again and said: "To the Lord is salvation, your blessing is upon your people (Psalm 3:9)." "To the Lord is salvation": This is what we teach, that Israel is meritorious, for to every place to which they were exiled, the Shekhinah was exiled with them. So when Israel is redeemed from their exile, for whom is the redemption—for Israel or for the Holy One? This [answer] has been established by various verses, such as here: "To the Lord is salvation." When? [When] "your blessing is upon your people." When the Holy One extends blessing upon Israel, delivering them from exile and treating them kindly, then "To the Lord is salvation," surely. And regarding this we learn that the Holy One will return from exile with Israel, concerning which it is written: "The Lord Your God will return with your captivity." (Deuteronomy 30:3)

The Zohar is a kind of Midrash (a creative re-reading of scripture), one that often radically re-reads Scripture against its simple meaning. Psalm 3:9 actually says (in a proper English translation) "salvation is the Lord's..." (meaning salvation will come from the Lord). But here the Zohar reads it as

## 112  EMBRACING EXILE

if it says "to the Lord is salvation [when] your blessing is upon your people." The "blessing" for the people is their redemption, and the salvation awaited by the Lord—salvation that *God* needs, not God's power to save Israel—is contingent upon the salvation of the Lord's people. God, or at least God's Shekhinah, experiences exile with God's beloved Israel. God will be reunited with God's self only when Israel is reunited with God.

Making the picture of God's separation and reunification more explicit is this section of Zohar, *Veheyi*:

> Since we are in exile, oppressed among our enemies, and the Matron has been separated from the King and distanced from Him, He causes the Shekhinah to dwell among us and He will redeem us.

"King" is a reference to the top *sefirah*—Keter = crown. "Matron" refers to the female partner of the king, that is, the Shekhinah = divine presence. A direct parallel is drawn here between the separation of the king's partner from the king and the exile of Israel from God. In effect, the text claims, on account of Israel's exile, God is diminished, for God experiences what Israel experiences. Only through what later Kabbalah would call a "*tikkun*"—a repair—would God and Israel both one day be healed. In the meantime, God does what only the most committed lover would do, that is, God subjects part of Godself to the same fate as the beloved.

The Zohar's longest and most playful elaboration of these ideas is found in *BeHukotai*:

> "And I will set My tabernacle [*mishkani*] among you (Leviticus 26:11)." My tabernacle is the Shekhinah. My deposit [*mashkona*] was mortgaged by the iniquities of Israel because she goes into exile with them. There is an allegory about a man who loved his friend. He told him, "Certainly, because of the sublime love that I have for you, I wish to dwell with you." His friend replied, "How will I know that you will dwell with me?" He went and took all the good things in his home and brought them to him and said, "My deposit is with you, so I will never part from you."
>
> So is the Creator. He wished to dwell with Israel. What did He do? He took His treasure, [the Shekhinah], and lowered it down to Israel. He told them, "Israel, here is My deposit with you, so I will never part from you." And although the Holy One was distanced from us, He left the deposit in our hands [because Shekhinah is with us in exile] and we keep His

EXILE, MYSTICAL TRADITION, AND THE SEPHARDI    113

treasure. And when He asks for His deposit, He will come to dwell with us. This is why it is written, "And I will set My tabernacle among you." "I will give you a deposit so I will dwell with you." And even though Israel is in exile now, the Creator's mortgage is with them and they have never left it.

"And My soul shall not abhor you." This is similar to a man who loves his friend and wishes to dwell with him. What did he do? He took his bed and brought it to his house. He said, "Here, my bed is in your house, so I will not draw far from you, from your bed and from your vessels." Thus said the Holy One, "And I will set My tabernacle among you, and My soul shall not abhor you." Thus, My bed [Shekhinah] is in your home. "And since My bed is with you, know that I will never part from you." And for this reason, "My soul shall not abhor you," I will not part from you.

"And I will walk among you and will be your God (Leviticus 26:12)." Since my deposit is with you, you should know for certain that I am going with you, as it is written, "For the Lord your God walks in the midst of your camp, to deliver you, and to give up your enemies before you; therefore shall your camp be holy." (Chapter 8, 114a)

This section plays on the fact that the biblical word for the Tabernacle—the place where God dwelt in the midst of Israel during their travels in the Sinai wilderness—is *mishkan*, which uses the same root as the word for divine presence (*Shekhinah*) and deposit (*mashkona* in Aramaic). Since the root means "dwell," it is also associated here with "bed." In the linguistically flexible imagination of the Zoharic author, therefore, any one of these can stand in for the other. So the Mishkan—the place of the indwelling of the divine presence—is the Shekhinah, and "I will set my Tabernacle among you" means "I will deposit my treasure = Shekhinah = bed among you." The deposit of the valuable "object" serves as an assurance of the return of God in God's totality to Israel, for only by returning to Israel can God gather what is most valuable to God. But God never leaves Israel completely, for God wishes to dwell with Israel, a desire manifest in the "fact" that the divine presence = Shekhinah dwells in Israel's midst (as did God in the Tabernacle in Israel's midst) even when there is no Tabernacle in which to dwell.

The illustrative parable is extremely important for appreciating the Zohar's force here. The text claims that the deposit (Mishkan, Shekhinah) is deposited on account of the sins (in the original Aramaic: liabilities or obligations) of Israel, on account of which Israel is exiled. In the normal order of things—say, according to the typical biblical pattern—Israel, having sinned, would have to pay what it owes (= repent, offer sacrifice) to restore itself to divine approval. Classical rabbinic midrash often embodies this dynamic by describing a king who becomes angered with his rebellious son and sends him away. But the king, the father, loves the son and so opens opportunities for the son to return. Biblically or rabbinically, it is the child who is expelled, even if the parent is eager for that child to return. In the Zohar's illustration, though, the dynamic is virtually the opposite. In this version, God, the parent, so loves the expelled child that He longs to continue dwelling with the child, unable, apparently, to bear their separation. To assure their ongoing connection, the parent (God) takes the best of the (divine) household and deposits it with the child. Because of the depth of the parental/divine love, it is the child/Israel who is in the stronger negotiating position, demanding of the parent/God an assurance of ongoing cohabitation.

The deposit is presumably the Shekhinah = the manifestation (*sefirah*) of God that in Kabbalah sometimes goes by this name. Applying the parable to its intended reference, this means that God so loves Israel that God "deposits" part of Godself with them when they go into exile. But there is another possible meaning here. The parable speaks of "all the good things in his home" as being deposited by the parent/God with the child/Israel. In context, the "good things" are likely to be the Shekhinah. But they could also be the Torah and commandments ("all good things"), which God gave to Israel to accompany them in all their wanderings. As we noted earlier in connection with the Torah itself, Torah offers Israel a portable homeland, or, in the language used here in paragraph 32, an ever-present resting place (= bed). Whichever of these directions we take in our interpretation, the implication is clear: as paragraph 33 says explicitly, God's most valuable part or possession will accompany Israel through all her wanderings.

The Zohar's teachings affirm that Israel is not alone in exile. Exile does not distance Israel from God. Quite the contrary. God loves Israel so much that God assures intimate contact between Israel and the divine even in exile. Going further, the Zohar claims that exile is an earthly expression of what God experiences—God's exile from Godself—and that heaven relies on the earthly condition of Israel for God's restoration of Godself. If what Israel experiences is no worse than what God experiences, and if God insists on being with Israel whatever her experience, then what anguish can Israel possibly experience? If exile means to be cast out by and distanced from God, then how can Israel ever be in true exile if God is exiled with Israel? In this scenario, "exile" takes on a whole new meaning, and it is certainly not the meaning it had in the Hebrew Bible.

In fact, one may rightly argue that, for the Zohar, "exile" is at the same time "blessing." Consider *Veyehi* 3 (213a): "And he said, 'send me off, for it has dawned (Genesis 32:27).' And he [Jacob] said, 'I will not release you unless you bless me.' What is 'bless me'? He [God] gave us Exile and assured us that he would redeem us from it." It is not just redemption that is called blessing in this teaching but exile too. And how could it not be? If there is no exile without God's accompaniment, then exile must simultaneously be blessing. There is no other way to understand it.

In light of these teachings, the Zohar's imagined Galilee takes on new colors. In R. Shimon (the Zohar's fictional main teacher) and his disciples, the Zoharic masters see themselves. In their Galilee, they see their Castile. Let us recall that the second-century Galilee of R. Shimon is no redeemed Galilee. Under the domination of the forces of Rome, it is—like Daniel's Land of Israel long before—a Holy Land in exile. But it is also the site of redemption, so to call it "exile" alone will not suffice. By the same token, for the kabbalists of the Zohar, Spain is "exile," an undeniable reality of Jewish life under a Christian regime whose identity was built by conquering infidels. But at the same time, it is not just exile, because—as they also experience—God is there with them. In fact, given their new mystical powers, they are arguably closer to God than any Jew has been for a very long time. So they are with God, at home, in exile. In the landscapes of Castile, they see windmills—the windmills of the ancient Promised Land.

The Jews of Spain, mystics or not, found their lives becoming more and more difficult in the late fourteenth and into the fifteenth century. In 1391 anti-Jewish riots led to the taking of numerous Jewish lives, and some in the Jewish population felt that the only way to escape the cycle of violence and hatred was to convert—to become "New Christians." Not all Jews took this path, and many continued to live as Jews. Jewish writers and thinkers continued to express themselves, some gaining reputations that long outlasted their lifetimes. The surviving material artifacts from this period also support the conclusion that Jewish life in Iberia, though increasingly challenged, had not lost all its richness.

But the seeds for the downfall of the centuries-long Jewish experience in Spain had been planted. Crucially, conversion under force rarely leads to genuine new belief, and many of the New Christians maintained Jewish

116  EMBRACING EXILE

practice in private. Soon, the newly established Spanish Inquisition sought to root out such "heretics," hoping to purify Christian belief and observance. Not only were hidden Jews punished under this regime, but Jews who maintained their identities and convictions came under increasing pressure, for the mere presence of active Jews might tempt former Jews, now New Christians, to return to their former ways. Something needed to be done with this tempting Jewish "pollutant."

The solution was to expel Jews (and, in short order, "Moors" = Muslims) from Spanish lands. In the famous royal decree of 1492, Jews were forced to leave, to undertake a new exile. The first stop for many was Portugal, but a mere five years later, Portugal, too, expelled her Jews, and the former Sephardic Jewish nation found itself (mostly) fleeing to whatever lands would take them. Some, having had enough of running, converted to Christianity, making it possible for them to remain in Portugal. Needless to say, their Christianity was often half-hearted, and many preserved diluted Jewish observances in private. Others fled to territories controlled by Venice or elsewhere in northern Italy, and a considerable number accepted the invitation of the newly powerful Ottoman empire, which saw Jewish refugees as a source of vitality. Various cities, particularly Salonika (more on which later), became veritable new Jewish "homelands."

In these new homelands, Sephardic Jews not only continued the traditions and habits of diaspora Jews through the ages, but they also added a new level of diaspora to their consciousness and expressions—that of the Sephardic diaspora. So when, beginning in the late sixteenth century, Portuguese New Christians—including the family of Spinoza—emigrated to Amsterdam to resume their Jewish lives, they did not, as we would expect, immediately take up Dutch as their primary language. Instead, they preserved their Portuguese and Spanish (Portuguese as their vernacular, reserving Spanish—the "high" literary tongue—for translation of sacred texts), even printing prayer and other sacred books with Spanish translation on pages facing the Hebrew original (or sometimes in translation only, without the Hebrew). This linguistic identity is an expression of a larger identity, one on which Sephardic Jews would insist for centuries.

The Spanish diaspora had assumed a special diaspora identity for generations. Long before the expulsion in 1492, they were accustomed to referring to themselves as "the exile of Jerusalem that is in Sepharad," a quotation taken from the prophet Ovadiah, verse 20 (the book has only one chapter) and appropriated as a description of the Jewish nation in Spain. We hardly need comment on the meaningfulness of a prophetic statement now applied to a diaspora community that understood itself as the fulfillment of the prophecy; their place and fate, they believed, was biblically ordained. And this phrase continued to serve the Sephardic community as a self-reference during the expulsion and beyond, when "exile of Sepharad/Spain" took on a new meaning—referring not only to the Jewish exile in Spain, but now also to the Jewish exile from Spain.

One of the outstanding figures of the era of the Spanish expulsion was Don Isaac Abarbanel. Abarbanel was born in Lisbon, settled in Toledo, was expelled with his compatriots, and ultimately settled in Venice, where he died. Abarbanel's family was wealthy, a factor which, combined with his own distinction as a scholar, led him to service of the royal houses in both Portugal and Castile. Though he knew, both through his family history and his own experience, the growing troubles of Jews in Iberia, he also witnessed the surviving richness of even diminished Jewish life there, particularly in Toledo, whose main synagogue still announced the grandeur of Jewish Sepharad.

Abarbanel wrote works of philosophy and apologetics, but he is particularly renowned for his biblical commentaries, which are studied to this day. One of his comments on Moses' final song in Deuteronomy is relevant to our exploration. According to Deuteronomy chapter 32, verses 26–27, God considered destroying the Jews (known in the Torah as "Israel") on account of their sins, but instead scattered them to their enemies. The biblical text makes it clear that this exile is a punishment. But, explains Abarbanel, it is not only punishment, for the scattering of exile actually offers evidence of God's ongoing care for the Jewish people. How so? As Abarbanel remarks, not only is it true that exile is a milder form of punishment than destruction, but:

> If the Jews all were together in one corner of the world, an enemy who ruled over them wrathfully would be able to wipe all of them off the face of the earth, as Ahasuerus intended to do...but while they are scattered to all corners, if one king becomes angry with them another king will show compassion, and they might flee from nation to nation and from one kingdom to another, finding some of their fellow Jews there. (Trans. Alan Cooper)

Unfortunately, it is impossible to know whether Abarbanel wrote these words before or after the expulsion he himself experienced. Abarbanel's commentary on Deuteronomy was composed over the course of two decades. He began the commentary in the 1470s while still in Portugal. He then abandoned the project because of deteriorating conditions and consequential demands on his time. He completed it only after the expulsion, while living in Corfu.

But whether before or after, already in the latter half of the fifteenth century, Abarbanel and other Jews felt the pressures of increasing Catholic intolerance, and expulsion could not have been beyond their imaginations. Besides, whenever these words were originally written, Abarbanel let them stand in the final version of his commentary, which was indisputably finished after the expulsion. So it is reasonable to read these words as a knowing reflection on an experience that Abarbanel and his Sephardic Jewish brethren knew too well.

What, then, does Abarbanel say about the Jewish experience of exile? His emphasis is on the scattering of Jews to various lands. Hearkening back to the book of Esther, he explains that a scattered exile is a protected diaspora, for whatever anti-Jewish action a king may take in one place, Jews in other places will be safe. Moreover, royal cruelty in one place will be answered by royal compassion in another, and Jews cast out from one home will be welcomed by their brothers and sisters elsewhere. On their face, his words seem to be purely pragmatic. But Abarbanel was a Jewish theologian, and there can be no doubt that he viewed all this as being part of God's desire—particularly since it is an explanation of the words of scripture, the words of God. Hence, Abarbanel is undoubtedly speaking of God's care of Jews in exile. In fact, Abarbanel may be understood to be offering an early answer to the travails of Iberian Jews during his lifetime, suggesting that such difficulties are not evidence of God's abandonment. On the contrary, in preparation of such an exile, God has assured that as one door closes, the next will be open. This theme, we will see, becomes a common one among Jewish writers, a much-repeated defense of diaspora.

Whatever the chronology of Abarbanel's comments, the passing of but a few years would lead to a multitude of writings and creative outbursts that may be seen as undeniable responses to the expulsion, at least in part. For example, many scholars have seen the new and particular form Kabbalah took in Safed (Palestine, the Ottoman empire) in the sixteenth century under the influence of Isaac Luria as an attempt to understand the brokenness of the world to which the expulsion testified.[6]

## EXILE, MYSTICAL TRADITION, AND THE SEPHARDI   119

To explain the world's imperfections, and by implication the rupture represented by the Spanish expulsion, Luria offered the idea that there had been a flaw in creation itself, a flaw that perpetuated exile and made territorial redemption impossible. At the time of creation, the energies of the divine contracted to make room for creation (if God is "without end," then there is no room for anything but God, so God had to contract Godself to make room for something other than God). These energies were contained in vessels, but the power of the concentrated energies caused the vessels to shatter, scattering sparks of the divine energy throughout creation. In this scenario, God is actually separated from Godself, and God's power is compromised by that separation. Only when the divine sparks are reunited will God be re-empowered to redeem Israel. How would this reunification happen, according to Luria? Through acts of *tikkun*, of "repair," to be specific, through performance of the mitzvot (divine commandments) by both mystics and common Jews. In the meantime, God is exiled along with Israel, with each dependent on the other for redemption.

If God is in exile, it is difficult to say what the meaning of the exile of Israel—either the original exile or subsequent exiles, such as that from Spain—might be. After all, Israel in exile is living the same life that God lives—scattered and "weakened." But if the repair of the divine is in the hands of Israel, then Israel has the power to effect its own redemption—a redemption with a cosmic map, not one centered on a particular piece of land. Some kabbalists, such as Luria himself, made their home where they could breathe the magical air of the Holy Land. But others insisted that Israel in exile was part of God's plan, as "natural" as natural could be.

The irony of Luria's solution, formulated in the Galilean city of Safed, should not be missed. Luria's system posits a profoundly unredeemed world, one that can only be redeemed through acts of *tikkun*. Crucially, the unredeemed state of the world is present everywhere, even in the Holy Land. Cosmically speaking, there is no difference between the Holy Land and other lands—or, one might say, between exile in the Holy Land and exile in the diaspora. This recognition may be a mirror of the geopolitical reality: The Ottomans control Safed just as much as they control Constantinople/Istanbul. Extending the irony is the fact that, while Luria experiences "exile" in Safed, other Jews, living at the same time, experience "Jerusalem" elsewhere in the Ottoman empire.

For testimony to the latter, we turn to Samuel Usque's response to the Spanish expulsion, recorded in his *Consolation for the Tribulations of Israel*.

120    EMBRACING EXILE

Usque was born about 1500 to a family that had fled Spain in 1492 to settle in Portugal, only then to confront the Portuguese decree of 1497, in the face of which they converted to Christianity. His writings show that he was educated in traditional Jewish subjects, including Talmud, Midrash, and Maimonides. His family must, therefore, have been, to some extent, Hidden Jews. This would explain Usque's abandonment of Portugal after the establishment of the Portuguese Inquisition in 1531. At this point, Samuel began a series of travels, first to Naples, then to Ferrara, and thereafter to places like Constantinople, Salonika, and even Palestine. Ultimately, he made his home in Ferrara.

Ferrara at the time had an established Jewish community, like Venice and other cities in the Italian north. These Jews often lived well, and some were wealthy. They dressed like their Italian-Christian neighbors, spoke the same language (though Sephardic Jews also preserved Castilian and Portuguese), ate the same foods (most Jews—but not all—observed the restrictions of Kashrut), and admired the same culture. Jews had widespread access to Jewish and other classics through volumes produced in Venetian and other printing presses (some Christian), and they continued to create fine manuscripts, the decoration and illumination of which signaled their comfortable status. In the fifteenth and sixteenth centuries, select Italian Jews were ennobled by local authorities, and others even created unofficial "coats of arms" for their families, expressing their high estimation of their station. Crucially, Venice during this period was tied to the Ottoman east through active Mediterranean trade-routes, creating a partially blended cultural world both ends of which Jews could enjoy.[7]

Usque's composition is a kind of history of the sufferings of Jews through the ages, the ultimate purpose of which is to comfort Jews for those sufferings. The work is composed as a dialogue between the Jewish patriarch, Jacob (here called Ycabo) and an interlocutor named Numeo. Jacob can view all of Jewish history from his transhistorical perch, and his catalogue of Jewish sufferings is quite daunting. But the purpose of his recitation— Usque significantly writes all of this in Portuguese—is to offer comfort to Jews. Both the way Ycabo comments on the sufferings and his final offer of comfort are significant for our discussion of Jewish defenses of exile/ diaspora.

Most of the chapters recounting the sufferings of Israel are introduced in roughly the same manner: the long-term comfort and security of the community of Israel in this or that diaspora setting comes to an unfortunate end. For example, Usque's account of a calamity in France begins by reporting that "During the time that Henry VII ruled as Holy Roman Emperor, I [= Ycabo] found myself [= Israel] wallowing in riches. My children in the kingdom of France were thriving materially and were secure spiritually."[8] Concerning Naples in 1240: "I saw my children, who had been thriving in population and wealth." Concerning England in 1242: "I saw the Israelites increase their numbers; and in London alone, the capital city of the kingdom, there were two thousand very rich families tranquilly spending their time in exile as the Jews did elsewhere in the kingdom." And so forth.

What is crucial to notice about this catalogue is that it is as much a recounting of Jewish flourishing in exile as it is an account of Jewish suffering. In fact, though the narratives focus on the suffering—that is, on the interruption of the normal conditions that had preceded the suffering—viewed chronologically, Jewish peace and comfort in exile far outweigh Jewish suffering. Ironically, the catalog of Jewish suffering belies its main narrative by emphasizing that suffering is not the main exilic condition. This is surely factually correct, for any history of Jewish catastrophes in diaspora focuses on the chronologically limited drama of abuse and persecution. Concerning the far less dramatic realities of everyday life, there is less to say.

Equally as interesting in the catalogue is the reasons for the disruptions of the peace Jews enjoy. Not unexpectedly, outbreaks of suffering are often described as divine response to Jewish sin. But Usque also, in many cases, suggests more natural causes. In the French case it is Christian envy of Jewish flourishing, which the Christians, as common folk, do not enjoy in the same measure. In the Naples case, the cause is a misunderstanding on the part of the grateful son of the grateful king, who wishes to grant Jews the "gift" of Christianity. In the England chapter, Jewish suffering is instigated by a friar who falls in love with a beautiful Jewish girl, converts to Judaism to make marriage possible, and is still spurned by the girl. In Spain in 1456, envious resentment of Jewish power with the court is again the cause. There is anti-Judaism, but it is generally not represented as a free-floating hatred. When Christians act against Jews, there is an immediate and particular reason.

The case of Jewish suffering in Salonika, where many Sephardic Jews settled after the expulsion, is particularly notable for the way the story is told. Usque/Ycabo begins by observing that Salonika is, in his day, "a true mother-city in Judaism," for many who have been persecuted and exiled

## 122    EMBRACING EXILE

from other homes have settled there. "She embraces them and receives them with as much love and good will as if she were Jerusalem,"[9] Usque/Ycabo adds. Salonika, in the mid-sixteenth century, is effectively a new Jerusalem. Following the pattern established long ago, Zion has moved elsewhere.

But this idyllic picture would come to an end, as God communicated God's wrath with the community (for unknown reasons!) by sending fire to the Jewish quarter of the city and inflicting great damage—the loss of one hundred Jewish lives, the destruction of property, including the synagogue, and so forth. Now, we would say that this is what happens in densely built, pre-modern cities. There was Jewish suffering here, but not suffering that originated with a non-Jewish population. Jews suffered, like all other peoples, because of the unfortunate dangers of everyday life. That Ycabo interprets this as an expression of divine wrath is evidence of his traditionalism—suffering is God's punishment for sin says the Hebrew Bible, along with much of Jewish tradition to follow. That Ycabo lists this with all the other "catastrophes" in his catalog tells us that, in his (Usque's) mind, this is not a narrative of anti-Semitism but one of divine justice. Such justice can use human or natural means to obtain its goal.

This is all affirmed in Usque's proffered comfort for the sufferings of Jews, at the end of his exposition. His first two sources of comfort are thoroughly traditional, going back to the Talmudic period. First, Usque writes, "He meted out your punishment gradually, so that your full punishment might not consume you and destroy you." Second, "he punished you immediately after each sin, so that your unrequited iniquities should not accumulate."[10] Translated for the present context, this means that the sufferings of exile are evidence of God's love and concern for Israel, for those sufferings, coming regularly, allow Israel to pay the account of their sins without massive suffering. With other people, presumably, God is not so concerned, so their suffering is sudden and catastrophic. In fact, Usque argues, there is no doubt that the other nations ultimately suffer more than we do; one after the other of the leaders who allowed our persecution or nations who supported our oppression found their ends in far more gruesome circumstances.

Crucially, Usque goes on to say, exile is primarily not a punishment but an act of mercy, one that God has granted to Jews alone. He writes:

By scattering you among all peoples, He made it impossible for the world to destroy you, for if one kingdom arises against you in Europe

EXILE, MYSTICAL TRADITION, AND THE SEPHARDI    123

[he has in mind Spain and Portugal] to inflict death upon you, another in Asia [as he will make clear, he is thinking of Turkey] allows you to live. And if the Spaniards burn you in Spain and banish you, the Lord wills for you to find someone in Italy [where Usque himself found refuge] who welcomes you and lets you live in freedom. And if the Lord had not dispersed you but instead, as your iniquities merit, had isolated you in one corner of the earth, like your brethren, the Ten Tribes, your life would be in jeopardy and the die for your destruction cast. You would long ago have perished from the wrath of only one of the peoples who had subjected you.[11]

In this paragraph, obviously reminiscent of the argument of his Sephardic compatriot, Abarbanel, Usque has set the stage for his ultimate claim. Echoing earlier teachings, Usque suggests that God has a plan in scattering Israel to the four winds. And what is that plan? Survival. Unlike other, normal nations, Israel cannot be destroyed. Understood properly, therefore, exile is a great gift from God. As he goes on to say:

Therefore, what you regard as an injustice from the Lord is a supreme mercy and a special favor which he has employed with you alone....He dispersed you among the peoples and did not herd you together. Therefore acknowledge that heaven has sent you this secret and sublime boon.

If we are honest in our evaluation of the trials of human history, we will admit that survival is not easy. All nations, all peoples, are challenged, and many ultimately meet their end. The only nation not subject to this danger, according to Usque, is Israel, for God has, in God's supreme mercy, done Israel "a special favor," dispersing her in all directions and thereby assuring that she can never be destroyed. Exile may have originated in sin and punishment, but that was not its sole, nor even its primary, purpose. Even in light of Israel's sufferings—and what nation does not experience sufferings?—exile is arguably the best thing that could ever have happened to her.

Usque has in mind not just the general exilic experiences of Israel but particularly the most recent ones, those that affected his family directly, driving them from Spain to Portugal, from open practice of Judaism to at least feigned conversion to Christianity. He has in mind his own wanderings and those of *his* people, not Jews in general but the Sephardic nation, then establishing new homes outside of Sepharad, and particularly in the

124   EMBRACING EXILE

Ottoman east. Concerning this latest entry on the Jewish itinerary of wanderings, he writes:

> You will rise to a higher degree of consolation…in the great nation of Turkey. This country is like a broad and expansive sea which our Lord has opened with the rod of His mercy, as Moses did for you in the Exodus from Egypt, so that the swells of your misfortunes…might cease and be consumed in it. Here the gates of liberty are always wide open for you that you may fully practice your Judaism; they are never closed. Here you may restore your true character.…
>
> This is a sublime mercy from the Lord, for He has granted you such abundant freedom in these realms that you may now take the first step toward your belated repentance.[12]

Usque's consolation comes to a climax by focusing on the new home of so many of his compatriots of the Jewish Sephardic nation, that is, Ottoman Turkey. This new realm he analogizes to the Red Sea split by God for Moses and the Israelites fleeing Egypt; like the sea, the path to various Ottoman ports is the path to freedom. This new Jewish home is a gift from the Lord, an expression of God's mercy, for in this home Jews can freely practice their Judaism in utter freedom and in peace. Their freedom in their new land is so complete, in fact, that they now have the luxury of examining their acts, identifying the sin at the root of their sufferings, and returning to the Lord.

It is not going too far to insist that we take Usque's analogy to its logical conclusion. If the gift that awaited the Hebrews on the far side of the sea was ultimately the Promised Land, Zion, then Turkey may be seen as the Promised Land, the new Zion. Now, to be fair, the actual Zion was, during Usque's lifetime, within the Turkish realm, and some Jews did, in fact, settle in Palestine (though rather few altogether, with more in the north and fewer in Jerusalem). But this is not Usque's point here. Recall Usque's description of Salonika, the new Ottoman "mother city," the new Ottoman "Jerusalem." The gift, the blessing, is the Ottoman realm as a whole. For Usque's Sephardic nation, this was the new Zion. For other Jews, in other times and places, it was other lands and their regimes that served the same function. What Usque's comforting words help us understand is that, however many diaspora homes Jews have been forced to abandon, there are at least as many others that welcome them. Poland welcomed Jews fleeing from

## EXILE, MYSTICAL TRADITION, AND THE SEPHARDI    125

western Europe, America welcomed Jews forced to flee the Russian empire. Other cities become "mother cities," Jews survive and flourish, and memory and experience make it clear: never is a threat a threat of true extinction, for God's gift of dispersion assures survival.

In the end, we should not forget the Sephardi-specific quality of Usque's experience. He was, as much as anything else, a spokesperson for the Sephardic exile from Sepharad/Spain. He wrote in Portuguese because many Sephardic Jews maintained the Sephardic language as their special tongue. They also founded Sephardic synagogues so that they could maintain uniquely Sephardic rites and liturgies. To this day the Jewish exile from Spain retains its special identity, an exile from an exile-turned-mother land, in many new mother lands. The Sephardic diaspora echoes the general Jewish diaspora, showing just how much at home Jews are in their diasporas. This, Usque insisted, should be a source of comfort.

The other Sephardic diaspora community that demands our attention is that of Amsterdam. Sephardic crypto-Jews who had resided in Portugal began to relocate to Amsterdam in the late sixteenth century. This was the beginning of what is known of as the Dutch "golden age," the age of Rembrandt and, later, Spinoza. Amsterdam was a flourishing international seaport at this time, blessed with policies of openness and freedom— religious and intellectual.[13] As Spinoza himself commented, "We have the rare good fortune to live in a commonwealth where freedom of judgment is fully granted to the individual citizen and he may worship God as he pleases, and where nothing is esteemed dearer and more precious than freedom."[14] It is not a coincidence that we find close connections between Jews and golden ages; it is the openness that makes golden ages possible that also attracts Jews seeking a welcoming diaspora home.

The new Sephardic community in seventeenth-century Amsterdam quickly established itself, building a large new synagogue and related buildings, accumulating a rich community library, and opening a cemetery distinguished for the beauty of its monuments. These Jews were largely comfortable (this can be seen to this day in the images of Jews preserved in Rembrandt's paintings), many engaging in trade and shipping. Like other comfortable Amsterdam residents at the time, some Jews owned slaves who had been brought on ships from Africa; these slaves were "converted" into Jewish households according to rabbinic interpretations of biblical laws pertaining to "Canaanite" slaves, and some were buried by the side of their owners in the community's cemetery.

## 126    EMBRACING EXILE

It is no accident that the best-known Amsterdam Jew from this period is Baruch (or Benedict) Spinoza. Spinoza was the son of a Portuguese family of hidden Jews who fled the Inquisition and resettled in the lowlands. He grew up in Amsterdam, within the Sephardic community but exposed to the ideas and ways of the world. He developed a rigorous, radical philosophy that posited a distinctly untraditional God and offered critique of the accuracy of Scripture. As a result of the ideas he espoused, he was, as a young man, excommunicated by the Jewish community in which he had been raised. It would appear that he never looked back.

On the one hand, we must admit that it is problematic to hold up Spinoza—alienated as he was from the Jewish community—as an example of a Jewish response to the diaspora condition or any other Jewish question. But on the other hand, it was precisely his diaspora time and place that made his apostasy possible, for it was only a relatively enlightened Netherlands that permitted the formation and expression of such ideas. Besides, against the background of our exploration, it hard not to notice that Spinoza's God was a God who is present everywhere—much like the God imagined by other Jewish diaspora commentators. Furthermore, the state Spinoza explores in his political writings is a universal or generic state, one that may support religion as a regulator of peoples, but one that must also respect the diversity of religious beliefs and practices, the specifics of which lay beyond its legitimate realm of state oversight. Admittedly, these may not be the views of a diaspora Jew, as Spinoza himself left the Jewish community, but since his time they have been and will continue to be the views of many diaspora Jews.

This account of the Sephardi exile offers only one side of the diaspora Jewish experience during these centuries, and only one source of opinions regarding that experience. At that same time that the Sephardic population experienced its tumultuous travels through exile and resettlement, the Ashkenazi diaspora was growing and strengthening, emerging into what would become its greatest period, a true golden age. This realization of unprecedented possibilities demanded that it too re-consider the meanings of life in "exile."

# 7

# The Great Theorizer of Diaspora

## The Maharal of Prague

One of the most important and profound theorists on the question of exile/diaspora in the history of Judaism was the sixteenth-century rabbi, Rabbi Judah Loew, known as the Maharal of Prague. Very little is known about the intimate details of the Maharal's life, as he wrote nothing about his teachers or influences and little about his personal life more generally. But one thing is clear: his stature was immense and his influence on others great. Why else would the Golem of Prague—the legendary Jewish equivalent of Frankenstein's monster—belatedly have come to be associated with him, two hundred years after his death?

Rabbi Loew was not a systematic thinker, and much of his wisdom was, as far as we can tell, self-taught. He embraced mysticism, and his writings are populated by the influence of a broad range of thinkers, Jewish and not. The tensions and paradoxes that emerge from these multiple streams can be dazzling, and his reader should not expect logical consistency from his arguments. Indeed, it is fair to say that his brilliance is expressed in the crosscurrents of his thinking as much as anywhere else.

The Maharal's association with Prague was powerful but partial. His longest residence as chief rabbi was in Moravia, from 1553 to 1573. He resided in Prague for two separate periods, first from 1588 to 1592 and then from 1596 to the end of his life (either 1604 or 1609), and only during the latter period was he the chief rabbi of the community.[1] Prague at the time was a thriving city, the capital of Bohemia and largest city in the Hapsburg Commonwealth, with somewhere between 50,000 and 60,000 residents. Earlier in the sixteenth century, Jews were twice expelled from Prague for short periods, but Emperor Maximillian II (r. 1564–76) affirmed Jewish rights in the city, making possible considerable growth of the community. His successor, Rudolf II (r. 1576–1611), ruled in a spirit of religious tolerance and was particularly generous in bestowing rights to Jews—supporting Jewish self-rule in Jewish Town, exempting Jews from customs and toll

128  EMBRACING EXILE

duties, and confirming affiliation of Jews to the imperial court. During most of his reign, he was served by a court Jew who also served as his banker. Contemporary testimony confirms that Jews flourished in Prague at this time as their number increased, and though there is scholarly debate concerning the precise size of the Jewish population, in the sixteenth- and seventeenth-century context, this probably meant some 500 or so souls (some estimates go as high as 6,000). The Jewish population included those whose families had lived comfortably in Prague for generations, along with newcomers—Sephardic Jews—who sought new homes after their old homes in Iberia had been taken from them. Jews lived in the Jewish Town of Prague, where they had their own government, led by two distinguished members of the community. There were also a considerable number of Torah scholars who populated the city's synagogues and study halls.[2]

In such a context, and with the aid of the growth of book-printing in Bohemia, Rabbi Loew published prolifically, writing books that are studied to this day. The most important of these for our purposes is *Netzah Yisrael* ("The Eternal One of Israel" or "The Eternity of Israel"), devoted to explicating the process that would ultimately lead to Israel's final redemption.

Maharal's exposition begins by laying a theoretical groundwork for the discussion of exile and redemption that follows. His first words already suggest that exile and redemption are intimately entwined, as "exile itself is a clear proof of redemption." Every concept is defined, at least in part, by what it is not, and a state called "exile" only has meaning if there is a corresponding state called "redemption." Or, as Maharal explains his assertion, exile could not be termed exile unless it represented a diversion from an original or natural order, and diversions from the natural will inevitably be corrected, in this case through redemption. Maharal continues:

> There is no doubt that exile is a change and divergence from the normal order, for God, may God be blessed, set every nation in the place appropriate to it, and set Israel in the place appropriate to them, which is the Land of Israel....And all things, when they leave their natural place, and they are out of their place, they have no survival in the place that is unnatural to them, rather they return to their natural place. And if they were to remain in their unnatural place, the unnatural would become natural, and this is impossible....And Israel themselves, if they stayed forever in exile, which is not their appropriate place, for their appropriate place, according

THE GREAT THEORIZER: THE MAHARAL OF PRAGUE    129

to the order of reality, is for them to be in the Land of Israel under their own control and not under the control of others....And if they were to remain in their exile forever, this thing—that is, survival outside of their place, which is unnatural—would become natural, for only natural things survive forever....

Similarly, dispersion is not a natural thing...and for this reason, all dispersions will be gathered together. Therefore, the dispersion of Israel among the nations is a divergence from nature, for since they are one nation, it is fitting that they be together...and from this it appears that dispersion is, particularly for them, not at all natural...and the unnatural dispersion would become natural if it lasted forever. (*Netzah Yisrael*, chapter 1)

Maharal here makes what we might call a "scientific" argument (scientific, that is, in the pre-modern sense), though we might also call it tautological. Everything belongs in its natural place, and nations too, the Maharal claims, have their natural places, assigned by God, who created them. Israel's natural place is the Land of Israel (precisely as the name of the land suggests). Expulsion from the Land brings Israel into an unnatural condition, one that must eventually be corrected, since the unnatural cannot last.

But it will be evident to every reader of Maharal's argument that it carries the seed of its own subversion. If an unnatural condition cannot be sustained, then any condition that lasts for a long time must be "natural." The only question is how long that "long time" must be. At the time Maharal wrote these words, Jews had already lived in "exile" (the term implies unnaturalness; hence the scare quotes) for over 2,000 years, from the time of the Babylonian exile. Is 2,000 years a long time? Do 2,000 years, in the scope of human history, approach "forever?" It is hard to avoid these questions, as the Maharal must surely have realized. In the midst of arguing that exile is, for Jews, unnatural, he is at the same time suggesting that it is perfectly natural.

In chapter 8, he makes this suggestion more explicit:

When God brought them out of the Land of Egypt, God brought them out to give them the Land [of Israel]. And had those who left Egypt come to the Land, they would have remained there forever....But because they cried a meaningless cry [lamenting leaving Egypt behind] and didn't want to enter the Land, and the Holy One swore that He would not bring that

130   EMBRACING EXILE

> generation to the Land…their coming to the Land was not eternal, but could be nullified or interrupted.
>
> Moreover, all things in nature long for their natural place. And if the Land were the natural place for Israel, and they longed for the Land, this would remain forever. But the opposite was the case here, for they cried a meaningless cry and didn't want to come to the Land. Therefore, this teaches us that the Land is not the natural place for Israel, and for this reason they didn't remain there.…For the cry they cried teaches that the Land doesn't belong to them completely.

This section is part of a longer argument claiming that, as the Exodus from Egypt was eternal (there was no going back), so too the inheritance of the Land could have been eternal, but only if it were accomplished by the generation that experienced the Exodus. Lamenting the change in their condition and clearly not longing for entrance into the Promised Land, the Exodus generation instead showed that the Land was *not* their natural place. It was not theirs, at least not completely. Connecting this observation with the conclusion intimated in the selection from chapter 1, we may say that, as far as the Maharal is concerned, the Land is not the natural place of Israel and exile may well be. True, he seems to say the opposite as well, but that opposing opinion doesn't diminish the power of the one just made. Indeed, only selective reading allows one to say that the Maharal was a "proto-Zionist," as some modern readers have claimed. More accurately described, he may well be an "anti-Zionist," whose opinions are at least as often contrary to those who think of the Land as Israel's natural home.

Consider this characterization of his opinion by a contemporary religious Zionist thinker, Rabbi Shagar. "At the end of the day," writes Shagar, "Redemption itself, i.e., the ingathering of the exiles to the Land of Israel, is perceived by the Maharal as unnatural to the Jewish people. The Jew's authentic place is, in fact, in exile…exile is the ideal Jewish condition."[3] This is a startling claim—the Maharal is indeed making a radical claim for the relationship of Jews with their diasporas. Even if one day they will be redeemed from their present homes, in our day, their homes are perfectly natural; their diasporas are their homelands, their birthplaces, their ancestral houses.

What does the Maharal say about the Jewish condition in exile? To begin with, he often admits the difficulties of the exilic experience; he will not permit any "whitewashing" of that reality. But he also builds upon earlier notions to insist that exile is not a breach in the covenant between God and Israel. On the contrary:

> It is fitting that the divine presence should be with Israel to an even greater extent when they are in exile, for when they are in exile they are like a sick person who left his natural state, for it is not natural for one nation to be dominated by another. Therefore, God, may He be blessed, is with them in exile. (Chapter 10)

The vulnerability of Israel in exile demands that God be with them to protect and care for them. In the protection of their own home, they could have been "left alone." Away from home, God must assure closer contact.

The most important part of Maharal's commentary on exile appears in chapters 24–25. To begin with, he reiterates and expands upon his comments concerning the natural order from chapter 1:

> It is perfectly clear that the exile of Israel and the destruction of the Temple is a change in the order of the world, and it is well known that a matter that is against the order of the world can last only temporarily, for it is impossible that it should be outside of the order of the world and survive, because then the out-of-order would be ordered....And since, according to the order of reality, it is fitting that everything should exist in the place that God, may He be blessed, arranged for it, and how much the more so the nation of Israel, which is a unique nation, having no essential connection with any other nation, it is not fitting that it [= the nation of Israel] exist among them, and the existence of Israel among the nations is therefore considered unnatural.

But then Maharal goes on to offer observations concerning Israel's condition in exile, observations that lead us down an entirely new path:

> If Israel had a special land, since they left the land that was special to them, this would be their loss. But they are scattered throughout the world, and God did not give them a special land, rather, the whole world is their land. And this is fitting for Israel, for it is already known that everything has a place that corresponds to its qualities. And since without Israel the world would not have been created, for this reason the whole world is their place. Therefore, when they were exiled from the Land [of Israel], they

## 132   EMBRACING EXILE

were exiled throughout the world. And if so, even if they dwelled in a particular land, it is not theirs, for they are not in their place.

Israel's exile is not to a single place but a dispersion to many lands. The "special land" in the opening comment apparently refers to a special land in exile, which Israel does not have. Why not? Because "the whole world is their land." According to the well-known rabbinic tradition, the world was created for the sake of Israel, whose acceptance of the Torah made the creation of the world possible. If the world was created for Israel, then the world is Israel's *natural* place. For this reason, Israel is scattered throughout the world. From this perspective, the scattering of Israel is not evidence of their debased quality, but just the opposite. As Maharal says elsewhere in this treatise (chapter 56), "the exile, the fact that [God] scattered them [= Israel] to the four winds, is evidence of Israel's loftiness."

This is a complete reversal of earlier expressed opinions. The Maharal has moved from a claim that the Land of Israel is Israel's natural place and exile—the rest of the world—unnatural, to the claim that the world as a whole is Israel's natural place. In fact, in light of this reversal, the opening sentence of this section becomes a kind of double-edged sword. The statement "if Israel had a special land," that is, a land set aside for them, implies that they do not—not even in the Land of Israel. In fact, at first read it is difficult not to interpret the meaning this way, particularly since the Maharal is here arguing against "Haman's" argument that the dispersion of this people is proof of their lowliness. "On the contrary," Maharal writes, Israel's dispersion is proof of their special status, as the people upon whom the world's creation depends. Despite anxious statements to the contrary, Maharal's meaning is hard to miss: if the world as a whole is Israel's land, then Israel has no special land, not even the Land of Israel.

If exile is (or has become) Israel's natural home, then it would be improper for Israel to leave it. Indeed, this is precisely what Maharal goes on to say, but in a particular and significant way: "If Israel were to leave what God, may He be blessed, decreed for them, that is, exile, it would be Israel's destruction." Articulating the view adopted later by such groups as Neturei Karta (see Chapter 10), Maharal indicates that Israel may not leave their exile—presumably until God redeems them. But Maharal goes one step further. If Israel were to leave her exile, he says, "this would be Israel's destruction." Israel requires exile to survive. In this world, at least, exile is Israel's natural place, and Israel should not seek to overthrow the natural

THE GREAT THEORIZER: THE MAHARAL OF PRAGUE    133

order, for anything that tries to live outside the natural order cannot hope to survive.

Continuing his articulation of his theory of exile, Maharal remarks:

[25] God, may He be blessed, who put Israel in exile, decreed the survival of exile as well. For something that represents a change, going outside of the order of reality, requires special guarding and strengthening for it to survive. For this reason, God, may He be blessed, decreed the manner of their survival... [which is the separation from their neighbors required by the laws of the Torah].

Repeating his earlier observation that Israel in exile requires special strengthening—to assure the survival of the exile the survival of which God assures—Maharal suggests that God gave Israel the Torah, the observance of which would separate Israel from her neighbors and thus support her survival. To be specific:

The survival of Israel in exile is [made possible by] their uniting with one another and separating from the nations...they are separated from the nations in their eating and their dress and their flesh [= circumcision] and their doors [which are marked by *mezuzot*].

Drawing on ancient teachings concerning the distinctions between Israel and her neighbors, Maharal endorses the power of these practices to keep Israel distinct.

But what is it that unites the people of Israel with one another? Maharal suggests:

And that which the Talmud said—"pray with the congregation" (Berakhot 8a)—there is no doubt that when there is a slight measure of leaving exile, as when Israel [in community prayer] unite and are no longer divided, that is considered their leaving the exile. For in their exile they are scattered among the nations, and when Israel unites, this is considered to be their leaving exile.

This remark is pregnant with possibility. One might imagine that just as observance of the commandments of the Torah separates Jews from their neighbors, so too does their common observance of the Torah unite Jews with one another. But here Maharal focuses on a single Talmudic teaching to propose that certain practices—in this case, the practice of reciting one's prayers not alone but with the congregation—are especially efficacious in uniting Israel and removing them, at least to a certain extent, from the condition of exile.

How does this work? According to Maharal's interpretation, exile is the condition of being scattered, disunified. Hence, if there is a practice that unifies Israel, such as praying with the congregation, with a minyan, it removes Israel from her exilic condition. By defining "exile" in this reasonable but particular way, Maharal allows exile to be defined away. The promise of all this is that exile need not be exile. If Israel is united in the observance of the commandments God gave her, then she is by definition not in exile. By the same token, we may imagine that disunity in the Land would be "exile." So, Jews can be in exile in the Land and enjoy a largely non-exilic condition in exile.

None of this should be taken to suggest that the Maharal rejects the concepts of exile and redemption. Undeniably, the entire treatise from which we have been quoting is devoted to laying out how redemption from exile will one day be achieved. The key, however, is that redemption is in the future. "Exile" is in the present, and for the present, it is the natural place for Israel. It is so natural, in fact, that it is hard to call it full exile, because in this long-term, currently natural home Israel is cared for by the Shekhinah and protected by God's commandments. What was once unnatural has become natural. What was once natural—Jewish residence in the Holy Land—would today, before redemption, be unnatural.

Looking back on the world in which the Maharal lived diminishes only a little the shock of what he wrote. Bohemia in his day offered Jews a mostly comfortable, culturally rich, and accepting home. It is no wonder, then, that the Maharal, and other Jews with him, considered it genuinely to be home. But Maharal said out loud what many Jews probably felt but would have hesitated to express: that redemption wasn't an urgency but a future hope, one not of this world but of another; that Jewish life in this diaspora was perfectly natural, the summit of what it meant to be a Jew at *this* time; that acts of Jewish practice both protected Jews in exile and removed them from it, not literally but spiritually. This was all a brave and bold message, but one that perfectly expressed the affirming side of the Jewish relationship with their diasporas.

# 8

# Hasidism and the Eastern European Diaspora

If early modernity was a time of extraordinary change and growth for Europe at large, it was a period of particularly significant transformation and opportunity for Europe's Jews. From the latter part of the sixteenth and on into the nineteenth century, Jewish eastern Europe (including Greater Poland, Lithuania, the Russian empire, and beyond) became a veritable new Jewish homeland. In the words of Abraham Joshua Heschel, "In Eastern Europe, the Jewish people came into its own. It did not live like a guest in somebody else's house.... There Jews lived without reservation and without disguise, outside their homes no less than within them."[1] In these territories, Jews lived in larger numbers, with greater self-regulating author- ity, than at any time since the war with the Romans in the first century. They spoke their own language (called "Jewish" = Yiddish) and created their own culture. And it was in these lands that was born one of the most original, creative, and influential of modern Jewish movements: Hasidism— a movement of self-described "pietists," followers of charismatic *tzaddikim* ("righteous" rabbinic leaders).

What was the dynamic that led to this development? Poland and Lithuania were territories where Jews had resided in large numbers for cen- turies, and the conditions of their residence were often quite favorable. In the words of a papal diplomat, writing in 1565, "In those principalities, one still comes upon masses of Jews...they possess land, engage in commerce, and devote themselves to medicine and astrology.... They possess consider- able wealth and they are not only among the respectable citizens, but occasionally dominate them.... In general, they enjoy equal rights."[2] Their presence was so immense, and their place in society so significant, that, beginning in the sixteenth century and continuing for generations, Jews were granted a considerable degree of autonomy, making laws for their own communities, adjudicating their own disputes, and conducting "diplomacy" with local monarchs and nobles. Jews even organized their own regional

136 EMBRACING EXILE

legislature-government, known as the Council of the Four/Five Lands, which was recognized by authorities in these territories.

The right of Jews to build community institutions and engage in trade was protected during much of this period by local law, and despite the opposition of the church, local nobility often granted Jews privileges that their Christian neighbors could only envy. To be sure, Jews and Christians were often suspicious of one another, but there was also cooperation between members of the different communities. Jews and Christians had not only business relations with each other, but even partnerships, and there are even reports of Jews who ate and drank with others in gentile taverns, sometimes setting aside their distinctive dress and customs to fit in with the larger commercial society.[3]

Central to the development of Jewish society in this region was the increasing number of great yeshivas, academies for advanced study of the Talmud and related texts. In those academies, the "portable homeland" that is the Talmud became the center of scholarly devotion as never before, thanks to its increasing availability as a product of that most revolutionary of modern inventions, the printing press.[4] Over time, the academies gained great prestige and their leaders considerable authority, as the law of the community was Jewish law, which was rooted in the Talmud and its commentaries. Scholars of the Talmud had both legal and cultural power, and they were admired as heroes who had attained what was considered to be the height of Jewish achievement.

The yeshiva's society of scholars excluded most Jews, who had to earn a living and therefore could not devote themselves to the scholarly life. The consequent imbalance of power and prestige between normal, pious Jews and yeshiva scholars resulted in resentment, which contributed to the growth, in the eighteenth century, of a new "populist" movement—Hasidism. Reacting, as it did, against the extreme intellectualism of the yeshiva, Hasidism set out to offer new paths to Jewish fulfillment.

Hasidism identifies as its founder R. Israel Ba'al Shem Tov, known as the Besht. By reputation and legend, the Besht was a charismatic holy man, one who sought spiritual uplift in local forests, in the company of God's more modest creatures. But recent research has shown that he was no recluse or rebel. On the contrary, he was a respected member of the established Jewish community, as much a preserver of current realities as he was an innovator.[5] The city in which he lived and taught, Medzhybizh, was a large one, with a population of 5,000, of whom approximately 2,000

HASIDISM AND THE EASTERN EUROPEAN DIASPORA    137

were Jews.[6] Still, for all his conventionality, his promotion of joy in Jewish practice and intensity in Jewish worship had considerable influence, an influence carried by his disciples to large swathes of the local Jewish population. The power of the movement that emerged was centered on these disciples and those who followed them, for they became the *tzaddikim* (the "righteous ones") of the Hasidic world, a virtual royalty in the eyes of common Hasidim in local communities throughout these territories.

It is significant that the first several generations of Hasidim lived in lands saturated with Jews and Jewishness. Though Jews shared their towns and small cities with Christians, in many of these communities they constituted 40, 50, or even a larger percentage of the population. Living this way, side by side, Jews and Christians generally saw one another as the "other," and while common contact often led to cooperation and even limited affection, Christian anti-Judaism certainly informed the attitudes of many Christians. Jews, in turn, fashioned themselves as "foreigners" relative to the local populations.

But, as Heschel suggests, even as "foreigners" Jews in these places were very much at home. How so? The prominence of Jews in these towns allowed them to take their situation for granted, to give them a sense of self-confidence. They had a significant footprint in their marketplaces and on their roads. And when they retreated into their own districts after the day's affairs had ceased, they felt a sense of ownership, living unimpeded in their generally modest homes. The notion that all Hasidim were simple, poor Jews has been rightly challenged by modern scholarship; in fact, Hasidism attracted all kinds of Jews. But it is still fair to say that Jews of this place and time were—along with the general population—mostly of modest means. This does not mean, however, that Jewish life was a life of deprivation and suffering (at least no more than was true in general). In significant respects, Jewish life was extremely rich, and Hasidism enriched it even more.

This picture provides the context for an understanding of Hasidic teachings pertaining to exile. On the one hand, the perceived impoverishment of Jewish life in Poland and Lithuania might lead us to expect an emphasis, in Hasidic thought and commentary, on the exilic quality of the lives of Jews scattered in these lands. On the other hand, the rich personal, communal, and spiritual lives of Jews, now enhanced by Hasidic imagination and creativity, would make it difficult to experience Jewish life as dominated by the "sufferings of exile." It would be a mistake to expect one view only, and an even greater mistake to expect consistency (Hasidic masters were not

138   EMBRACING EXILE

systematic thinkers). What did Hasidic leaders teach in this regard, and what message did their followers hear?

Of the *tzaddikim* of the early generations, the teachings of R. Elimelekh of Lizhensk, R. Menachem Nachum of Chernobyl, and R. Nachman of Bratzlav stand out in their comments on exile as in many other matters.

Elimelekh was an early Hasidic master who made his court in a small, poor town in the hills of Galicia, in what is today southeastern Poland. Elimelekh was a confident proponent of the emerging hierarchies of Hasidism, and his teachings emphasize the crucial place of the *tzaddik*—the righteous master—for common Jews, who must rely on the *tzaddik*'s merit and powers to assure their own welfare. Elimelekh is best known for the book *Noam Elimelekh* ("The Pleasantness of Elimelekh"), in which his teachings are gathered.

In this work, Elimelekh does not have a lot to say on the question of exile. What he does say, however, is of significance. Consider, for example, a teaching from his comments on the weekly Torah portion, *lekh lekha*, in which Abraham is directed to leave his ancestral home for the Promised Land. The teaching begins by quoting and commenting upon the Talmudic claim that "one who dwells in the Land of Israel *as though* has a God, and one who lives outside the Land *as though* has no God" (Ketubbot 110b). Elimelekh spells out the implications of this claim: If the one who lives in the Land "as though" has a God, this means that in reality they do not have a God; and if one who lives outside the Land "as though" has no God, this means that in reality they do have a God. In other words, logical analysis of the teaching actually leads to the opposite conclusion of the one we might expect. In reality, this analysis suggests, God is available to those outside the Land but not to those within it. This is not the intention of the original Talmudic teaching. But Elimelekh does here what the Talmud does, that is, he undermines a teaching that favors the Land by reading it in a way that eliminates that preference.

Still, how can it be that the Talmud, even in Elimelekh's understanding, asserts God's real presence outside the Land but not in it? To answer this question, Elimelekh takes his direction from another Talmudic passage:

> It is said in the gemara (Berakhot 30a), "one who stands outside of the Land of Israel and prays should direct his heart toward the Land of Israel…." So a person who wants his prayer to be heard should have the intention that he is, as it were, praying in the Land of Israel and the Temple is built and

the altar is in its proper place, and it is as though he lives now in the Land of Israel, and in this way he comes to a clarity and complete cleaving (to God), praying with complete intention and love and fear, as though he is standing in the Holy of Holies. (Noam Elimelekh, *lekh lekha* 15)

In the view expressed here, being in the Land of Israel is not a geographical state but a spiritual one. One who is outside the Land but prays with full and proper intention is as though in the Land, while (presumably) one who is in the Land but does not pray with the same intent is effectively in exile from God. From this perspective, the implications of the paradoxical passage with which Elimelekh begins his exposition are not problematic at all.

Prayer was (and still is) of extreme importance to Hasidim, and Elimelekh was no exception in his appreciation of its importance. His emphasis on the centrality of the prayer experience makes this comment particularly important. Building on the Talmud's teaching that the praying Jew should always "direct his heart toward the Land of Israel," Elimelekh offers an entirely new notion of what this means, one with considerable import for our exploration. In the Talmud, the instruction is a purely geographic one—the pray-er should direct his heart, and with it his body, toward the Holy Land. Enacted this way, the prayer ritual would highlight the centrality of the Land. But in Elimelekh's reading, the teaching is transformed into something quite contrary to this original purpose. In his mind, the person praying should have the intention of mind/heart to pray as though he is in the Holy Land, even in the Holy of Holies itself. If he does so "with complete intention and love and fear," then it is as though he is actually there—actually in the Land and even in the Temple. From this perspective, the adept Hasidic pray-er, the one who prays with full and proper intention, will essentially be in the Land and the Temple. He will experience no distance from Land and Temple because he will have created them around him, in his personal place of prayer. If the experience of the Land, and even of the Holy of Holies, is available in the prayer space in Galicia, then it is difficult to imagine what the liability of "exile" might be. With the most intimate of contact with the divine always available to him when he prays with proper intent, the Hasid will effectively find himself in the Holy Land, even in the hills of eastern Poland.

This in not to say that Elimelekh and his followers did not experience exile—which Elimelekh insistently calls "bitter exile" (given the reflexiveness of this formulation, it is reasonable to ask whether he actually experienced exile as "bitter" or whether this was simply the conventional way of referring

140 EMBRACING EXILE

to exile). But even while admitting the condition of exile, Elimelekh draws upon ancient rabbinic teachings to moderate the "bitterness" of that experience. So, in his comments on the Torah-portion *vayigash* we read: "Now, in this bitter exile, even though our 'servitude' is difficult, along with the yoke of exile, even so, the divine presence (*shekhinah*) is among us, and we have the strength to cleave to the divine presence." Even though Jews are subject to the control of the nations ("servitude"), they nevertheless live in the presence of God, fully capable of "cleaving" to God despite their exilic condition.

Crucially, for Elimelekh, cleaving to God accomplishes more than succor or even comfort. He goes on to say that "in this bitter exile we have playfulness with the Shekhinah," for "the one who listens to me [= the Shekhinah] to hold fast to me and my holiness can come to [experience] play and joy and gaiety even in the bitter exile"—or, perhaps better, "bitter" exile. In this statement, Elimelekh makes it clear that the phrase "bitter exile" is a mere traditional tic. As the Shekhinah is available in exile, and cleaving to the Shekhinah leads to joy, there is no reason that exile need be "bitter" at all. The Jew may enjoy the same joy anywhere, for the only distance that matters is the distance from God. If your relationship with God is unbroken, then where you reside—whether in the Holy Land or in exile—makes little difference.

In light of the ability of the pious Jew imaginatively to construct the Holy Land and Temple around him, even in exile, and recognizing the close relationship with God he may achieve in that exile, what is the meaning or force of "exile" as Elimelekh understands it? An answer is suggested in Elimelekh's comments on the Torah portion *vayishlach*: "The holy Torah teaches us how to conduct ourselves in this bitter exile, in which we are subject to the hand of the nations, and we must accept exile with love until God has mercy on us and redeems us." Exile is God's will, a will Israel must accept. One day God will deliver Israel from exile, but the Jew should anticipate that future without urgency. In the meantime, the Jew should live in exile according to the teachings of the Torah, conjuring Zion in his prayer house (and, we might add, study hall). In the future, Israel will, with God's help, return to Zion. In the current world, Zion will come to the Jews.

A contemporary of R. Elimelekh, R. Menachem Nachum of Chernobyl, expresses a conception of the Land of Israel that overlaps almost exactly with the former. He teaches:

Even though the Land of Israel has a physical reality, in any case its essence is spiritual and vital, and it is Life [or: the Life force] from the

Creator, blessed be He. And even though we are outside the Land, in any case we have the quality of The Land of Israel…because in all the synagogues and study halls there flows from the Creator, blessed be He, the Life force of the Land of Israel….When one stands in the synagogue or the study hall and stands and prays with the thought within the speech, then he is in the Land of Israel, that is to say, within the Life of the Creator, blessed be He.[7]

In this formulation, the essence of the Land is not to be found in its physical reality but in its spiritual one, as a container of the Life force of the Creator, who imbued it with special vitality. Since "the Land" is about that force, anywhere the force can be animated shares the essence of the Land of Israel. How can Life be animated, then? Through the acts of the common, pious Jew—his prayer and his study of Torah. Making sure there is no misunderstanding of what is intended here, Moshe Idel remarks that this represents a "neutralization of the importance of the Land of Israel," since the essence of the Land can now be manifest anywhere.[8]

Rav Nachman of Bratzlav offers a more subtle perspective on the condition of exile. Nachman was and continues to be one of the most influential Hasidic masters. A grandson of the founder of Hasidism, the Ba'al Shem Tov, Nachman attracted thousands of followers during his lifetime, and, because he left no successor, Bratzlaver Hasidim continued to be devoted to his personal spirit and teachings, even to this day. Suffering from bouts of depression, Nachman sought a remedy in the joy of Torah and mitzvot (observance of commandments), something he emphasizes frequently in his teachings.[9] Nachman's followers today are especially distinguished by their joyous observances, which they seek to spread to others. Nachman's ongoing influence is evidenced in the fact that his grave site, in Uman, Ukraine, is a popular site for pilgrimage, both for his Hasidim and for other Jews.

In his discussions of exile, Nachman teaches that the bitterness Jews experience in exile is a product of misunderstanding. In the words attributed to him:

All of the troubles and sufferings and exile are all on account of lack of understanding…and the nations know that the greatness they have had, and the lowliness we had during the exile, all of that greatness was [actually] ours. And even though it is impossible now to understand all of this, because one cannot deny one's experience, even so understanding will be

142  EMBRACING EXILE

increased, and all will understand that the greatness of the nations was actually our greatness and their lowliness. (Liqutei Moharan 21, 11)

Experience, Nachman admits, is difficult to deny, and the fact is that Israel has often experienced exile as bitter (to use Elimelekh's word). But experience also deceives, he insists. With greater understanding than they currently possess, both Israel and the nations will one day appreciate that the only apparent greatness of the nations is actually lowliness, and the apparent lowliness of Israel is actually greatness.

How so? Nachman does not specify. But a shift in perspective can yield a shift in experience. The people Israel, in this world, lacks the grandeur of government and power. But in this same world, Israel possesses Torah, God's unique gift, a truly divine and grand blessing. By studying and observing Torah, Israel achieves grandeur. At the same time, the nations, who on the surface exercise power and gather wealth, also abuse that power and wealth, thus degrading themselves. In other words, their apparent "greatness" is actually lowliness. We don't know whether this is how Nachman would have shifted our perspective. But he would have demanded a similar such shift to accomplish the same ends—a recognition that what Israel experiences in exile is, in fact, not degradation but greatness. If one truly believes in Israel's special place in the world, then how could one imagine that Israel, in reality, experiences anything else?

In an even bolder teaching (61, 2), Nachman effectively takes Elimelekh's claim for Jewish prayer space and extends it to the entirety of Israel's home, even in exile. He notes that, according to one of the Talmud's teachings, "the air of the Land of Israel makes one wise" (b. Bava Batra 158b). This he takes to mean that wherever Jews are wise there must be "the air of the Land of Israel" (if A = B then B = A). This is true, he recognizes, wherever Israel is well established, because wherever Jews make a home, they build study halls, study Torah, and offer new insights into Torah. The consequence? "A place where Jews have dwelt for a while, even outside the Land of Israel, has the quality of the sacredness of the Land of Israel, the quality of 'the small sanctuary' (Ezekiel 11:16)." Wherever Jews dwell for a while has the sacredness of the Land of Israel. Zion alone is not Zion because, on account of Israel's relationship with its Torah, Zion may be found in all the dispersions of Israel.

Supporting this same conclusion, Nachman elsewhere (55, 2) teaches that "the sacredness of the Land of Israel is now in exile." Now, Nachman knows that the "bitter exile" doesn't feel like the holy Land of Israel. But this, he

says, is because exile is now subject to the domination of the "*sitra achra*"—
the evil "other side" of the divine force. Consequently, the "sacredness of the
Land of Israel" now in exile cannot be fully revealed. Still, that sacredness
can be "drawn out" in exile, through the "sparking of the light of the merit of
the ancestors [*zekhut avot*]." The "merit of the ancestors" is a treasury of
merits upon which Israel can draw when seeking God's mercy, and it has
worked on Israel's behalf throughout the generations. It still does so in
Nachman's exile. Completing the logic of his argument, Nachman then
declares, "In the place where there is [the merit of the] ancestors, there is the
divine presence [the Shekhinah]." If the divine presence is in exile (which
we have known since the period of the Talmudic rabbis), then the sacredness of the Land of Israel is in exile, partially hidden though it may be. And
if Jews in "exile" already dwell in the Holy Land, then the notion of exile,
with its implied dichotomy between exile and the Holy Land, loses its force.

In what is perhaps his baldest statement of the extension of the holiness
of the Land of Israel to territories of the diaspora, R. Nachman builds upon
Rashi's first comment on the Torah and the verse Rashi cites there: "the
power of His ways He revealed to His people, giving them the inheritance
of the nations" (Psalms 111:6). For Rashi, this verse declares that God, as
creator, has the power to designate a land, including the Holy Land, to one
nation and then to another, and so Israel cannot be accused of stealing the
land previously held by the Canaanite nations. Extending this notion,
Nachman claims that "the essence of the power of the Land of Israel is an
aspect of... 'the power of His ways,' for on account of this Israel could go
and conquer the Land of Israel." The same is true, he says, outside the
Land. How so?

> Israel, the holy nation, sometimes comes to places that are very, very far
> from the holiness of [the people of] Israel, such as a place that originally
> belonged to idolators, and even now they may be under the authority of a
> nation that is distant from the holiness of Israel. But Israel comes there,
> and conquers the place, and sanctifies it as a Jewish place, and this [terri-
> tory now] too has the aspect of the Land of Israel... and on account of this
> we have the right to conquer the entire world and to sanctify it with the
> holiness of the Land of Israel. (*Likutei* II, 78)

"Conquer," in Nachman's usage, clearly does not mean "military conquest."
What Nachman is describing is the creation of new Jewish spaces by

144 EMBRACING EXILE

populations of Jewish refugees in the diaspora, in areas that were not previously Jewish. As illustrations, we may think of towns in Poland or Ukraine where Jews settled and became a large component of the population—in their side of town, the overwhelming majority. "Conquering" such spaces and sanctifying them as Jewish, Jews made them, Nachman argues, an "aspect" of the Land of Israel. Again, Jews do not need to go to the Holy Land, for the Holy Land comes to them.

It is impossible not to see these teachings as an expression of Nachman's evaluation of his own diaspora. R. Nachman's world—Poland, Lithuania, Ukraine—was a world filled with Torah and its students. It was, moreover, "a place where Jews have dwelt for a while," filled with spaces that Jews "conquered" and sanctified. Partaking of these qualities, it was, according to Nachman's formula, a sacred land, precisely like the Land of Israel itself. In R. Nachman's system, Exile becomes Zion and Zion is rendered unnecessary. Diaspora is fully justified because it is fully holy, lacking nothing essential a Jew might need.

It is well known that Nachman himself travelled (briefly!) to the Holy Land, which was theoretically unnecessary according to the teachings we have just reviewed. Why, then, did he make this effort, undeniably a dangerous one in his time? In Elon Goshen-Gottstein's interpretation, Nachman did not deny the special quality of the physical Land of Israel, which he understood (like Menachem Nachum of Chernobyl before him) to contain the sacred energy of God's creative power. But Nachman was of the opinion that the *tzaddik*—in this case, himself—could serve as a conduit to extend that energy beyond the borders of the Land, to all places where Jews dwelt. In his trip, Nachman took responsibility for bringing this energy to his own followers.[10]

Indeed, Nachman saw the *tzaddik* as having a unique power in drawing the sacredness of the Land of Israel to wherever he was. Consider just the following teachings:

- [Concerning the true *tzaddik*] the one who sees him... at the time that the world gathers to him, coming to hear the word of God, in particular on Rosh Hashana, at the time of the great gathering... then any place he looks is made an aspect of the Land of Israel (Likutei Morharan II, 40).[11]
- The rule is that the words the *tzaddik* speaks, of Torah or of prayer, are called the Land of Israel (Torah 81).[12]

## HASIDISM AND THE EASTERN EUROPEAN DIASPORA   145

- True *tzaddikim* inherit the Land of Israel, for they merit that the place of their burial is literally sacred with the sanctity of the Land of Israel (Torah 109).[13]

Seeing the *tzaddik* allows one to "see" the Land of Israel. Hearing the words of the *tzaddik* allows one to be "in" the Land of Israel. The burial-place of the *tzaddik* brings the Land of Israel to him, "literally" ("*mammash*"). The Land of Israel, drawn away from its physical source, is available to the common Jew anywhere, thanks to the *tzaddik*, because, as scholar Goshen-Gottstein remarks, "the *tzaddik* is equivalent to the Land of Israel."[14]

Nachman's teachings were transmitted to subsequent generations of Hasidim, who were much influenced by them. For example, his own disciples put together his teachings on the Great Rosh Hashana Gathering and the magic of the grave of the *tzaddik* to create the groundwork for the Rosh Hashana pilgrimage to Uman. But it is not only Bratzlaver Hasidim who were thus influenced. So, in a remarkable restatement and extension of Nachman's message (whether intentional or not), an "editor's note" printed in the *Chabad Journal* of May 7, 2013, recounted:

> Over 150 years ago, there was a pious and devoted Jew who desired to apply himself to Torah study and prayer in the Holy Land. When he shared his plan with his rebbe, Rabbi Menachem Mendel of Lubavitch, he was taken aback by the rebbe's response, "Make Israel here." He did not need to go to Israel; rather, he was to bring Israel where he lived.
>
> Every time we do another mitzvah, we [im-]port a bit of Jerusalem to wherever we are. And when the world is full of such mini-Jerusalems, we will all gather in our homeland—for real.

The writer here does not deny the future redemption, when Jews will be gathered into their ancestral homeland. But, according to the original Lubavitcher Rebbe and his latter-day disciple, in the pre-redemption world, Jews should not go to Israel. Jews should instead bring Israel to where they are. They should do one mitzvah, then another, turning their cities and villages into "mini-Jerusalems." In this simple, persistent Hasidic view, Zion is not one place; it is—potentially at least—many places. If one's place is, on account of one's pious deeds, already Zion, then one need not return to Zion. If every place the Hasid lives may be rendered a Jerusalem, then for that Hasid, at least, redemption has already occurred.

# 9

# Haskalah, Reform, and Early Zionism

Modernity challenged Jews to re-evaluate their relationships to the lands in which they made their homes. The European enlightenment, which gained full political momentum in the eighteenth and nineteenth centuries, led to new configurations of the relationship between church and state, and new definitions of citizenship. Both developments opened the prospect of Jews gaining more equal roles in the modern nation-state. But the prospect generated challenging questions: Did Jews want to give up on their traditional status as resident "foreigners" who to some degree conducted their own affairs? Would claiming modern citizenship require them to give up on their hope of redemption to Zion? Would diaspora still be "exile" if Jews were accepted as equal citizens of the secular nation-state? And so forth.

Even before the political revolutions of the late eighteenth century, enlightenment currents had a profound impact on beliefs, from high philosophy to popular opinion. Beginning in the seventeenth century, modern philosophy accorded priority to human reason, changing the ways the learned few, and even the less-educated many, thought about humans and their relationship to God, the place of religion in society, and the construction of just human societies. Theories of natural human rights emerged to challenge received views of the place of "man"—different kinds of men, and, we would add, women—in the hierarchies long believed to have been ordained by heaven. The purposes and powers of societies and their governments were now open to question.

Jews who found themselves in centers of the European enlightenment—relatively few though they were, at this stage—could not avoid these developments. Among them was Moses Mendelssohn, who, though born in Dessau to a poor family, in his mid-teens followed his teacher to Berlin, where he was exposed to the flowering culture of enlightenment, one that included Jews. Though they were few in number, at the time of Mendelssohn's arrival in 1743, most of Berlin's Jews were already well-to-do. At least the younger among them were strongly attracted to general German culture, and the Jewish community in general was reputed to exhibit a high level of culture. According to one account, penned later in Mendelssohn's lifetime, Berlin's

HASKALAH, REFORM, AND EARLY ZIONISM    147

Jews "socialize a good deal with Christians.... They love reading more than ever. They pay equal attention to the weekly journals and the theater.... The mania for novels has proven particularly contagious ... but they love the theater above all else." Another writer reported that Jews (including Mendelssohn) played a leading role in "matters of taste and philosophy."[1] Suffice it to say that Mendelssohn, an observant Jew, had entered a new world, one he quickly embraced.

Indeed, Mendelssohn educated himself in the philosophies of his time, becoming a leading figure in Berlin's cultured society. Yet, unlike others who followed him, he refused to grant that Jewish tradition and enlightenment philosophy were essentially at odds, and, writing in German, he sought to reconcile the demands of each with the other. His central work in pursuit of this goal is his major work of political philosophy, *Jerusalem* (1783).

Focusing on questions of the state and its relationship to religion, Mendelssohn had little to say about Jewish diaspora as such. But his argument supports and defends the place of Jews in their Christian European home, insisting that the Jew's Jewish obligations present no irreconcilable conflict with full citizenship. Referencing the advice of that ancient "Jew," Mark (as in the Gospel of Mark), who represented Jesus as directing that we "render unto Caesar what is Caesar's and unto God what is God's" (Mark 12:17), Mendelssohn writes, "No better advice than this can be given to the House of Jacob: adopt the mores and constitution of the country in which you find yourself, but be steadfast in upholding the religion of your fathers too." Quoting a Christian source in an apologetic for a Christian audience, Mendelssohn really does little more than reiterate Jeremiah's old advice— make yourself at home there, for that is now your home—as codified in the Talmudic dictum: "the law of the land is the law."[2]

What is perhaps most notable about Mendelssohn's political treatise is its lack of comment on an imagined Jewish polity. Mendelssohn writes in the European idiom of his day about political theory in general, not about a particular manifestation thereof. This perspective is quite different from the political writing of an earlier Jewish philosopher, Maimonides, who, in his *Mishneh Torah*, describes the executive, legislative, and judicial branches of an ideal Jewish state, one that never existed but one day (he surely hoped) would. For the medieval Jewish philosopher, the state worthy of discussion was the ideal Jewish one; for the enlightenment Jewish philosopher, it was the modern state that would soon emerge. For even the traditional Jew in the modern European mode, there is no Jewish state, just a state of citizens among whom the Jew may count him- or herself.

148  EMBRACING EXILE

All these questions came into greater focus in France after the Revolution, which opened up possibilities for citizenship that Prussian Berlin could not yet fully imagine. In 1806 Napoleon gathered an assembly of 71 distinguished Jews to respond to a series of questions relevant to the question of offering full citizenship rights to Jews in the emerging French polity. It was Napoleon's sixth question that raised the question of the Jews' relationship to their diaspora homes. "Jews born in France and treated by law as French citizens," Napoleon asked, "do they consider France their country? Do they have the obligation to defend it? Are they obliged to obey the laws and to conform to the dispositions of the civil code?"[3]

The gathered Jewish Assembly, or "Sanhedrin" (after the ancient Jewish legislative and deliberative assembly), was not exactly free to offer an unvarnished answer to the questions with which it had been addressed; the fate of Jews in France hung on the answers of this body to these questions. At the same time, the question about loyalty and status challenged Jews to ask themselves who they truly were, for the potential advantage of full citizenship came at a cost, one felt more by France's Ashkenazi Jews than by the Sephardic community. The "medieval" arrangement accorded Jews the right to conduct their own affairs within their communities, provided that they paid their taxes and submitted to general regulations of the crown. Ashkenazi Jews had for years enjoyed the fruits of their corporate autonomy, and they recognized the cost of giving up this status in favor of individual rights, according to the modern social constitution. They might have hesitated, therefore, to provide an uncompromisingly affirmative answer.

Against the background of these tensions, the Sanhedrin's answer to Napoleon's sixth question is of considerable interest:

> Men who have adopted a country, who have resided in it these many generations—who, even under the restraint of particular laws which abridged their civil rights, were so attached to it that they preferred being debarred from the advantages common to all other citizens, rather than leave it—cannot but consider themselves as Frenchmen in France; and they consider as equally sacred and honorable the bounden duty of defending their country.[4]

The first sentence of this response bears a faint echo of Reb Nachman's "a place where Jews have dwelt for a while," but this hardly resembles the kind of affirmation found in Nachman's words. Admitting the disadvantage

HASKALAH, REFORM, AND EARLY ZIONISM    149

that had, to this point, defined Jewish status, the assembly's opening statement is honest, and thus begrudging.

The more affirmative answer, if there is one, resides in what follows:

> Jeremiah (chapter 29) exhorts the Jews to consider Babylon as their coun-
> try, although they were to remain in it only for seventy years. He exhorts
> them to till the ground, to build houses, to sow, and to plant. His recom-
> mendation was so much attended to, that Ezra (chapter 2) says, that when
> Cyrus allowed them to return to Jerusalem to rebuild the Temple, 42,360
> only, left Babylon; and that this number was mostly composed of the poor
> people, the wealthy having remained in that city.
>
> The love of the country is in the heart of Jews a sentiment so natural, so
> powerful, and so consonant to their religious opinions, that a French Jew
> considers himself in England, as among strangers, although he may be
> among Jews; and the case is the same with English Jews in France.[5]

The argument, hearkening back explicitly to the biblical prophet, is that
Jews are biblically encouraged to plant roots in the lands in which they find
themselves, so much so that even when they have the option of returning to
their Land, the best of them ("the wealthy") choose to remain. Making a
home in a new land, they develop a love of that land, a love both "natural"
and conforming to Jewish religious teachings. In other words, "do not doubt
our loyalty," these Jewish representatives declare. We are in every respect
devoted citizens of this country.

This response is notably less bold than many of those in more explicitly
religious sources. Still, it does convey something that is indisputably true.
Jews living in France or Italy or Egypt or Turkey—speaking the languages of
those lands while sharing material and other culture with their neighbors—
really did develop love of those lands. They came to be *of* them, even while
remaining Jews. Perhaps ironically touching on the truth, the writers recognize that Jeremiah's advice had long-term, powerful consequences. By
planting and building, while praying for the welfare of their neighbors,
Jews, in virtually all their exiles, made themselves at home.

The French Revolution was only the first of numerous European
revolutions (and counter-revolutions), movements that changed European
governments and societies forever. The ideas planted by the French
Revolution—celebrating liberty, equality, and the rights of the citizen—and
spread across the European landscape by Napoleon's armies would be

150    EMBRACING EXILE

repeatedly challenged, but they would never retreat completely. Modern Europe, centered in its cities, would flourish despite the setbacks, and Jews were attracted to these centers as much as others.

Jews modernized quickly in their new urban homes. An increasing number enjoyed university educations, and they joined the ranks of educated society, becoming (depending upon the land and its laws) doctors, lawyers, bankers, writers, and artists. Despite scattered restrictions and setbacks, Jews often thrived in these settings, rising to the cultured middle class with surprising swiftness. The ways of modernity influenced Jewish study and practice, spawning the first modern studies of Jewish history, religious tradition, and the like. At the same time, Jews were increasingly attracted to the culture and arts of their Christian neighbors, whether music in Berlin, opera in Paris, or architecture in various European cities.

These developments led many Jews to deny their Jewish particularities, for various reasons. Where restrictions on Jews continued to limit opportunities, some sought acceptance through baptism. Others found this path abhorrent, though they still strived to acculturate—to become "good citizens"—in the fullest way possible. This was particularly true in Germany, but such trends were not restricted to any one place. Reformers, fighting the attractions of full assimilation, instituted unprecedented changes in Jewish liturgy and practice to attract their increasingly secular audience. Others would not go as far as the Reformers, but many would at least critically question the tradition as received, including the hope for territorial redemption.

German Jews during this period often spoke of their German homeland. The great German Jewish poet Heinrich Heine declared in 1820 that the German language was his true fatherland. A writer in the Jewish magazine *Der Orient* announced: "The savior for whom we have prayed has appeared. The fatherland [= Germany] has given him to us. The messiah is freedom."[6] And a liberal rabbi in Magdeburg, Ludwig Philippson, insisted, "We are and only wish to be Germans! We have and only wish to have a German fatherland!"[7] Diaspora was good to them; hence, the messiah had come. One who already lives in his fatherland has no need for another.

Remarkably, one of the most popular nineteenth-century German writers, and the inventor of a new genre of fiction called *Heimat* ("homeland") literature, was a Jew, Berthold Auerbach. The first volume of Auerbach's *Tales from the Black Forest* was published in 1843; this was quickly followed by five additional volumes. In Amos Elon's description, "The tales idealize simple peasant life in Nordstetten, a peaceful place where Jews...and Catholics coexist harmoniously side by side."[8] These tales came across as so genuine—and so appreciative of the German *heim*—that none other than the composer and notorious antisemite Richard Wagner praised Auerbach as someone who truly understood the "innermost features of the German national soul."[9] A Jew, too, could be a German of the Romantic age, rooted, as others, in German life and soil.

One of the most significant representatives of the modern turn in Judaism was Heinrich Graetz, the first genuinely "modern" Jewish historian. Like many of his generation, Graetz began life as a traditional Jew with a traditional education, but he also pursued a modern education, eventually earning a Ph.D. at the University of Jena (not far from Weimar). His major work, produced according to the scholarly standards of the German-speaking world, was a multivolume *Geschichte der Juden* (*History of the Jews*, 1853–70). He offered his major statement on the diaspora experience, though, in his 1846 essay, "Construction of Jewish History."

In that essay, Graetz offered what might be described as a "romantic-tragic" picture of the Jewish diaspora experience, which he saw as an "eighteen-hundred year era...of unprecedented suffering, of uninterrupted martyrdom without parallel in world history."[10] Putting aside his unnuanced and highly problematic historical claim, we may nevertheless appreciate what he offers as "the other aspect" of the diaspora experience. The picture of the diaspora Jew, he suggests, requires a "two-sided image"—one of "humbled Judah with the wanderer's staff in his hand" and the other of the same figure. "Bearing the earnestness of the thinker upon his luminous brow, the mien of a scholar in the radiant features of his face; he is in a study filled with a huge library in all the language of mankind and dealing with all the branches of divine and human knowledge."[11]

The history of the Jew, then, is the history of a people "inquiring and wandering, thinking and enduring, studying and suffering." We need not detain ourselves with the question which side of each of these couplets is the more noble? Obviously, for Graetz, the inquiring, thinking, studying Jew is heroic and superior. Next to such an elevated quality, of what importance is suffering and wandering, particularly as the latter contributed to the growth of the former? As he writes further on, "Migrations brought the Jewish people new experiences; homeless, they exercised and sharpened their gaze. Thus even the plentitude of their suffering contributed to broadening the horizons of Jewish thinkers."[12]

## 152 EMBRACING EXILE

In fact, reflecting on the scattering of the Jews, Graetz spends considerable time lauding that very condition. On account of their dispersion, "there is likely no science, no art, no direction of the spirit in which Jews have not shared." Jews so thrived in their diasporas (Graetz does not use this language explicitly, but it is certainly implied) that "as soon as a new part of the world is invaded by a new people, scattered Jews immediately appeared." Leaving behind the lament of the earlier part of this essay, Graetz praises this scattering with high praise: "The Jewish people has become a universal people; being nowhere at home, it is at home everywhere."[13]

This final flourish is reminiscent of the teaching of the Maharal; in his framing, if the world was created on account of the Jews, then the entire world is their home. The implication of Graetz's formulation is reminiscent of what we suggested there, that is, if the Jew is at home everywhere, then the Jew has no need for a particular home anywhere. Zion, in other words, is unnecessary. Add to this the fact that it is diaspora life that contributes to the quality that makes the Jew ascendant—his (and Graetz surely thought only of "his") luminous learning and exceptional scholarship—and the superiority of the diaspora for what really matters cannot be denied. None of this should be taken to mean that the sufferings of diaspora should not be lamented. But, on the Jewish scale of priorities, the weight of those sufferings pales in comparison with what is gained in "Torah," understood by Graetz in the broadest possible terms.

During this same period, Jewish Reform began in Germany, soon spreading to other lands. Reformers asserted the legitimacy of modern Jewish life immersed in modern European culture, while simultaneously affirming their specific identities as German or French Jews, for example. These identities, coupled with ongoing anxieties over being considered "foreign" or "other," required the denial of dual loyalties. For Jews inclined toward Reform, therefore, traditional hopes for restoration to the Holy Land were problematic or worse. Besides being evidence of ambivalent loyalty, such hopes would have been tantamount to an admission of failure to make Germany (or another emerging European state) fully their home. Equally importantly, many such German Jews considered Germany their one and only home, while Zion had become a mere memory.

Reform resistance to the traditional hope of return to Zion found primary expression in newly formulated Reform prayer-books, particularly in passages that had in the past prayed for redemption and the ingathering of the exiles. Beginning with the very earliest Reform prayer-books, reformers struggled with how—and whether—to present these passages. At first, the Hebrew text of the traditional prayer was left intact while the German translation omitted such a passage. But soon, the Hebrew version was either modified or omitted, while the German—which was the only language accessible to the majority of the congregants—either omitted or masked the prayer for the ingathering of the exiles, which was not the actual prayer of many modern German Jews at all.

One of the most revealing passages found in a Reform prayer-book from this period is the product of the most radical congregation in Europe, a liturgy published in Berlin in 1848. The passage is its "Celebration in Memory of the Destruction of Jerusalem," that is, on the occasion of the Ninth of Av—the saddest day of the Jewish year, the day that commemorates the destructions of both Jerusalem Temples. According to this newly conceived passage, the Temples were not destroyed, nor the people exiled, on account of their sins, but because God chose these people for His service, so that His work could be "accomplished everywhere." Israel is meant to bear witness to God's truth, which can be accomplished only if they are scattered throughout the world. Exile, therefore, is an elevation, not a punishment. Furthermore, such scattering does not entail the loss of Temple, sacred city, or homeland. Why not? Because "the Temple is in the ears of all earth's children," cities are consecrated wherever God's name is consecrated, and the new homeland—in this case, Germany—replaces the ancient one.[14]

This feels like a radical reversal of much of Jewish liturgy, and even of Jewish tradition more widely considered. But when we recall the comments of medieval commentators who saw exile as the fulfillment of the Jewish mission, or the teachings of the Maharal, who saw the whole earth as the Jews' home, or when we consider the only slightly earlier comments of Hasidic masters who imagined the construction of the Holy of Holies in Galicia, we quickly appreciate that this is not nearly as radical as it has been described. The reformers chose certain traditional perspectives above others, but most of the sentiments they expressed were not without precedent.

Thus it occasions no surprise to recognize that, as Zionist ideology developed and won adherents, Reformers formed an opposition to it. For these Jews, deliverance had already been largely achieved, in the enlightened setting of post-emancipation Europe. Reform opposition to Zionism was explicit and loud (traditional Jews opposed Zionism, originally an overwhelmingly secular phenomenon, for other reasons). For example, in 1898 the organization of Reform Jewish congregations in the United States, the

154   EMBRACING EXILE

Union of American Hebrew Congregations (UAHC), declared, "We are unalterably opposed to political Zionism. The Jews are not a nation, but religious community.... America is our Zion."[15] This was a common sentiment of Reform Jews and their spokespeople, whether in Europe or in America. As one would expect, this sentiment had consequences for the shape of the liturgy in Reform prayer-books everywhere, as they, like their German progenitors, typically omitted or modified prayers expressing the hope to return to Zion.

Zionist thinkers themselves had views of the diaspora, not all of which were negative. In addition, the nationalistic impulse embodied in Zionism also found expression in diaspora Jewish nationalism. Zionism was a European development under the influence of European ideas. As the nineteenth century progressed, nationalism became a controlling European ideology. The notion of the modern nation-state, a state of all its citizens, resident on a single land, inspired peoples who had shared languages and cultures to fight both the domination of larger empires and the division of smaller cantons to create united, modern republics. Some Jews were taken with this spirit, and just as Italians vowed their loyalties to a united Italy and German peoples to Germany, these Jews dreamed of a modern "state of the Jews" (this being the meaning of the Hebrew "*medinat yisrael*"—commonly translated as "the State of Israel"—for "Israel" is the way Jews have traditionally said "Jew").

Zionist hopes were also generated by more troublesome factors. In the east (the Pale of Settlement, including Lithuania, Congress Poland, and Ukraine), where the majority of the world's Jews lived, imperial decrees promulgated by the Russian tsar diminished the quality of Jewish life significantly. The hated conscription of Jewish youth—some as young as their pre-teens—took a specified number of Jewish boys away from their families for years on end. And, particularly from 1881 onward, anti-Jewish riots (pogroms) threatened the lives of common Jews in community after community. None of this is to say that modernity did not affect and even benefit some Jews living under Russian hegemony. The cities of the Pale, where many Jews lived, were modern cities, where Jewish printing presses and businesses employed modern means to support vibrant flows of Jewish communications and commerce. Naturally, outlying rural communities lagged far behind in these matters. Yet even—or perhaps especially—in these latter settings, Jews often enjoyed neighborly relations with gentiles from the other side of town, with whom they traded in the market square and cooperated for common needs. So, on the one hand, there was, in these lands, undeniably a "Jewish problem" that had to be addressed, and for some the solution would be found (or so they hoped) in Zion. On the other hand, there were large Jewish populations who, like their forebears, continued to live Jewish lives in these territories, whatever the obstacles, and for them Jewish life would remain diaspora life, whatever the mix of troubles and small pleasures.

Antisemitism was not confined to eastern Europe, and it was the public resurgence of antisemitism in France—modern, enlightened France—that most provoked and energized Zionism in western Europe. It was the fraudulent trial and conviction of the fully acculturated French Jew, Colonel Alfred Dreyfus, for espionage that raised the alarm. The Dreyfus Affair, as it is known, was built on paltry or contrived evidence against the colonel. But the trial was about "loyalty," and it was a French Jew—and army officer—who had been accused of disloyalty. The popular response, fueled by beliefs that a Jew could not be a thoroughly loyal citizen of France, raised anti-Jewish feelings to a boiling point, leading to outbursts of virulent antisemitic protest. The battle over Dreyfus and the question of his guilt went on for years.

Crucially, a journalist from Vienna, one Theodor Herzl, was present at Dreyfus's military degradation in Paris in January 1895, following his conviction. The antisemitism Herzl witnessed in the crowds of the city horrified him. In response to what he saw, Herzl concluded that the only solution to the "Jewish problem" was a Jewish state, his conception of which he formulated in his groundbreaking work, *Der Judenstaat*. This work laid out in detail a pragmatic plan for the creation of such a state, infused with the spirit of modern nation-building.

Recognition of the untraditional quality of modern Zionism is critical to understanding why it was, at its inception, so controversial. Jews through the ages expected that they would remain in their exiles until God would send the messiah, heralding the redemption of Jews from their dispersions. In fact, from the Talmud onward, Jews understood a mass movement of Jews to the Holy Land before they were "called" by God to be prohibited. Zionists ignored this prohibition—ignored the traditional counsel to wait—and, relying on modern secular analysis of the Jewish condition in the international setting, called on Jews to solve their own dilemma by building a Jewish state in Palestine. Such a state would, they thought, normalize the Jewish condition, in the context of other modern nationalisms, as Jews would cease to be a homeless people, dependent on the good graces of others to protect their lives and livelihoods.

Many Zionists, relying on this analysis, concluded that building a Jewish state would lead to a diminution and even disappearance of the diaspora. In fact, for many Zionists, "negation of the diaspora" became an article of faith. But not all Zionists agreed, and the writings of one of the earliest and most influential "Lovers of Zion," Ahad Ha-Am, are of particular interest for their affirmation of diaspora as part of the Jewish condition.

Ahad Ha-Am, born Asher Ginsberg in Ukraine in 1856, had a traditional upbringing and education. But his exposure to modern writings drew him away from his pious roots, and his awareness of early Russian pogroms around 1881 provoked him to identify with the Hibbat Zion movement, the eastern form of political Zionism. His commitment to the cultural revival and modernization of Jews was, from that point, unwavering, and he became a leading thinker among cultural Zionists. His orientation did not triumph in Zionist circles in the twentieth century, but the wisdom of his approach has gained considerable appreciation over time.

Ahad Ha-Am's opinions regarding the Jewish diaspora begin with the sober recognition that "'the ingathering of the exiles' is unattainable by natural means. Even with the establishment of a Jewish State," he admits, "the greater part of our people will remain scattered on foreign soils." If the negation of the diaspora will not be accomplished, then the question of the role and import of the diaspora must be addressed.

In an 1897 essay, Ahad Ha-Am opines that Judaism in his day suffers from a spiritual problem. Why? Because Judaism has come out of the ghetto:

> This contact with modern culture overturns the inner defenses of Judaism, so that it can no longer remain isolated and live a life apart. The spirit of our people desires further development; it wants to absorb the basic elements of general culture which are reaching it from the outside world, to digest them and to make them a part of itself, as it has done before at various periods of its history. But the conditions of its life in exile are not suitable for such a task. In our time culture expresses itself everywhere through the form of the national spirit.[16]

Later, in 1909, he expresses the challenge this way: "Jews cannot survive as a scattered people now that our spiritual isolation has ended, because we have no longer any defense against the ocean of foreign culture, which threatens to obliterate our national characteristics and traditions."[17]

What, for Ahad Ha-Am, is the answer to this challenge? A national project in the historical-spiritual center, that is, the Land of Israel. To be efficacious, such a project does not require negation of the diaspora; it does not even need an actual state. Gathering together and creating a Jewish society in Palestine, Jews will establish the conditions necessary for the revitalization of Jewish culture—the flowering of Jewish creativity conforming with modern standards. When this is accomplished, says Ahad Ha-Am, "from this center, the spirit of Judaism will radiate to the great circumference, to all the communities of the Diaspora, to inspire them with new life and to preserve the over-all unity of our people."[18] In other words, the national center will be the stage not only for solving the modern challenge to Judaism; it will solve the problem of the post-ghetto diaspora as well.

Lacking a developed sense of the complexity of Jewish history, Ahad Ha-Am seems to believe that the only thing that saved Jews and Judaism during years of exile was the ghetto—the isolation of Jews and their protection from the surrounding culture. Even if we forgive him the fact that there was no such thing as an actual ghetto until the early sixteenth century, we must still recognize that his observation and consequent diagnosis is based upon a fallacy, as he himself admits. Jews have often lived not in isolation from their neighbors but in meaningful contact, and Judaism has absorbed, and even been enriched by, elements from its surroundings. Ahad Ha-Am's analysis is built on his (partially romanticized) picture of more recent Jewish history in eastern Europe, which he seems to suppose provides the only conditions under which Judaism might flourish.

But this leads to a crucial observation. Jewish diasporas can and have flourished, he admits, when Jews have lived in "ghettos." In relative isolation, Jews created vibrant cultures of remarkable richness. Even if Jews sometimes suffered, they also lived, built, and created. How, we might wonder, did they succeed in doing so if their lives were so oppressive (and they so oppressed)? The answer is that, as Ahad Ha-Am admits, "we have been compassionately granted asylum by the nations of the earth."[19] So it is not diaspora life as such that is untenable for the Jew; it is diaspora life after emancipation.

But even under modern conditions, diaspora life is not, according to Ahad Ha-Am, completely impossible. On the contrary, though that life is challenged, it may thrive if informed by the contributions of Jews creating a new Jewish culture in a national center. Diaspora, supported by the fruits that flow from Zion, may indeed persist.

Why, though, must this happen in Palestine? Jews in Palestine, too, tasted the tempting nectars of modernity. They too emerged from the ghetto.

158 EMBRACING EXILE

Furthermore, Jews in Palestine also did not live alone (and, in Ahad Ha-Am's express view, they need not), having Arab and other neighbors. What was the real difference, then, between Palestine and Ponevezh? The answer must be that, as Ahad Ha-Am observes, "in our time culture expresses itself everywhere through the form of the national spirit." Ahad Ha-Am lived in the age of nationalism, of the unification of historically diverse territories under the flag of the modern nation-state. Moved and limited by the spirit of his own age, he could only imagine national fulfillment in the national territory. Jews must build their modernity in the image of the modern nations around them. Ironically, this solution itself is a concession to the secular (and non-Jewish) spirit of modernity.

Though we must read between the lines to glean these messages from what Ahad Ha-Am writes, the affirmation of diaspora in his words is undeniable. How could it be otherwise? Ahad Ha-Am knew traditional Judaism well. Steeped in its genius, he was alive to its beauties, even if some of them were, in modernity, outdated. And he knew that the Judaism he loved was in significant ways the product of diaspora. Diaspora was, therefore, not something he could imagine negating. That secular Zionists often failed to appreciate this wisdom of Ahad Ha-Am's is no surprise. There was little room for a "secular rabbi" in the contentious space between Zion and the ghetto.

The influential historian Simon Dubnow agreed with Ahad Ha-Am that nationalism is essential for the renaissance of the Jewish spirit in modernity but disagreed with his assessment that Palestine is the only place such a Jewish nationalism could be realized. Born in Belarus in 1860 into a traditional family, Dubnow turned to modern European culture at a young age, first as a journalist writing in Russian, then as a historian, and finally as a political theorist. In his theoretical writings, Dubnow elaborated a theory of Jewish diaspora nationalism, one that explicitly responded to Ahad Ha-Am and other Zion-centered nationalists.

Early in his essays on the subject, Dubnow argued for the supreme maturity of the Jewish nation:

> When a people loses not only its political independence but also its land, when the storm of history uproots it and removes it far from its natural homeland and it becomes dispersed and scattered in alien lands, and in addition loses its unifying language; if, despite [all this]...such a nation still maintains itself for many years, creates an independent existence, reveals a stubborn determination to carry on its autonomous

development—such a people has reached the highest stage of cultural-historical individuality and may be said to be indestructible.[20]

He elaborates:

> The nation without a state also became a nation without a territory…the source of vitality of the Jewish people consists in this: that this people, after it had passed through the stages of tribal nationalism, ancient culture and political territory, was able to establish itself and fortify itself in the highest stage, the spiritual and historical-cultural, and succeeded in crystallizing itself as a spiritual people that draws the sap of its existence from a natural or intellectual "will to live." All this came only because in the play of forces that sustained Jewish nationalism those elements not dependent on territory counted more than those dependent on territory.[21]

The highest stage of the development of a people, Dubnow asserts, is "the spiritual and historical-cultural." The Jewish nation has indeed achieved this supreme level, but only because "in the play of forces that sustained Jewish nationalism those elements not dependent on territory counted more than those dependent on territory."[22] In other words, in Israel's progress up the ladder of nationhood, the summit was accessed only by virtue of its diaspora life. Diaspora nationalism, which requires no territory, is nationalism at its finest. In Dubnow's view, only the Jewish people has truly achieved this.

In what does the supremacy of diaspora nationalism lie? The answer, Dubnow offers, is precisely in what diaspora makes impossible. He writes, "I know that my people, because of the special conditions of its existence in the Diaspora, is not able to aspire anywhere to primacy and dominance." This stands in contrast to conventional, territory-based nationalisms, which are "aggressive." Only when this kind of nationalism disappears will there no longer be any need for the concentration of power typical of "defensive nationalism." The Jewish nation has, since antiquity, exercised no nationalism of this kind. It is therefore, claims Dubnow, "completely ethical." Since this ethical, non-aggressive nationalism requires no domination or defeat of other peoples, it can live side by side with other nationalisms. Indeed, it "is fully compatible even with the ideals of universalism."[23]

Dubnow agreed with Ahad Ha-Am and others that nationalism—even diaspora nationalism—required some degree of autonomy; as a historian,

160 EMBRACING EXILE

he knew well the cultural and political achievements that relative Jewish autonomy in diaspora lands, and especially in eastern Europe, had made possible. He readily admitted "the tragic aspects of the Diaspora," and he granted that "we cannot hope to achieve in the Diaspora as full and complete national-cultural development as is possible for a nation living in its own independent state." But the majority of the Jewish nation lived, and would continue to live, in the diaspora, which in any case had the advantages articulated earlier. In their diasporas, Jews "must strive…to attain national-cultural autonomy for the majority of the nation."[24] The modern European view, to which Dubnow subscribed, was that nationalism was an essential quality of human community. But for Dubnow, nationalism was not identical with the nation-state. Indeed, it required no territory. It could therefore be realized in any diaspora in which Jews made a home.

Dubnow was not alone as a diaspora nationalist (or "autonomist"). His views were shared by others, who were often inspired by his writings. These thinkers and activists, raised in a Yiddish-speaking milieu, often (like Dubnow himself)[25] saw Yiddish and the culture it expressed as key to the national culture Jews would build in the diaspora. Chaim Zhitlowsky, for instance, was of the opinion that socialism would unite the poor, oppressed masses—including the Jewish masses—and that Yiddish was the tongue in which Jewish socialism was expressed. Crucially, Yiddish was not a language that the people "have long forgotten" (= Hebrew), nor was it (in its living form, at least) a language borrowed from European neighbors. It was, rather, the Jewish *mame-loshn* (= mother tongue), the language of the majority of the common Jewish nation in diaspora.[26] It is not an accident that Y. L. Peretz, who insisted that "the mission of the eternal people, the world-people…[was to build] the Jewish home, Jewish school, Jewish theater, Jewish books, and everything that is Jewish"[27] devoted his life, to a significant extent, to the flowering of a new Yiddish literary culture. Yiddish, the Jewish language of the diaspora (at least in the myopic view of Yiddish-speaking Jews), was the perfect language for an autonomous Jewish nation in diaspora. On this point, even Jewish nationalists who did not comment directly on diaspora agreed. Their arguments for a Jewish autonomy that did not require a land made this abundantly clear.

Modern Jewish culture was, of necessity, a diaspora phenomenon, one primarily centered in Europe. But in the late nineteenth century, the affairs of European nations and empires were birthing a new world, one that, in the east in particular, carried increasing hardships and risks for Jews. At the same time, the land over the ocean promised more "golden" opportunities, inviting many Jews to do what Jews have always done, that is, to follow the path toward a better life. By the outbreak of the Great War, New York was already the largest Jewish city in the world. In that city, and in the country that extended from its shores, Jews would once again take up the question of the meaning of exile when exile felt so much like home. As in the past, many would affirm their exilic home, leaving others to aspire to "ascend" to the actual, terrestrial Zion.

# 10

# Modern Jews on Diaspora

The early part of the twentieth century witnessed unparalleled Jewish growth and creativity in the western diasporas. Jews in Europe and the United States joined general society in a fuller way than ever before. As populations grew and Jews modernized, many moved to vibrant urban centers such as Warsaw and New York, where diaspora communities the likes of which Jews had never before known exerted their strength and expressed their confidence. Millions of Jews from the Russian empire and its communist successor escaped pogroms and hatred, finding their way overwhelmingly to American shores, where they settled in poor but vibrant neighborhoods from which they then dispersed far and wide, becoming Americans within a generation. The richness of their culture and the resourcefulness of their souls allowed them to flourish, becoming one of the most successful immigrant groups in American history and perhaps the single most successful diaspora in Jewish history.

Jews in these modern urban centers, in Europe and America, flourished as Jews and as citizens of their respective nations, particularly in America. Yiddish periodicals and publications proliferated; Jewish political parties multiplied. Powerful Jewish cultures, representing the spectrum from religious to secular, from conservative to socialist, flowered in these settings, as Jews found an increasingly confident voice despite their status as new immigrants. As they increasingly acquired advanced educations and greater affluence, Jews became prominent in commerce, the arts, and the sciences. Pursuing the traditional Jewish value of healing, Jews became doctors in disproportionate numbers, opening hospitals and supporting research. Extending the traditional Jewish commitment to law, Jews became jurists and attorneys in numbers well out of proportion to their share of the population. The long Jewish tradition of advanced education led many to become scientists and engineers.[1] Building on the role into which they had defaulted in Europe, they became bankers and financiers. In all these capacities, Jews benefited from the advancements of their neighbors and made their own contributions in return. Indeed, the Jewish contribution to broader society was often recognized (consider the number of Jewish Nobel Prize winners), granting dignity and legitimacy to Jews as citizens of the nations that were their homes.

But all was not idyllic. Antisemitism did not abate in Europe, and it was not absent in America; in fact, fueled by the "modern" science of race, Jewish difference was increasingly seen as racially inherent, and exclusion or fear of Jews was justified by reference to these "scientific" ideas. Ultimately, propelled by the horrors and humiliations of the Great War in Germany and beyond, these ideas provided fertile ground for the Holocaust itself. Even in the United States, Jews often felt the sting of antisemitism, along with the fear of its possible consequences, despite legal protections. These developments, nightmarish as they often were, made it clear how tenuous Jewish "at-homeness" could be. Indeed, by the mid-twentieth century, Jews could not ignore the fact that more Jews were murdered in this century (by far) than at any earlier time in Jewish history. How could this not be taken as an indictment of diaspora and a spur to human-fueled "redemption" = Zionism? How could a state in the land traditionally promised to Israel not be the answer?

The complicated and contradictory conditions that buffeted Jews in the early twentieth century provided modern Jewish thinkers with an exceptional opportunity to reflect and comment on Judaism and its diasporas. Perhaps the greatest Jewish philosopher of this period, and one who offered profound reflections on Zionism and diaspora, was Franz Rosenzweig. Born in Kassel, Germany, in 1886 to a secular Jewish family, he flirted briefly with the idea of converting to Christianity but experienced an awakening to Judaism when he was not yet thirty. His philosophical approach was influenced by the great neo-Kantian Hermann Cohen, whom he admired deeply. Rosenzweig's magnum opus was *The Star of Redemption*, a work studied to this day.

Rosenzweig was an opponent of Zionism, which was at this early stage an ideology opposed by many Jews—by traditional Jews because of its secular, anti-traditional quality, and by many modern, secular Jews because of its insistence that they uproot themselves from the modern cultures and societies they admired. In personal correspondence written in May 1917, Rosenzweig speaks approvingly of Hermann Cohen's "hate" of Zionism, while simultaneously approving of Ahad Ha-Am's recognition that "only by realizing its connection with Berlin, Lodz, or, someday if you like, New York...will Palestine remain Jewish and also make life in the Diaspora

164  EMBRACING EXILE

really possible." Rosenzweig's fullest reflections on the Jews and their land(s) are found in *The Star*.

Having witnessed the carnage—the voluminous shedding of blood—wrought by land-hungry armies during the First World War, Rosenzweig was extremely critical of the lust for land. "The peoples of the world are not content with the bonds of blood," he wrote in *The Star*. "They sink their roots into the night of earth, lifeless in itself.... Their will to eternity clings to the soil and to the reign over the soil, to the land. The earth of their homeland is watered by the blood of their sons, for they do not trust in the life of a community of blood."[2] Clearly, the trauma of the Great War had led Rosenzweig to condemn the folly—as he perceives it—of hinging one's life and the uniqueness of one's nation on land. Land only leads to death.

He continued "We [Jews] were the only ones who trusted in blood and abandoned the land." Rosenzweig distorts the facts here, for Jews did not actually *abandon* their land; they were expelled from it. But he permitted himself this distortion of the truth because of his confidence in a deeper truth. As he wrote:

> Whenever a people loves the soil of its native land more than its own life, it is in danger—as all peoples of the world are.... In the final analysis, the people belong to him who conquers the land. It cannot be otherwise, because people cling to the soil more than to their life as a people. Thus the earth betrays a people that entrusted its permanence to earth.[3]

It is the way of the world, Rosenzweig admitted, that a people stakes its claim to peoplehood on the soil on which it resides. Many nations, in fact, claim to reside naturally on their land—even, at their origins, to have sprung from it. Relying too much on land, they are inevitably betrayed by it, for ultimately that land will be conquered. If a people is a people only when they live on their land, then what happens when their land is taken? The answer must be that they are annihilated.

But the Jewish people are different, Rosenzweig claimed. "In contrast to other peoples, the earliest legends about the tribe of the eternal people are not based on indigenousness." The land promised Israel is not the land where they were born. "Thus in the dawn of its earliest beginnings, as well as later in the bright light of history, this people is a people in exile." To be a Jew means to be in exile, and this from the very beginning. Moreover, exile is, for this people, not a fate to be suffered but a noble journey. As Rosenzweig wrote:

> The eternal people...never loses the untrammeled freedom of a wanderer who is more faithful a knight to his country when he roams abroad, craving adventure and yearning for the land he has left behind....In the most profound sense possible, this people has a land of its own only in that it has a land it yearns for—a holy land.[4]

In Rosenzweig's utterly romantic vision, Jews are knights who travel the globe, their freedom unrestrained by attachment to their land. Pursuing their adventures, settling sometimes here and sometimes there, they long for their land. But the meaningfulness of the land to the people is in the yearning, not in the realization of return. And why is this so important? Because "only a community based on common blood [but *not* on possession of a land] feels the warrant of eternity warm in its veins."[5] Jews—the eternal people—have staked their eternity on blood, not land. Eschewing the foolish ways of other peoples, they have escaped the death sentence of land and assured their eternity, which will be transmitted through blood from one generation to another.

Rosenzweig understood all this to be fundamental to the teachings of Judaism. He cited, for example, God's insistence in the Torah that "the land is mine [and you are but sojourners with me]" (Leviticus 25:23). But at the same time, this is also a highly pragmatic analysis on Rosenzweig's part. In truth, people who live or die with their control of their land, people who cannot survive in exile, stand little chance of surviving long-term at all. In this respect, Jews are an exception. By theorizing and rationalizing (= making rational) exile, they have assured their survival under the same conditions where other peoples have disappeared.

Some would find Rosenzweig's arguments extreme, and an increasing number of modern Jews were attracted to Zionism—to a Judaism rooted in the land. Still, even while supporting the Zionist cause, there were influential scholars and writers who made room for a deep appreciation of diaspora. One such individual was Yehezkel Kaufmann, a Bible scholar and intellectual historian of Judaism. Born in Ukraine, Kaufmann studied in Odessa, Petrograd, and Berne, lived in Berlin for several years, and finally settled in Palestine in 1928. Kaufmann's first major work was his *Golah ve-Nekhar* (*Diaspora and Alien Lands*), published in 1929–30.

166    EMBRACING EXILE

In this work, Kaufmann devoted himself to solving the great puzzle of Jewish survival in exile. How or why did Jews survive after being scattered abroad when other nations did not? In addressing this question, Kaufmann—unlike many other ideologically driven writers—admitted that Jews acculturated and often flourished in their many dispersions. "Their God dealt charitably with them in that he scattered them among the nations and taught them to wander from land to land...many of them succeeded valiantly with their money, and others turned to intellectual disciplines."[6] There was indeed suffering in exile. But, on balance, their exile was "charitable." Furthermore, being often benign, exile encouraged scattered Jews to do what all scattered peoples do—to assimilate. As Kaufmann put it:

> When the people of Israel was scattered among the nations, it, too, went the way which was laid out for every scattered and dispersed people—the way of assimilation. The Jews were influenced by the culture of their neighbors, became attached and clung to the lands of their habitation, learned the ways of their neighbors, adopted their manners and customs, their clothing, food and drink...adopted their languages.[7]

For Kaufmann, assimilation (or perhaps acculturation), as he described it, is not a problem. Jews and Judaism were enriched through their immersion in diverse cultures. As he said, "More than once the Jews clung to the lands of their exile with a faithful love. They learned the foreign languages, spoke them, thought and wrote poetry in them."[8] The problem, for Kaufmann, was simply how Jews survived this assimilation when other peoples did not.

The answer, Kaufmann argued, is the religion of Israel. For Jews, the language they did not speak, using it only for prayer and religious writing, was the Holy Tongue; the land on which they did not live, hoping to return to it only in the messianic future, was the Holy Land. And, most importantly, their covenantal fate cast upon them a Holy obligation, for—they believed—they were "the sole bearer[s] of God's true teaching."[9] Their existence in exile, therefore, "has a clear purpose"—the maintenance, modeling, and even promulgation of the one true message of the one true God. As others had taught before, the dispersion was necessary because it was only by their living among the nations of the world that Jews could teach those nations the reality of God and God's plan for humankind.

Events of the 1930s and 1940s challenged any such affirmation of the Jewish diaspora, the horror of the Holocaust convincing many that diaspora was inescapably a place of danger for the Jewish people. For them, the lesson learned from the Holocaust was that only a Jewish state in the Land of Israel could truly guarantee the safety of the Jews. Even Jews who would remain in the diaspora agreed that Jews could no longer afford to live without a home and a refuge, again: a Jewish state in the Jewish land. When the State of Israel was declared, therefore, and when the vastly outnumbered Jewish forces defeated invading Arab armies, the Jewish world was electrified. Increasingly, it became a world in which to be Jewish meant to be a supporter of the State of Israel, in the imprecise parlance of the day: a Zionist. One way or another, from this point onward, it became virtually impossible to express an opinion about the Jewish diaspora without at the same time responding to Zionism/the State of Israel. And from the very beginning, because of a dominant Zionist ideology of "the negation of the diaspora," the relationship of the state and its citizens with the Jewish diaspora was fraught.

Against this historical background, the opinions of the influential but controversial political theorist and critic Hannah Arendt take on a particular sharpness. Arendt had very little to say directly about diaspora; her opinions on this subject must be gleaned mostly from a close reading of her comments on Zionism and the Jewish state, which are relatively abundant. They are also rather critical, at least with respect to Zionism and Jewish nationalism as they took shape during and following the Holocaust. But it is possible to read between the lines of her critique for its implications regarding diaspora, and, combined with her few explicit comments on the same, something like a coherent idea (though not much more than that) emerges.

Arendt was familiar with the broad contours of Jewish historiography from the century leading up to her writing, "according to which the Jewish people did not have a political history of their own but were invariably the innocent victims of a hostile and sometimes brutal environment."[10] However, while granting fundamental points of this approach she also expresses some degree of suspicion concerning its unnuanced vision, accusing the historians of ignoring "all those trends of the Jewish past which did not point to their own major thesis." In this suspicion, she was evidently much influenced by Gershom Scholem's work on Lurianic Kabbalah and the failed messianic movement inspired by Shabbetai Tzvi. The disappointment of messianic hopes, she writes, provoked, in the nineteenth century, a secularization of the notion of "the chosen people," freeing "that status from all observance of the Law and all hope for the Messiah."[11]

168  EMBRACING EXILE

Arendt's comments here (penned in September 1944, after she had fled Europe for safety in New York) are critical, for she deemed this secularized ideology a failed one, one that emerged from "the need to justify the Jewish Diaspora" in the absence of traditional hopes for redemption. Still, despite its failure, she was sympathetic to its possibilities. She wrote, "Here an authentic possibility presented itself of making every country in Europe home without at the same time surrendering Jewish identity." For reasons she went on to elaborate (the idea of how this balance would be accomplished was too varied, depending too much on the "accidental worldview" of the person interpreting and applying it), this possibility failed. But it offered a noble prospect, and, ironically, it accurately described the history of Jewish diaspora in Europe. It was also in harmony with certain non-secular Jewish notions following the Shabbetai Tzvi debacle, particularly those of Hasidic masters, which claimed Jewish homes in Galicia, the Carpathian Mountains, and elsewhere. Finally, in Arendt's formulation, it made a claim for the "Europeanness" of Jews even beyond Europe. This is an important claim, and Arendt elaborates upon it elsewhere.

In her lengthy 1944 essay "Zionism Reconsidered," Arendt described the "false notion of the non-European character of the Jews" as one of the biggest of Zionist misconceptions. (Zionists insist that Jews are a Near Eastern people.) In doing so, Zionists "break the necessary solidarity of European peoples," which "would even deprive the Jews of the only historical and cultural homestead they can possibly have," and "would deprive the Jewish people of its just share in the roots and development of what we generally call Western culture." This Zionist assertion is absurd, she insisted, because "Palestine together with the whole Mediterranean basin has always belonged to the European continent: geographically, historically, culturally."[12] Many people would respond that the latter claim is spurious—positing as definitive what is actually a matter of convention—if not actually absurd. Arendt surely must have known that her argument here was not "airtight." So what led her to make it? The answer is Arendt's rejection of the Zionist belief that the Jew is "other" with respect to the European and his/her culture. Even a Jewish homeland (not necessarily a Jewish nation-state) in Palestine will be an expression of this European fabric, meaning that the European diaspora was also, *always*, part of the fabric of Jewish life and home.

Earlier in the same essay Arendt offered a simultaneous critique of Zionists and assimilated Western Jews, one that begrudgingly allows for a romanticized vision of diaspora, now less explicitly European. Zionists, she said, "shut themselves off from the destiny of the Jews all over the world." This they do by rejecting the diaspora. At the same time, "assimilated Jewries of the western world had pretended to ignore the strong ties which had always connected Leningrad with Warsaw, and Warsaw with Berlin, and both with Paris and London, and all together with New York."[13] The strong ties that always connected international Jewries—there is no more frequently repeated, romantic idealization of Jewish diasporas in all their diversity than this. Scattered Jewish homes—fruitful, productive, creative, all in specific and various ways—are united precisely in their Jewishness. The monoculture of a Jewish Palestine would tragically undermine this reality. It is a reality to which the diaspora, over the course of its many generations, gave birth.

The "pessimism" of Zionism (to use Arendt's term) turned out to be misguided, and even after the Holocaust and the declaration of the State of Israel, surviving centers, including America in general and New York in particular, saw a surge in Jewish life and creativity. There was not a Jewish group—from liberal and secular to Hasidic and ultra-Orthodox—that did not see growth during this period, thanks to the peace and protection of a Jewish home like no other. In America, the lesson some drew from the Holocaust was answered with a counter-lesson: that only a land of human rights codified in laws, protecting its minorities and separating church from state, thus delegitimating the historical prejudice that had restricted Jews, could provide Jews (and other minorities) with a secure home. In this home, Jews began as students at the City College of New York and wound up teaching at Harvard. They became partners in America's most prestigious firms. They could eat kosher or *treif*, wear Hasidic garb or high fashion, and, over time, meet with ever-diminishing resistance. Their grandparents lived in crowded urban neighborhoods, but they could build large, comfortable homes in the suburbs. They could make their names in Hollywood or on Broadway, in publication or in business. And, thanks to new interpretations of a constitution that assured no privileging of a particular religious establishment, they could do all this while taking off from work on Yom Kippur and leaving the office early to attend a Passover seder. This was, in many ways, an unprecedented condition for Jews, and it offered a counter-lesson to the Holocaust that provoked an obvious question: How could Jews make sense of a world in which it was both "the best of times" and "the worst of times"?

170  EMBRACING EXILE

Musing on this question were contributors to a special issue of *Midstream*, published in March 1963. The contributors were asked to comment on "the Meaning of Galut in America Today," and the range of their opinion reflects well on the commitment of the editors to open dialogue. Two of the authors contributed meaningfully to the defense of diaspora—and the rejection of any traditional concept of Galut—at least in the modern American setting.

Jacob Agus, a Conservative rabbi, wrote of America as the "heartland" of the modern Western world. In his evaluation, it is in America that "the Jewish vision of the good life, the luminous core of the tradition, can be cultivated, developed, and made fruitful." He continued, "If it is for a high and universal purpose that our people endured martyrdom for two millennia, then here the purpose can be exhibited in the light of day, examined and evaluated."[14] For Agus, the Jewish historical experience, in bona fide *galut*, had a purpose—to lead Jews to a "heartland" (if not a homeland) where the Jewish purpose—a "high and universal purpose"—could be tested and evaluated. This purpose could not be properly evaluated in Israel, for it is a universal purpose, and so must be tested in a universalist setting—in an open society, in its universities and public platforms. If, say, the prophetic vision, the very foundation of Jewish ethics, could not survive the scrutiny enabled by the light of the nations, then how could Judaism ever have claimed to be a light to the nations?

The literary critic Alfred Kazin went still further. Kazin began by recalling that he had once planned to write a book about modern Jewish writers titled *In Praise of the Diaspora*. The book was never written, but Kazin went on to express his praise, much more briefly, in the essay at hand. His affirmation of diaspora began simply: "Dispersed we Jews are, in a sense always have been, and I hope always will be; dispersion is a condition of our existence, for we are not merely a people but peculiarly a people concerned with the world, a people that belongs to the world, that senses in itself a specific historical mission in and to the world."[15] The echoes in this sentence of earlier teachings, teachings the writer may not have known, are unmistakable. Like the Maharal of Prague or the Talmudic sage, Kazin asserted that Jews are citizens of the world at large, and they have an essential mission within it. He went on: "Dispersion, adaptation, cultural pluralism are indeed necessities for the Jew, who would long ago have died of boredom if he had been confined to one small corner of the earth."[16] So not only do Jews have a mission to the world, but they gain sustenance from it. Death can come from different sources. It can be the result of physical attack, as it was too often for Jews through the ages. But it can also be the result of spiritual famine, a famine that is the result of the impoverishment of one's environment. Diaspora, with its cultural pluralism and demand of adaptation, offered a rich menu of spiritual nourishment for the Jew. National isolation in a single land could not do the same.

Just a few years later, Gerson D. Cohen, one of the outstanding Jewish historians of his generation and chancellor of the Jewish Theological Seminary in New York from 1972 to 1986, offered a related argument "in praise of diaspora." As a scholar familiar with the breadth and depth of Jewish history, Cohen knew well the ups and downs of the Jewish diaspora experience. It is that mastery and intimate knowledge that makes his major piece devoted to diaspora, "The Blessings of Assimilation," so compelling.

Cohen's comments were offered as a commencement address at Boston Teachers College in June 1966. The graduating students were embarking on careers in Jewish education and communal leadership. What Cohen offered them was not cold historical analysis—though his argument is built on sound historical research—but an expression of his convictions concerning how Jews best live in the broader world. This was a period when American Jews were focused on the challenge of living as Jews and as Americans, or as Jews in America. Central to the concerns of Jewish leaders at the time was the problem (at least as they understood it) of assimilation. Would Jews not disappear, they feared, if they became culturally like everyone else? Was not some degree of Jewish separation or distinction necessary for Jews to survive? Cohen's counsel, based upon his analysis of the historical record, was to "calm down." Jews who acculturated would not disappear, because Jews who had acculturated in the past did not disappear.

A large part of what Cohen said was offered as a critique/response to a popular midrash declaring that the reason Jews survived in Egypt (a foreign culture) in biblical times was that they did not change their names, their language, or their clothing. In other words, they preserved their Hebrew names, spoke the Hebrew language, and dressed in Jewish garb. This was taken by many to offer counsel for how Jews would survive in other foreign cultures. But, as Cohen observed, what this midrash claims is, historically speaking, preposterous. Jews often took on local names: Alexander, Aristobulus, Antigonus, Hyrcanus, and Tryphon being variously the names of Maccabean kings or ancient rabbis. Jews almost always spoke the local tongue and not a Jewish language: Aramaic, Greek, Arabic, and so forth. And, though Cohen neglected this detail, abundant

172    EMBRACING EXILE

evidence, including contemporary accounts and illustrated Hebrew manuscripts, make it clear that Jews through history overwhelmingly dressed just like their neighbors.

But Cohen's argument was not merely that Jews "assimilated" (or again, "acculturated") in the past and therefore will again. He went further. In his most powerful expression of his thesis, he said:

> A frank appraisal of the periods in which Judaism flourished will indicate that not only did a certain amount of assimilation and acculturation not impede Jewish continuity and creativity, but that in a profound sense, this assimilation and acculturation was a stimulus to original thinking and expression, a source of renewed vitality. To a considerable degree, the Jews survived as a vital group and as a pulsating culture *because* they changed their names, their language, their clothing, and their patterns of thought and expression.[17]

In the end, Cohen assured the graduates he is addressing, "the phenomenon of assimilation also presents us with unprecedented opportunities to reinterpret the Jewish tradition so that it will be relevant to the needs of the twentieth century."[18]

Throughout this forceful expression, Cohen was speaking, on the explicit level, at least, about "assimilation." But assimilation, as he meant it, almost always takes place in diaspora—Egypt, Spain, Germany, Poland, etc. In fact, with the exception of the Hellenistic period in the Land of Israel, the opportunity to meet and engage the riches of foreign cultures, learning their lessons and absorbing, while "Judaizing," their beauties, is a diaspora opportunity. His essay could just as easily have been titled "The Blessing of Diaspora," for that is what it actually described. What Cohen was arguing, in fact, is that diaspora has often—though certainly not always—been a blessing for Jews, and Judaism is stronger and richer thanks to diaspora. For Cohen, this was a historical fact. But his essay also offered an ideological statement. Cohen was saying that Jews and Judaism are better off with diaspora, despite the "dangers" of assimilation. Correspondingly, he was implying that the "negation of the diaspora" would be a tragedy because Jews and Judaism would be culturally impoverished as a result.

The celebration and euphoria emerging from Israel's victory in the June 1967 Six-Day War had significant impact on Jews in Israel and abroad. There was a wave of new immigration of Jews from the diaspora to Israel in the period from 1967 to the next, less successful war in 1973. These Jews sought to wed their lives to the land where they saw the future of Judaism emerging. At the same time, in the United States, the pride of Israel's victory, combined with emergence of identity politics and identity studies in universities, empowered Jewish Americans to be more publicly vocal about their Jewish selves. Jewish Studies followed Black Studies, and the burst of creativity that emerged—from the counter-cultural *Jewish Catalog* and the Havurah movement to the Association for Jewish Studies—promised new strength and directions for Jewish life in America and beyond. Yet even as the American diaspora flourished, mainstream American Jewish movements and organizations overwhelmingly became "Zionist"—that is, they demanded loyalty to Israel and its security—and Israel came to be recognized as the center of gravity of Jewish identity worldwide.

But this euphoric period was not to last long, and diaspora Jewish identities built on the foundation of Israel quickly became more complicated. Religious politics in Israel became fraught for non-Orthodox diaspora Jews. Debates pertaining to the question of "Who is a Jew?" made it impossible to ignore the nonrecognition of Reform and Conservative rabbis in Israel, where their conversions were rejected and their practices and beliefs often ridiculed by the religious establishment. At the same time, idealized Israel—a "Jewish, Democratic state"—came to be perceived as being at odds with the reality. Holding on to West Bank territories captured in the 1967 war, Israel slowly went from being viewed as the underdog to the aggressor. Jewish settlements on formerly Palestinian lands proliferated and enlarged. To protect their Jewish populations, Israel had to take measures limiting Palestinian mobility. Sometimes, only the harshest measures protected the safety of Israeli settlers. Palestinians resisted, and violence often met violence. As images of Israeli brutality against Palestinians emerged, and Palestinian losses vastly outnumbered Israeli ones, the image of heroic Israel became harder to sustain, and differences of opinion developed even within the committed Jewish community. Needless to say, this led to rethinking on the relationship between Israel and the diaspora.

Bearing evidence of the tensions of the time, some of which would have been present even without immediate political considerations, was the "first collective 'statement of principles' ever issued by the Conservative Movement," *Emet ve-Emunah*, issued in 1988.[19] This collective statement contains whole sections on "The State of Israel and the Role of Religion" and "Israel and the Diaspora." The center of the former, not surprisingly, is the insistence that "the State of Israel, founded for the entire Jewish people, must in its actions and laws provide for the pluralism of Jewish life. The State should permit all rabbis, regardless of affiliation, to perform religious functions, including officiating at all marriages, divorces and conversions."[20] It is the latter section, though, that is of primary interest here.

The subsections of the statement on "Israel and the Diaspora" are "The Central Role of Israel," "Conservative Judaism and Israel," and "Various Centers of Jewish Life." Even the trajectory of these titles reveals the perspective this ideological statement will support: while Israel might have the central role in modern Jewish life, Israel is not the only such center. There are other, diaspora centers as well—maybe not *the* center, but centers nonetheless (the echoes of Ahad ha-Am are obvious).

The elaboration of the stated themes quickly makes it clear that this is not a one-sided affirmation of the centrality of the Promised Land in Jewish experience. So, for example, the authors (unidentified, as this is a collective statement) write:

> This zealous attachment to Eretz Yisrael has persisted throughout our long history as a transnational people in which we transcended borders and lived in virtually every land. Wherever we were permitted, we viewed ourselves as natives or citizens of the country of our residence and were loyal to our host nation. Our religion has been land-centered but never land-bound; it has been a portable religion so that despite our long exile (Galut) from our spiritual homeland, we have been able to survive creatively and spiritually even in the tefutzot (Diaspora). Indeed, there have been Jewish communities in the Diaspora from the days of the Prophets. The relative importance of the Land of Israel and the Diaspora fluctuated through the centuries. Whether the Diaspora was more creative than Zion or Zion was more vital than the Diaspora is of little importance. What is important is Eretz Yisrael enriched world Jewry even as world Jewry enriched Eretz Yisrael.[21]

As the day required, these American Conservative Jews affirmed the "zealous [Jewish] attachment" to the Holy Land throughout the ages. Nevertheless, they also affirmed that Jews have been a "transnational people" who "transcended borders." Though wanderers, Jews nevertheless saw themselves as loyal citizens or even natives in the lands where they made their homes. How was this possible? Because Judaism is a portable religion that (like other diasporas) is spiritually "land-centered but never land-bound." Most of those who contributed to this document were rabbis and scholars, so it is not surprising that we easily find centuries-old echoes of many of their assertions. What is new is the historical context in which they were made, a context in which many had been persuaded of the unambiguous centrality of the Land—and now State—of Israel in everything Jewish. To this belief, the authors respond explicitly:

> We view it as both a misinterpretation of Jewish history and a threat to Jewish survival to negate the complementary roles of Eretz Yisrael and the Diaspora. Currently there are various important centers of Jewish life in the Diaspora. Diaspora Jewry furnishes vital economic, political and moral support to Israel; Israel imbues Diaspora Jewry with a sense of pride and self-esteem. Some see the role of Medinat Yisrael [the State of Israel] as the cultural and religious center of world Jewry. Others insist that since the days of the Prophets, various foci or centers of Jewish life and civilization, in both Israel and the Diaspora, have sustained the creative survival of Am Yisrael and Torat Yisrael. Eretz Yisrael produced most of the Bible, the Mishnah, the Talmud of Eretz Yisrael, the major Midrashim, liturgy, and other great works while the Diaspora gave us the Babylonian Talmud, Hebrew poetry, philosophical writings, commentaries, law codes, and other lasting creations. The various communities interacted in a continual symbiotic process of mutual enrichment.
>
> Both the State of Israel and Diaspora Jewry have roles to fill; each can and must aid and enrich the other in every possible way; each needs the other.[22]

It is simply wrong, these writers claim, to claim the centrality of the Holy Land without at the same time recognizing the centrality of diaspora to Jewish history and life. Reference to the supreme spiritual-cultural creations of Jews through the ages demonstrates this unambiguously. If history is instructive, then even in an age when Jewish hegemony over the Land has been restored, the diaspora has an indispensable role to play in everything Jewish. Their argument is a well-constructed one, and its defense of the authors' place on the Jewish stage clear. If one insists on a substantive critique of their claims, it can only be directed at one of their apparent "facts," that is, that the Land of Israel produced most of the Bible. In the view of biblical historians, though many of the traditions that provide the

176   EMBRACING EXILE

building blocks of the major biblical texts originated in the Land of Israel, most of the canonical books as we know them—including the Torah itself—originated in Babylon.

What we see in *Emet ve-Emunah* may be taken as representative of contemporary defenses of the diaspora enunciated not only by America's Conservative movement but of other diaspora movements as well.[23] And how could this not be so? Should we expect that people engaged in the building of vibrant Jewish lives (their own or those of their community), wherever their choice has landed them, would negate their own choice? Would they not seek to justify it? Indeed, this is, as we have seen, what diaspora Jews have done for centuries, and it is what they continue to do, despite the existence of a State of Israel.

The complications of Israeli policies as they pertain to the security of its people and their relationship with neighboring Palestinians has also provoked abundant response, some of it taking the form of reflections on the advantages of diaspora. One individual who commented perceptively on the Israel-diaspora conundrum was the internationally renowned novelist Philip Roth. Roth, born in 1933, was a child of the Weequahic section of Newark, New Jersey. This was a modest neighborhood, with a heavily Jewish population that included immigrant Jews and their children. The parent generation of Weequahic's Jewish families tended to be less-educated business people; their children aspired to, and succeeded in, higher education and the professions. Perhaps the greatest mark of success for these Jews was acquiring the resources to move to the suburbs, and most of the neighborhood's second generation did just this. Their Jewish identities were built on education, professional accomplishment, and being good Americans. Their Jewish citizenship was expressed in support of synagogues through membership; for most, attendance was rare outside of the High Holidays.

Roth's Jewishness, complex as it was, was in many ways typical of the Jews who were raised in these circumstances. He rejected religious belief as such, and he rejected the label "Jewish writer." But despite his protestation, that is precisely what he was, not only technically (he was Jewish and he was a writer) but also in terms of literary concerns and representations. Jewishness was, in fact, a regular focus of his writing, literally inescapable.[24] Even a work as notable as *Portnoy's Complaint*, infamous for its masturbation scenes, is as much about the challenges of growing up in a Jewish family of his time and place—with the attractions of the non-Jew being only one of many such challenges—as anything else. Roth's Jewishness was important to him. He resented the lack of embrace of his writings by many prominent Jews and Jewish organizations, particularly early in his career, and he took great joy in the honorary degree awarded him by the Jewish Theological Seminary late in his life. However irreligious he was, he was a profound thinker of Jewishness. For that reason, and because of his immense legacy and influence, his reflections on diaspora are essential to consider.

Roth's Newark was his diaspora homeland, and as his career progressed, he continuously commented, via the indirect vehicle of his fiction, on diaspora as he knew it and its relation to Israel. He was an extremely astute observer, and his *Operation Shylock* (1993), written during the period of the first Intifada (Palestinian uprising against Israeli occupation), is his most challenging and perceptive writing on this topic.

*Operation Shylock*'s two main characters are Philip Roth and Philip Roth. One of these characters is a famous author by that name and the second his doppelganger. The doppelganger, a self-fashioned "diasporist," takes advantage of the fame of the author, and of his near-exact similarity to the appearance of the author, to promote his diasporist ideas. The creator of this fiction is the famous author Philip Roth, who writes a novel about a famous author named Philip Roth and his doppelganger, Philip Roth.

The first scene laying out the diasporism of Philip Roth the doppelganger—henceforth known as Pipik, the nickname given him by Philip Roth the author in the book—is one in which Aharon Appelfeld, the Israeli author, calls the author Roth to report that there is a story about him in an Israeli newspaper. The article is about his diasporism, as expressed during a visit to Lech Walesa in Poland. Walesa, it appears, has invited him to cooperate in a project to restore Jews to Poland, an effort Roth the diasporist supports.

Roth the diasporist is quoted in the story as saying that "Europe…was the most authentic Jewish homeland there ever has been, the birthplace of rabbinic Judaism, Hasidic Judaism, Jewish secularism, socialism…of Zionism too." Having already remarked that it would be tragic to judge the Jewish experience in Europe on the basis of the few years of the Holocaust, Pipik asks, "who and what is to prevail in Europe: the will of this subhuman murderer-brute or the civilization that gave to mankind Shalom Aleichem, Heinrich Heine, and Albert Einstein? Are we to be driven for all time from the continent that nourished the flourishing Jewish world of Warsaw, of Vilna, of Riga, of Prague…?" and so forth.[25] The argument is

178 EMBRACING EXILE

simple and compelling: Europe produced a Jewish civilization unrivalled in history. Why, then, should it not be considered the Jewish homeland?

But the character Roth the author knows that none of these words attributed to him in the story are his. He had not even been in Poland with Walesa. So Roth searches out the person masquerading as him and finds that he is staying at the King David Hotel in Jerusalem. Pretending to be a French journalist, Roth connects with Pipik and begins to question him. Pipik, still pretending to be Roth, explains that he has given up writing novels and is now devoting himself to diasporism. Why? Because "Israel is no longer in the Jewish interest. Israel has become the gravest threat to Jewish survival since the end of World War Two."[26] A short time later in the "interview," Pipik adds, "the great mass of Jews have been in Europe since the Middle Ages. Virtually everything we identify culturally as Jewish has its origins in the life we led for centuries among European Christians…for the European Jews, Israel has been an exile and no more, a sojourn." For this reason, "the time has come to return to our real life and our real home, to our ancestral Jewish Europe."[27]

In basic detail, Pipik is right in these statements: Jewish civilization did grow and flourish in Europe, and much of what Jews of European background know of as "Judaism" in fact originates in the European encounter (Pipik is wrong about the origins of Rabbinic Judaism, unless he means the particular rabbinic-halakhic culture that arose in Europe during the Middle Ages). Moreover, it is fair to say, in 1988 (the fictional setting of the narrative), that Jews have survived, and even been reborn, following the Holocaust, and that Jewish lives are "today" more imperiled in Israel than abroad. Hence, the hope of a restoration of European Jews to Europe is not in principle foolhardy. For them, at least, Israel has perhaps been the "exile" and temporary "sojourn."

Later in the novel, another voice is introduced, speaking about the contrast between the Israeli and diaspora Jew from a very different perspective. That voice belongs to George Ziad—Zee—a Palestinian who had been a friend of Roth's when they were both graduate students at the University of Chicago. Roth's conversation with Zee takes place in Zee's home in Ramallah.

Zee's comments begin with a critique of Israeli culture and what it has created. "I've lived in Chicago, in New York, in Boston, I've lived in Paris, in London, and nowhere have I seen such a people in the street. The *arrogance*!" He goes on: "What have they created like you Jews out in the world?…Nothing but a state founded on force and the will to dominate." The focus on power has led to an impoverished creative culture, says Zee: "Dismal painting and sculpture, no music composition, and a very minor literature."[28] (The author of this novel, Philip Roth, would have disputed at least this last claim.)

So far, the reader has heard only Zee's opinion of the Israeli Jew. But what about the diaspora and its Jews? He continues: "There is more Jewish spirit and Jewish laughter and Jewish intelligence on the Upper West Side of Manhattan than in this entire country—and as for the Jewish *conscience*, as for the Jewish sense of *justice*, as for the Jewish *heart*…there's more Jewish heart at the knish counter at Zabar's than in the whole of the Knesset."[29] Now, one need not insist that Zee's words are true for them to be important. Zee is a Palestinian intellectual who speaks from the bitterness of recent historical experience. But even if Zee is overreaching (and this is not obvious either), the power of his rhetoric emerges from the fact that what he says is at least partially true, and possibly more than that.

A few minutes later in his conversation with Philip, Zee returns to further the contrast between Israel and diaspora Jews and their respective accomplishments. "Jews without tolerance, Jews for whom it is always black and white…these are the Jews who are superior to the Jews in the Diaspora? Superior to people who know in their bones the meaning of give-and-take?" He continues, then, with observations concerning the attitudes of Israeli Jews regarding their diaspora brethren. "What they teach their children in the schools is to look with disgust on the Diaspora Jew, to see the English-speaking Jew and the Spanish-speaking Jew…as a freak, as a worm, as a terrified neurotic.…And what these so-called neurotics have given to the world in the way of brain-power and art and science and all the skills and ideals of civilization, to this they are oblivious." While this attitude of dismissal is certainly not true of all Israeli Jews, it is true of many, and such an evaluation of diaspora Jews is not only without justification, Zee insists, but a despicable distortion of Jewish values and accomplishments.

Sharpening his comments as he approaches the finale of his soliloquy, Zee adds, "Oh, what an impoverished Jew this arrogant Israeli is! Yes, they are the authentic ones," he says with what I imagine to be a mocking tone, "the [A. B.] Yehoshuas and the [Amos] Ozes, and tell me, I ask them, what are Saul Alinsky [American-Jewish left-wing writer and organizer] and David Riesman [author of *The Lonely Crowd*] and Meyer Schapiro [art historian] and Leonard Bernstein and Bella Abzug and Paul Goodman and

180   EMBRACING EXILE

Allen Ginsberg, and on and on and on and *on*?" Whatever one makes of the details of Zee's argument, the fundamental point is unmistakable and undisputable: diaspora Jewish culture has been at least as rich as Israeli culture. Diaspora Jewry in its various promised lands has contributed at least as much to the world—Jewish and general—as Jewry residing in Zion.

Whose opinions do these statements represent? Pipik is a fraud (claiming, as he does, to be the author Philip Roth) and Zee a Palestinian intellectual— a sympathetic "other," but still an "other." What would Philip Roth, the real-life author of this novel, have to say about the diaspora question? By projecting the comments quoted above onto characters of this sort, does Roth mean to distance himself from them—to say, "I don't myself believe what they are saying"—or would he own them? The arguments attributed to Pipik and Zee are cogently, even convincingly expressed, so it is difficult to dismiss them out of hand. Moreover, each character is rendered sympathetically (even Pipik), even if we readers are left with reservations. Is this evidence of Roth's sympathy for what they say? Are we, his readers, meant to be sympathetic to what they say?

In the end, the answers to these questions do not really matter, for we can judge the statements of Pipik and Zee independently of their narrative context. It does not matter what Roth thinks about the statements he has ventriloquized. The statements demand to be considered seriously, whoever speaks them. And without engaging the question of the value of Israeli Jewish culture or politics, we may in any case readily assent to what both Pipik and Zee say about the Jewish diaspora. This diaspora has been and continues to be a powerful engine of Jewish life, culture, and creativity. Moreover, to the lists of past Jewish homes offered by Pipik, and of Jewish geniuses offered by Zee, we may add many others. Not only would Jews and Judaism be impoverished without their contributions, but so too would the world more broadly. Saying this in a world in which many Jews assume the centrality of Israel is not easy. But the push-back against this assumption is important. Whether he believed it himself or not, Roth has made the point extremely well.

Roth was far from alone in formulating fiction that celebrates the Jewish diaspora. Ironically, the writer who perhaps most powerfully made the case for the European home of Jewry was one of Israel's greatest writers, creating masterpieces in modern, Israeli Hebrew, S. Y. Agnon. His late, monumental story cycle about the Galician town of his youth, Buczacz—titled *A City in Its Fullness*—was written after the founding of the state of Israel in 1948, during the years the state was being built, and published only in 1973, following his death. The stories are not historical, in the literal sense of the word, being instead the product of Agnon's re-presentation of the world he left behind.

The Buczacz Agnon creates is truly a remarkable Jewish place, a thriving home for human triumph and squabbling that lasts for centuries. So full and so Jewish is Jewish life in Buczacz that even the Zionist has a hard time dismissing it. In fact, in Mintz's interpretation:

> the entire project of A City in Its Fullness can be taken as an effort to re-spatialize Diaspora Judaism by making a single, concrete place come to life. In this sense, Agnon is practicing a kind of inverted Diaspora Zionism. He espouses the need to reconnect soul to body and spirit to place, but he demonstrates that that unity, in its own way, was found in a place like Buczacz in its heyday well in anticipation of the later fulfillment in Eretz Yisrael.[30]

Diaspora Judaism was never detached from space, necessitating that it be "re-spatialized," nor was it ever possible actually to disconnect soul from body (except, in traditional belief, after death) or spirit from place. But Zionists argued that this had been the case in the diaspora and that a restored Zion was the only place that unity could be re-formed. Yet, as Agnon shows, such unity was also found "in a place *like* Buczacz"—that is, in the many Jewish towns and cities of eastern Europe in early through recent modernity—and it was for such places that many Jews longed even when they were forced into exile from them. This was the "inverted Diaspora Zionism" that so many felt, even if they could not express it.

Agnon's "Diaspora Zionism" is already evident in his story inventing the founding of Buczacz—"inventing" because in his very first words, Agnon puts us on notice that his tale will not be a historical one. He commences by asking: "When was our city founded, and who was its founder?"[31] "Our city," he says, referring not to the Jewish part of the city but, as the tale with which he answers his question makes clear, to the city as a whole. Contrary to any conceivable reality—even to one who knows nothing about the actual history of Buczacz—the city is imaginatively constructed as a Jewish city, founded by Jews who were then joined by others. But this is not just a common Jewish city. As Agnon's tale makes clear, it is a veritable Zion.

Agnon's answer concerning Buczacz's origins begins, "There once was a band of Jews who were moved by their own pure hearts to go up to the

## 182  EMBRACING EXILE

Land of Israel...." But "they did not know the road to the Land of Israel, nor did anyone they met along the way know where the Land of Israel was." Travelling safely through many towns and villages as they headed east, unharmed and even supported by the gentiles they met, they arrive, at the beginning of the season of the High Holidays, in "a place of forests and rivers," where they are forced to stay because of the early arrival of winter. Facing the prospect of a brutal winter, the Jews accept the invitation of local gentile noblemen to enjoy their hospitality and shelter. Having taken the Jews in for the season, the noblemen find themselves flourishing in all their endeavors, for which they credit the Jews. They therefore encourage the Jews to stay, offering local land on which to build. In scenes reminiscent of Jeremiah's famous "Letter to the Exiles," they build homes, a synagogue, a house of study, and a ritual bath; women become pregnant and have children, the elders find themselves comfortable and at home. Relations with their gentile neighbors are good. Soon, "the whole place came to be settled by Jews." The place came to be known as Buczacz.[32]

This story describes the founding of a rich, flourishing Jewish home, one that mostly avoids the travails of Diaspora until its final years. What is most significant about the story is its directionality: the Jews who founded Buczacz were headed to the Promised Land, which, arguably, they found, though not in Palestine (the location of which, notably, no one knew). Their preconceived aspiration cut short, they built a Jewish city in the image of traditional Judaism, as Agnon would have understood it. Establishing all the crucial institutions of such a city, they created what is unambiguously a Jewish home. As the stories unfold, it becomes more and more clear that this is a relatively ideal Jewish place, despite the flaws of any such place. It is, furthermore, a place to which the Jewish heart aches to return, again, even despite its flaws.

Buczacz is depicted, in Agnon's stories, as having a kind of redemptive quality. For example, in the tale of "The Brilliant Chandelier," R. Shalom, a merchant, shares "a repast of fruit" with a friend—a gentile merchant—in the city of Trieste. While in his home, R. Shalom notices a huge chandelier, unlit, hanging from the ceiling, and inquires about it. The merchant reports that the chandelier had not been lit since the time of his great-grandfather, when it had been lit on Sabbath and festival eves. R. Shalom reacts, "Surely you are Christians, you and your ancestors?" Actually, replies the merchant, his great-grandfather had been a Jew who was forced to convert to Christianity "because of a mistake in his business caused by one of his

MODERN JEWS ON DIASPORA    183

Christian workers." As R. Shalom is about to leave on his return journey to Buczacz, he discovers the Sabbath chandelier crated and wrapped for the journey, having been gifted by the Trieste merchant. In Buczacz, the chandelier is hung in the synagogue, lit and brilliant for Sabbath and festivals. There it remained, shining ever more brightly, "until the arrival of the depraved and reviled one, with his cursed and polluted gang [the Nazis], and then the light went out."[33]

This magnificent Sabbath chandelier, once bright but dark when discovered, had, as it were, gone into "exile" among Christians with its owner and his descendants. In exile it sat until it was seen by the merchant from Buczacz. But thanks to the relationship he made—thanks to his willingness to share a convivial repast with his gentile friend (something he could easily do only in exile)—he was able to effectuate its release from exile, its redemption. It returned to the holy land—which Buczacz, as we saw in its origin story, surely was—and found a place in the synagogue, redeemed and "restored" (spiritually) to its holy home. As the tradition teaches, at the time of redemption, the holy vessels will return to the Temple, or, as this story would have it, to the synagogue in Buczacz.

Similarly, in story after story, Agnon conveys how good relationships frequently were between Jews and their gentile neighbors and rulers. This warm acceptance, together with the factors already enumerated above, led to a clear affirmation of the sense of Buczacz Jews that they were at home. Thus, "The Tale of the Menorah," recounting the long history of the menorah of the synagogue of Buczacz, begins by emphasizing that the Jew, R. Nahman, "keeper of the royal seal," was beloved to the Polish king. To reward R. Nahman for his good advice, the king had a menorah made, to be given to the synagogue. There was only one problem—the menorah was made in the image of the menorah of the Temple, with seven branches, and Jewish law forbids the creation of exact likenesses of the Temple's vessels. So the community broke off the menorah's middle branch, creating a space that would be key to events in subsequent generations.

During the Khmelnitski uprising (1648–49), the synagogue was converted to a church, but the menorah was hidden at the bottom of the local river, where it was later rediscovered. This later generation was troubled by the gap created by the removed central branch, so they filled it with the national insignia of Poland, a Polish eagle. "Now we will let Poland know," they said, "how truly attached we are to our country and homeland, the land of Poland. Out of love for the homeland, we have even placed the

184   EMBRACING EXILE

national insignia of Poland in our house of worship!"[34] Later, after Polish Buczacz was captured by Austria, many Jews joined the Polish uprising against Austria, affirming their loyalty to and love of it. Polish territory, as is well known, passed from one conqueror to another, but, as the story concludes, "Israel remains forever,"[35] meaning, in this context, Jews in Poland, whoever may rule the territory in which they reside, remain in their homeland—a condition that would come to tragic end only with the catastrophes of the twentieth century.

More than anything else, what coveys the sense of "home" in Agnon's Buczacz stories is the very ordinariness of a rich, textured, Jewish life in that place, from generation to generation. Jews pray, study, observe the Sabbath, support one another, fight one another, live in harmony with their gentile neighbors, find themselves the targets of the enmity of their neighbors, and so forth. They experience "exile," but their exile is at the same time their homeland. And it had been their home, we are told, for 800 years, so even after the catastrophe of the Great War, they sought to return there.[36] Facing this longevity, one cannot help but recall the comments of the Maharal of Prague, who wrote that exile is "unnatural" for Jews, but the "unnatural" cannot last, so if the "unnatural" condition persists, it must be (or must have become) natural. Buczacz was a natural home for Jews, a true home, a true homeland. When, in the end, they were exiled from Buczacz, they found themselves in a new exile, even if they were among the few who "went up" to the Land of Israel.

An earlier, Yiddish story by Sholem Asch anticipated the spirit of Agnon's stories of Buczacz, particularly its founding. In the story "Kiddush Hashem" (1919), Asch proposed that at the time of the destruction of the Jerusalem Temple, God took a piece of the Holy Land, hiding it in heaven until the day God's people needed a haven, at which point God sent the parcel to earth to form the ground of Poland/Po-lin = "dwell here." "That is why," Asch's character goes on, "Satan has no power over us here, and the Torah is spread broadcast over the whole country." In light of its holiness, Jewish Poland will never be abandoned (little did Asch know what would soon come!). Rather, "when the Messiah comes, God will certainly transport Poland with all its settlements, synagogues and yeshivas to Eretz Yisroel. How else could it be?"[37]

In this legend and others, tellers of Polish Jewish tales appropriate Talmudic teachings regarding Babylonia and apply them to Poland. Stones from the Temple become part of a synagogue in Poland. Underground tunnels connect Poland to the Holy Land. Polish synagogues and study halls will be magically transported to the Land at the time of the messiah.[38] But Asch, in this story, goes even further, claiming that even "all its settlements" will relocate to the Land, for, after all, as Bar-Itzhak makes clear in her analysis of this story, "Poland is a piece of the Land of Israel." This claim was never made of Babylon, however sacred that diaspora home was imagined to be. What we see here is, then, an answer to the question we might have asked when we witnessed the Talmudic elevation of the status of its Diaspora-homeland: is Babylonia, which was biblically endorsed, a special case? Jews in Poland answered "no." Poland was equally elevated as a Jewish homeland, perhaps more so.

Unexpectedly similar to Agnon's Buczacz stories is Ruby Namdar's great Hebrew-American novel, *The Ruined House*.[39] Namdar's novel tells the story of Andrew P. Cohen, "a professor of comparative literature at New York University, who is at the zenith of his life. Admired by his students and published in prestigious literary magazines, he is about to receive a coveted promotion—the crowning achievement of his enviable career." What this jacket copy fails to add is that Cohen resides on Manhattan's Upper West Side, near Riverside Drive—a privileged location in a privileged neighborhood, disproportionally occupied by professional, intellectual, often committed Jews, whose Jewish identities range from "modern" but completely Orthodox to secular but Jewishly engaged. The author lives in the neighborhood he describes, and in his novel he captures the textures of the neighborhood in all of its rich detail.

Let there be no mistake about it: Namdar's Upper West Side (the real one, much of which he does not describe) is a Jewish "promised land," filled with diverse synagogues, Jewish day schools, yeshivas, delis, establishment institutions such as the Jewish Theological Seminary, innovative new groups attracting the unaffiliated, and much more. It is a promised land in which Jews are comfortable, excel in matters of culture and academe, and need have virtually no anxiety about their Jewishness, however it is expressed. Not surprisingly, there are many Israelis who have relocated on the Upper West Side, much like Namdar himself. But Namdar does not write for the English-speaking Jews of the Upper West Side, nor for the Hebrew-speaking immigrants. Writing with a visceral flare that bears resemblance to Philip Roth, Namdar nevertheless writes his book in Hebrew, for the larger Hebrew-speaking audience, the vast majority of whom are in Israel. In other words, Namdar is representing a diaspora

186 EMBRACING EXILE

Jewish homeland for contemporary Israelis in the Land of Israel. Perhaps it is the wonderful perversity of doing so that instigated the controversy and backlash when *The Ruined House* won Israel's most prestigious literary award, the Sapir Prize.[40]

Namdar's assertion of the Jewish holiness of early twenty-first-century New York is found not primarily in his language of composition, but in the structuring of his narrative, as well as in its most startling, puzzling, and shocking element. The novel is structured in seven "books," each labeled as such. This structure is unmistakably reminiscent of the five books of Moses—the Torah—or the six books of the Mishnah, though it is also different from those works, being divided according to a number that no traditional Jewish book models (the same was true of the Mishnah's six "orders" when compared with the earlier tradition). Notably, each book is separated from the others by several pages of traditional and invented "traditional" text, which is made to look, in its layout on the page, like the printed Talmud; these pages are printed on gray paper (this is more obvious in the English edition than in the Hebrew) to make their presence unmissable. Part of this "Talmud" is an invented representation of the order of the priestly service in the (destroyed) Jerusalem Temple on Yom Kippur, written in rabbinic Hebrew, and other parts are direct quotations from the Mishnah and Talmud on the same subject. So the novel interweaves "Torah," other traditional text, and commentary to create a unique tapestry, with the "Torah" being the Torah of diaspora, in New York City and environs.

Also clearly defining the progress of the novel is its dates, given according to both the common world calendar and the Jewish calendar. Mostly, the Jewish dates are merely a reminder that there is another, sacred Jewish way of counting the days, a way that is evidently as relevant in New York as in the Holy Land. But the Jewish dates also add meaning to the events that transpire in New York. For example, the 25th of Kislev, 5761 (December 22, 2000)—the first day of Hannukah—provides the occasion for the narrator to remark, "How easy it sometimes was to love New York!";[41] here, the joy of common experience echoes the joy of the holiday. Or later, the 17th of Tammuz, 5761 (July 8, 2001)—the day on which, according to Jewish tradition, the walls of Jerusalem were breached by the Romans and the quick decline toward the destruction of the Temple had commenced—is, in New York, a day "faint with heat," a day when "the walls have been breached, the besieged city has fallen."[42] Because it was 2001, it could also be the day on which the countdown toward September 11 commenced, and though the latter date does not correspond with a significant Jewish date that year, the beginning of recovery begins—in the novel at least—on the first of Tishrei, that is, on the Jewish New Year, Rosh Hashana.

The element of the narrative that most directly states the status of New York as "sacred precinct" is the startling, unsettling visions that punctuate Cohen's experience. Most of these are what might be described as a "priestly breakthrough"—huge visions of the High Priest in Jerusalem conducting the Yom Kippur sacrificial service, or of the sacrificial animal, covered with blood, on its frightening final journey. In parallel, Cohen—the priest—relishes the barbecued flesh of his steak, or recoils from an encounter with a found piece of loin—his own "sacrificial" experiences in the contemporary "sanctuary." Even more directly, the novel opens with "the gates of heaven...opened above the great city of New York, and behold: all seven celestial spheres were revealed, right above the West 4th Street subway station."[43] Or near the end, just before the 9th of Av (Tisha Be'Av), "through a portal in the ceiling, he [= Cohen] saw the gates of heaven open over the great city and all seven celestial views come into view."[44] The sacrificial service is not taking place in Jerusalem in the year 2001, but, according to Namdar, it is in New York. And no one knows whether the gates of heaven open over contemporary Jerusalem, but they do over the great city of New York. What had once occurred in the Holy City in the Holy Land now occurs in a new "Holy City." The book does not explicitly declare, as did R. Judah in the Talmud so long ago, that the diaspora location supersedes the promised location. But perhaps it does not have to.

One might object to this characterization of the message of Namdar's book on the grounds that his narrative is ultimately a narrative of decay and decline, one that ends with the ruin of Cohen's house. Perhaps, one could argue, this is a way of saying that diasporas lead to destruction. But such a conclusion cannot be defended, for, as the novel makes clear, Jewish homes are left in ruin in all Jewish homelands—including the homeland that is the Land of Israel. In fact, the entire novel is built on the parallel between the decline and destruction of the ancient Jewish home (or God's home) in Jerusalem and the decline of Cohen's house in contemporary New York. Crucially, the ancient destruction leaves ruin and exile—if not of the people then at least of God's presence. By contrast, Cohen's destruction leaves not ruin but almost a total return to normalcy. The new diaspora homeland remains a home.

188   EMBRACING EXILE

It is not only in writings such as those of Agnon or Namdar that the Land of Israel has, in recent times, been "drawn" into exile/diaspora. New Jewish rituals have done the same. An example of this phenomenon is the great annual Rosh Hashana pilgrimage to the tomb of R. Nachman of Bratzlav, which has become an event of major proportions, during which thousands of Israelis of various religious (and non-religious) orientations "go up" to the tomb,[45] in Uman, Ukraine. As Zvi Mark—who has studied this phenomenon in detail—reports:

> In recent years, an aerial caravan leaves the land of Israel on the eve of every Rosh Hashanah, airplanes filled with thousands of Jews–Hasidim and non-Hasidim, Sefardim and Ashkenazim, religious and secular—on pilgrimage to Rabbi Nachman's gravesite to celebrate Rosh Hashanah with him. Most of these pilgrims come from Israel, but groups travel as well from the United States, Canada and France. The broad range of those who come, which is expressed in their clothing and manner of speech, is clearly represented on the streets of Uman on Rosh Hashanah. Besides the principal prayer groups that meet in the New Kloyz ("Synagogue")—an Ashkenazi group and a Sefardi group, in which thousands of Hasidim participate—there are many other groups: those of Eastern communities, two in Yemenite style, a gathering of Chabad Hasidim and one of Satmar Hasidim, and so forth. Young secular Jews participate alongside famous rabbis as well as celebrities from the fields of entertainment and politics.[46]

According to Alla Marchenko, who has conducted interviews with these pilgrims, Israelis (and others) who make the pilgrimage do not view their trip as a "roots trip" to an ancestral home (though many could trace their families to Ukraine), but as a pilgrimage to a "holy land." Given that, for Jews, Holy Land = the Land of Israel, it cannot be due only to the origin of a large part of the pilgrim population that, during the holiday in Uman, the area around the tomb is "Israelized,"[47] with Hebrew as the dominant language, housing developments catering to Israelis, advertising in Hebrew, Israeli-style groceries, and the like, all conveying the message that "Israel is here," in the diaspora.[48] The notion that "Israel is here" is an affirmation of, or, at least, an extension of, teachings of R. Nachman—that (in Zvi Mark's paraphrase) "the holy person forms a new holy place, a new portion of the Land of Israel, for after the death of the Zaddik, his place of burial is sacred with the sanctity of the Land of Israel," or, in the words of his disciple,

R. Nathan, "the place of the burial of the true Zaddik has the aspect of the Land of Israel."[49] Mark adds, "The fundamental Bratslaver view sees the burial place of the Zaddik as having the sanctity of the Land of Israel, and even of the Holy of Holies [= the most holy precinct of the Temple]."[50] Indeed, based upon this same ideology, R. Abraham Sternhartz (1862–1955), the great-grandson of R. Nathan, insisted that the sacredness of the Land and the place of the Temple has been annulled and is to be found, in our day, only at the place of the burial of the Zaddik—in his case, of R. Nachman.

It is crucial to note that Mark and others, in their Hebrew writing about this phenomenon, employ the term "*aliyah la'regel*" ("going up for the pilgrimage"). One may argue that this is simply the Hebrew term for "pilgrimage," and, in the absence of another term, the writers have no choice. But the Hebrew has clear connotations: "aliyah" means to "go up," a term Jews have always used for traveling to the Land of Israel, and one that has the unmistakable connotation of ascending to the Land that is superior to other lands. "*Regel*" refers to the three biblical pilgrimage festivals—Passover, Shavuot, and Sukkot—all of which were to be celebrated by pilgrims at the Temple in Jerusalem. To use this term of pilgrimage-ascent for a mass gathering at a tomb in Uman admits that that place has taken on the status of the Holy Land, and even of the Temple. Whatever the conscious intent of the writers who use this term, they cannot but admit that, for those who attend the Rosh Hashana pilgrimage, the Holy Land is not restricted to its historical location. Their actions speaking more loudly than their words, the thousands of Israeli pilgrims who "go down" from Israel, only to "go up" to the tomb of R. Nachman, declare which territory is truly sacred—where the closest bond to God is to be found.

Not only has the sacredness of the Land of Israel been conveyed to the diaspora, but sacred diaspora sites have also been brought to the Land of Israel—to the modern State of Israel. One example of this is the full-scale replica of Chabad world headquarters, the original located at 770 Eastern Parkway in Brooklyn, built in 1986 in Kfar Chabad, in central Israel. The Brooklyn headquarters was the home of the last Lubavitcher Rebbe, where he taught and offered blessings to his followers and others. As we saw in an earlier chapter, this branch of Hasidism believed that the sacredness of the Land of Israel was to be found wherever a rebbe and his disciples learned and worshipped; there is, therefore, no need for Lubavitcher Hasidim to go to the Land. But there was a group who felt inspired to lay down roots in

190 EMBRACING EXILE

the actual biblical Holy Land, and they built a whole community for themselves and their like-minded colleagues. Ironically, though, upon making a home in the Land of Israel, they felt distant from the site that was most sacred to them—the headquarters of the rebbe in Brooklyn. To correct this circumstance, they brought the site to them. The building, which fits nicely into its Brooklyn surroundings, is, in Israel, an unmissable testament to their yearning for their true, sacred home—a home in the diaspora. For Jews who have made sacred lives in diaspora, the sacredness of the Land is just not enough. (The Rebbe's tomb in New York City is also a pilgrimage site, attracting pilgrims from Israel and elsewhere, though not in nearly the same numbers as R. Nachman's tomb in Uman.)

Another significant case of "drawing" the sacred diaspora site to the Land of Israel is the grave (and more) of Baba Sali in Netivot, in the northern Negev. Baba Sali (= Rabbi Yisrael Abuhatzeira) was a revered Moroccan rabbi, believed to be a miracle worker, who resettled with his community in Israel in 1964 (he had settled in Israel earlier but returned to Morocco to strengthen the spirit of Jews there as their fortune declined). When he died in 1984, his grave became a pilgrimage destination, drawing thousands of pilgrims a year on the anniversary of his death and at other times. What is notable for our purpose is not the grave, though, but the architecture that surrounds it.

Netivot was a common Israeli "development town," established in 1956 for new immigrants (to be sure, of certain populations and not others) to Israel. These towns were characterized by a simple, modern architecture. But in Netivot, buildings along the thoroughfare leading to Rabbi Abuhatzeira's grave—the street itself named Abuhatzeira—are characterized by ornamentation reminiscent of Morocco. This style was replicated in Netivot, according to one witness, "in order to symbolize the past."[51] But this is not just an act of nostalgia. It is also a way of "transporting" the diaspora home into the new Israeli environment. It is a way of saying that Morocco is a genuine homeland for Moroccan Jews, both those who immigrated to Israel and those who remained behind.[52] Immigrants to Israel, former citizens of familiar and even sacred diasporas, experience their move to Israel as not only a homecoming (this feeling may be more theoretical, even obligatory, than real) but also an exile. To overcome the gap, they take steps to re-locate some of the former home into their new environment.

The outstanding Jewish intellectual George Steiner was born to Viennese Jewish parents in 1929 in Paris, where his family had relocated on account of his father's prescient fear of the rise of Nazism. Staying one step ahead of the

MODERN JEWS ON DIASPORA    191

growing danger, in 1940 the family moved to New York (shortly before the Nazi occupation of Paris), where Steiner attended the Lycée Français through high school. He graduated from the University of Chicago and spent his academic career in a variety of distinguished positions in the United States and Europe. His life was therefore punctuated by the Jewish twentieth century's "worst of times" and "best of times"; he was haunted by the depth of Jewish suffering while knowing the height of Jewish accomplishment.

Steiner offered personal confessions and analysis of his relationship to Israel and the Jewish diaspora in an interview that appeared in *The Forward* on March 27, 2017 (itself an excerpt of an interview of Steiner by French journalist Laure Adler, which appeared in a book of their conversations titled *A Long Saturday*).[53] In that interview, Steiner describes himself as an anti-Zionist. His anti-Zionism is, he says, a product of the fact that Jewry in exile, without a land and an army, "did not have the wherewithal to mistreat, or torture, or expropriate anyone or anything in the world." He goes on, saying that "for me, it [Jewry in this condition] was the single greatest aristocracy that ever existed. When I'm introduced to an English duke, I say to myself, 'The highest nobility is to have belonged to a people that has never humiliated another people.' Or tortured another."

For Steiner, Israel is not a fulfillment of the mission of the people of Israel but its failure. In his view, the mission of the Jews is to be "the guest of humanity." This is not a concession to the condition of diaspora but an assertion that Jews, in their diaspora, have accepted responsibility for realizing the truth of the human condition, which Steiner, citing Heidegger, defines as being "the guests of life." What does this mean? Steiner elaborates:

> Neither you nor I could choose the place of our birth, the circumstances, the historical time to which we belong, a handicap or perfect health. We are *geworfen*, to use the German word, "thrown" into life. And in my opinion, whoever is thrown into life has a duty to that life, an obligation to behave as a guest. What must a guest do? He must live among people, wherever they may be. And a good guest, a worthy guest, leaves the place where he has been staying a bit cleaner, a bit more beautiful, a bit more interesting than he found it. And if he must leave, he packs his bags and leaves.

No human is fundamentally anything but a guest, Steiner says. We find ourselves thrown into these circumstances and not others, and we may claim no

192    EMBRACING EXILE

responsibility for that reality. What if I were writing about diaspora as a Jew in thirteenth-century France as opposed to twenty-first-century America? I would be writing with a quill, not a keyboard—if I could afford the writing materials in the first place. Each paragraph would mechanically take me many minutes to write, not a few, and who knows if I would have the privilege of sufficient time to record what I want to say. Besides, if I had lived in that world as opposed to the one in which I now find myself, I would likely already be dead, having succumbed to one of the many illnesses that can now easily be treated. Realizing these things, I must take responsibility for my "guesthood," refusing to assume my right to my privilege, whatever it may be.

But the condition of guesthood is not merely a burden or responsibility. To be a good guest means to be grateful for the many gifts one has, as a guest, received. As Steiner comments, "I haven't visited or lived in any place in the world that hasn't been fascinating, whose language hasn't been worth learning, whose culture isn't worth understanding, where one can't try to do something interesting. The world is incredibly rich." If people fail to pursue their guesthood, to live only as though they are at home (though they never really are), then they will be impoverished. Moreover, if people live as though they own their particular worlds, believing that they have what they enjoy by right and not as guests, they will do great damage. As Steiner continues, "If people don't learn how to be guests of each other, we will destroy ourselves, we will have religious wars, terrible racial wars." Jews, in their diasporas, learned this lesson—learned to live with others as guests, learned that their "hosts" were also, whether they realized it or not, guests. This led to a Judaism that lived and survived in the world, Judaism at its best. "If Israel were to disappear," Steiner affirms, "Judaism would survive; it is much greater than Israel."

At this point in his reflections, Steiner naturally turns to the diaspora. He begins by focusing on certain specific diasporas:

> Judaism goes far beyond Israel. The 500 years in Spain were one of the greatest periods in Jewish culture. The 500 years in Salonica were a period of immense spiritual and intellectual glory. American Jews dominate a large portion of the sciences and the economy of the planet. Not to mention their importance in the media, literature and so on.

Having affirmed the strength and qualities of at least some diasporas (and there were many more he could have listed), Steiner returns to imagining the scenario he hopes would never be realized: "Let's imagine that Israel disappears....I haven't the slightest doubt that Judaism would survive. Not the slightest doubt. Nor about the fact that the mysterious continuity of what I call the guests of life would go on." Israel's destruction would be traumatic, he admits, but Jews and their culture can flourish in diaspora, as they have many times before.

This is not merely a concession to a worst-case scenario. For Steiner, diaspora is not merely "making the best" of an unfortunate historical reality. On the contrary, for Steiner, "wandering is a wonderful destiny." Wandering, one can be a guest anywhere, and since being human means to be a guest, wandering allows for the fullest realization of the human condition. This affirmation of wandering guesthood = diaspora comes hand in hand with a diminution or negation of the nationalist alternative. As Steiner explicitly states:

> I'm fiercely anti-nationalist. I totally respect what Israel is, but it isn't for me. You need a Diaspora to balance things. And I also refused to consider it [= moving to Israel] because I was proud to such a degree, to an almost absurd degree, to be stateless. Proud. That's what I've been proud of all my life. To live in several languages, to live in the greatest possible number of cultures, and to abhor chauvinism, nationalism—which has been the guiding principle in Israel for a long time and is still dominant.

For a proud wandering Jew, any nation-state is a problem, including the Jewish nation-state. States narrow horizons, separate peoples, and negate the other, demanding of their citizens that they settle, not wander. This clearly is not the sort of humanity to which Steiner aspires. For him, therefore, Jewish fulfillment is best realized in the wanderings of diaspora.

Steiner thinks diaspora is "good for the Jews." An intellectual himself, he sees the best of diaspora Jewishness finding expression in "Jewish intellectual excellence." He points to some of the evidence of this excellence:

> In the sciences, the percentage of Jewish Nobel laureates is stunning. There are areas in which there is almost a Jewish monopoly. Take the creation of the modern American novel by Philip Roth, Joseph Heller, Saul Bellow and so many others. The sciences, mathematics, the media, as well; Pravda was run by Jews.

Steiner's focus here is modern. But he knows as well as (or better than) we do that the intellectual excellence of Jews covers all of the centuries and

194    EMBRACING EXILE

places of their diasporas. Working backward, and including only some of the best-known names, one could cite the Vilna Gaon, Moses Mendelssohn, Spinoza (born a Jew, though he converted out at a young age), Isaac Luria, Joseph Caro, Maimonides, Judah Halevi, Alfasi, Saadiah Gaon, and so on (this list is, regrettably, limited to men; unfortunately, the prejudices of earlier ages made it virtually impossible for women to realize and be recognized for the same intellectual achievements). And this, following Steiner's bias, is only in the intellectual disciplines.

If the topic is creativity more broadly, one must add to this list the extraordinarily skilled and often artistically gifted scribes who created the magnificent Hebrew manuscripts of the Middle Ages and beyond; the often unknown artists who decorated those manuscripts, and the craftspeople who gilded them; and the musicians who composed the melodies that accompanied synagogue services and the poets who composed its liturgical poetry. This list, too, is potentially endless, because the product of Jewish productivity in Jewry's various diasporas is virtually infinite.

Asking why the Jewish diaspora has been so extraordinarily creative, Steiner wonders whether this is "the fruit of the terrible pressure of danger? Is danger the father of invention and creation?" He answers that "I dare to believe that is true, quite often." In Steiner's thesis, diaspora is equal to danger, and it is danger itself that energizes the creative impulse. This explains, he submits, why Jews have so excelled in their various diaspora homes.

Here, Steiner fails to be sufficiently rigorous, accepting, as he does, the facile—and often erroneous—equation of diaspora with danger. Just look at the list or authors he offers. Roth, Heller, and Bellow did not write under conditions of danger. Einstein's groundbreaking work did not emerge from the depths of threat. Maimonides lived in a generally accepting and peaceful part of Cairo (the old city of Fostat). The ancient Babylonian rabbis, too, experienced no substantial threat of which we know. Though it is certainly true that Jewish diasporas were sometimes threatened, and Jews sometimes experienced the hatred of their neighbors, the fact is that Jewish communities in their diasporas lived as much in peace as under threat, and it was the relative comfort of those conditions that often provided the stage for the Jewish creative impulse. No one who sees a magnificently decorated manuscript will imagine that it could have been produced under oppressive conditions. No one who reads Maimonides' philosophy or jurisprudence could imagine that they were the product of danger.

In this detail, Steiner's thesis is unsupportable. The frisson of otherness? Perhaps. Danger? Not likely. But Steiner is certainly right that diaspora homes were creative homes for Jews. And he is equally correct in noting the degree to which the riches and range of diaspora host cultures contributed to Jewish creativity. Combine this reality with an ideology that celebrates wandering and guesthood and rejects isolating nationalism, and one has a powerful ideology of diaspora. Steiner's is a weighty argument, and one to which many modern diaspora Jews might assent.

Offering a far more detailed argument for such a defense of diaspora is Yuri Slezkine, in his book *The Jewish Century* (2004). Slezkine is a professor of history, and the book offers a kind of history of Europe and its Jews in recent centuries (primarily the twentieth). But the book is heavily theorized, and the author offers a bold, sweeping claim regarding Jews, their place, and their influence on modern Europe.

Slezkine divides human groups into two categories: those who live on and from the soil, on the one hand, and service nomads, "nonprimary producers specializing in the delivery of goods and services," on the other.[54] This second group Slezkine labels "Mercurians," after Hermes/Mercury, and the former group he terms "Apollonians," after Apollo.[55] Refining the difference between the two groups, Slezkine adds, "The difference between Apollonians and Mercurians is the all-important difference between those who grow food and those who create concepts and artifacts."

In Slezkine's view, Jews are the "quintessential, extraordinarily accomplished Mercurians."[56] Why? Because they practiced "service nomadism" in their many diasporas, and particularly in Europe, where they influenced the shape of modernity itself.[57] In Slezkine's interpretation, for Europe to become modern, they "had to become more like the Jews: urban, mobile, literate, mentally nimble, occupationally flexible, and surrounded by aliens." The rest of the book is devoted to examining the dynamics of European modernity, in which Jews flourish, non-Jewish Europeans become more like diaspora Jews, and tensions arise as groups that earlier lived while tolerating one another, side-by-side, now become competitors.

Valorizing, as he clearly does, the characteristics and qualities of the Jewish diaspora, Slezkine takes a very critical view of Zionism. In his first extended description of Zionism, Slezkine writes:

> It was nationalism in reverse: the idea was not to sanctify popular speech but to profane the language of God, not to convert your home into a

196  EMBRACING EXILE

Promised Land but to convert the Promised Land into a home. The effort to turn Jews into a normal nation looked like no other nationalism in the world. It was Mercurian nationalism that proposed a literal and ostensibly secular reading of the myth of exile; a nationalism that punished God for having punished his people....Zionism was the most radical and revolutionary of all nationalisms. It was more religious in its secularism than any other movement....[58]

In in a later, sharper characterization of Zionism, Slezkine captures his critique more clearly. "The Land of Israel," he writes:

stood for unrelenting Apollonianism and for integral, territorial, and outwardly secular Jewish nationalism. The world's most proficient service nomads were fit into the Age of Universal Mercurianism [the modern age] by becoming Apollonians. The world's strangest nationalism was to transform strangers into natives. The Jews were to find their true selves by no longer acting Jewish.[59]

Slezkine is clear: Zionism sought to "normalize" the world's outstanding "Mercurians," the Jews, by making them just like most of the world's other nations—residing on their own soil, working it, living off its produce, controlling its boundaries, and so forth. But, in Slezkine's view, this entire effort was perverse (my word, not his), because it insisted that Jews could only find their "true" selves "by no longer acting Jewish." What does this mean? Slezkine clearly equates Jewish with diaspora, and he believes that to act Jewishly, Jews must conduct themselves according to the habits they developed in their long, diverse diaspora. In his view, these diaspora skills, wisdoms, and affections are what make them Jewish, and they are positive qualities all. They are also almost all the opposite of the Zionist ideal—the Jew of the clever mind as opposed to the Jew of the strong body, the Jew of the study house (read: university) as opposed to the Jew of the soil. Diaspora is justified because of the Jew it has created. Negation of the diaspora would be the negation of everything Jewish.

Slezkine's discussions of Zionism focus on the Jewish nationalist movement that emerged late in the nineteenth century, not on Zionism as it has been realized and transformed in the state of Israel in the second half of the twentieth century and beyond. The success of Israel's high-tech industries has brought considerable affluence to the more secular, predominantly

Ashkenazi population that occupies Israel's coastal urban clusters. This Israel is a cosmopolitan, international Israel, whose citizens are as fully Slezkine's "Mercurians" as any other population—mobile, "connected," working in information and finance, barely tied to the land. One of the ironies of this Israel is the fact that many of these Israeli Jews are now living in major diaspora communities around the world, including not only New York and Los Angeles but also Berlin and Tokyo. This means that there is now a meaningful Israeli diaspora.

The persistence of a flourishing diaspora, side by side with a troubled and subjectively insecure Jewish homeland, has demanded still further reflections and reformulations of received ideas on the relationship between Zion and exile. This work of re-consideration is ongoing and diverse—though too often politicized. In addition, "re-consideration" is often not re-consideration at all, but simply stubborn restatement of entrenched positions. There is one particularly thoughtful recent reflection on the Zion-exile tension, though, that is neither political nor stubborn, that of Rabbi Shimon Gershon Rosenberg, known as Shagar. By virtue of his personal religious profile, and his increasing posthumous influence on at least one school of religious-Zionist dialogue, Shagar's work is immensely important. Shagar was an unexpected sort of religious Zionist. Born in Jerusalem and formed in religious Zionist institutions, Shagar was attracted by postmodern thought, in which he was self-taught. The yeshiva he founded encouraged eclectic influences and sometimes unconventional (from the perspective of traditional religious Zionism) thought, and his own ideas are often the source of surprise. One area where he surprises most is in his comments on Zionism and diaspora.

Shagar's most focused comments on diaspora begin by noting that the pilgrimage festival of Sukkot—Tabernacles—has, according to the prophet Zechariah and the Talmud, a universal aspect, its 70 required animal sacrifices corresponding to the "seventy nations of the world." This leads Shagar to ask about the balance of universalism and particularism in Judaism. To do so, he focuses on the comments of the Maharal of Prague.

Expanding upon the Maharal's teaching that "the Jewish people is the crux of the world...that is why the Jewish people was dispersed all over the world," Shagar comments:

Because the Jews lack a single place that is unique to them...the entire world is their place, they are cosmopolitan, and their state of dispersion is

198  EMBRACING EXILE

a function of their virtue. According to the Maharal, the exile...is...
evidence of the virtue of the Jewish people....

The ingathering of the exiles to the Land of Israel is perceived by the
Maharal as unnatural to the Jewish people. The Jew's authentic place is,
in fact, in exile, and the Land of Israel is outside the sphere of this
natural state.[60]

On a related teaching of the Maharal, Shagar rephrases: "This passage
implies that exile is the ideal Jewish condition."[61] He remarks:

The path to the Land of Israel...passes through exile. That exile is more
than merely historical, a punishment for past sins; it cultivates the ability
to gain a foothold in the land and take root in it. The Diaspora, befitting
the Jewish people by virtue of its unique character, is what constitutes its
connection to the world, and what enable the Jews to hold fast to their
land without being confined to narrow-mined parochialism and staunch
patriotism.[62]

This is an extraordinary statement, one that expresses the sober conclusions of his experience in the state of Israel. Building upon Maharal's teachings, Shagar admits—nay, insists—that diaspora is not only natural for the
Jewish people, but essential. Jews who do not "pass through exile," who
imagine they can be fully Jewish without incorporating within themselves
their exilic home, will come up short. Jews in exile are ever reminded that
they are, first and foremost, citizens of the world. When they are in the land,
they must preserve the same lesson and sensibility. Why? Because without
their exilic qualities, Jews in the land will be parochial and "staunchly patri-
otic" (not a good thing). Cut off, committed to Jewish life on the land alone,
they will lose an important part of what they are meant to be. How does
Shagar know this? Because in Israel he sees all around him the ills of a
Judaism that has forgotten its exilic ideal.

Shagar's assertion of the need for what one might call "Israeli diasporism"
goes further, as is evident in his comment that "the insecurity of the
Diaspora must deeply inform our confidence as inheritors of the land.
Otherwise, confidence will degenerate into hubris....Such a state of mind
precludes faithful devotion to God and sensitivity to the suffering of the
strangers in our midst—a quality we were dispersed to the ends of the earth
to acquire."[63] The danger of Israel—the modern State of Israel—is that

power on one's own land, a land on which also live many "strangers" (better: "others"), can easily lead to hubris, and such hubris will lead to insensitivity to "strangers in our midst." It is for this very reason, says Shagar, that the people of Israel [= Jews] were dispersed—to acquire sensitivity to the suffering of the stranger, a sensitivity Israel would need when she returned to her land in the mundane, nationalist future (before the messianic age). In other words, Zionism needs diaspora, without which it becomes cruel and hubristic. Jews who have left the memory of exile behind have left their very roots. Only by returning to "exile" can those who dwell in Zion recover their more ideal selves. Exile, diaspora, is good for the Jews.

Ironically, the author whose thesis perhaps comes closest to that of Shagar is a person who is in many ways his opposite, Judith Butler. Butler, an influential gender theorist and critic, was raised in a Jewish household. Butler had a Hebrew school education and was much influenced by a tutorial in Jewish ethics in which they participated as a teenager. Though Butler's work has not primarily focused on Jewish questions, such questions were never ignored.

In 2012 Butler, who is an outspoken critic of Israel and its policies (supporter of the movement to boycott, divest from, and sanction Israel), published an extended critique of the common contemporary equation of Jewishness and Zionism.[64] In this work, Butler insists that the only defensible "Jewish" state in Palestine is a binational state, and that binationalism can only be an outgrowth of the incorporation of the experience of the diaspora. To be specific, Butler argues that "the diasporic—is built into the idea of being Jewish (not analytically, but historically, that is, over time); in this sense, to 'be' a Jew is to be departing from oneself, cast out into the world of the non-Jew.... The diasporic... depends upon cohabitation with the non-Jew and eschews the Zionist linkage of nation to land."[65] Because of the historic linkage between Jews and diaspora, "there are Jewish values of cohabitation with the non-Jew that are part of the very ethical substance of diasporic Jewishness."[66] Life in diaspora required that Jews develop not only strategies of survival next to their non-Jewish neighbors, but an ethic of living with the "other."[67] For that reason, Butler argues, diaspora ethics offer a foundation for a binational future in Palestine.

It is in this final statement, and others like it, that Butler comes close to Shagar. Unlike Shagar, Butler rejects the Zionist state, which Butler views as colonialist. But this does not mean that Jews cannot make a home, by the side of Palestinian neighbors, in the land they share. What will make this possible,

200   EMBRACING EXILE

Butler offers, is retaining the lessons of diaspora—recalling what it means to live as an "other," recalling the value and incorporating the ethics of living side by side. As with Shagar, in Butler's view, diaspora saves "Israel," or, more correctly in Butler's case, the nation of Palestinians and Jews in Palestine.

The traditional Jewish opinion, still held by many ultra-Orthodox Jews, is that exile is where most Jews are meant to be, returning to the Holy Land only at the time of the messianic redemption. Such Jews are concentrated in self-restricting neighborhoods in greater New York, as well as in the "Land of Israel" (in their view, not in the nation-state named "Israel"). Given the shortness of human memory, the majority of Jews today consider these groups to be extremist oddballs. Not too long ago, they would have been considered merely traditional Jews.

In fact, until the middle part of the last century, "religious" and "Zionist" would have been deemed by most a contradiction in terms. Still in 1967, in his popular fictional work, *The Chosen*, Chaim Potok could represent the religious camp of the late 40s as believing that Zionism was a movement of "Jewish Goyim" who ignored the traditional Jewish belief of redemption through the agency of the messiah. Declares Reb Saunders, as Potok formulates his views: "Better to live in a land of true goyim"—that is, in exile— "than to live in a land of Jewish goyim!"[68] Now and until the coming of the messiah, it is God's will that Jews live in exile.

As soon as Zionism began to gain adherents, more traditionally minded Jews began to push back. For example, in 1904, less than a decade after the publication of Herzl's *Der Judenstaat*, Rabbi Joseph Rosen—a great Talmudic scholar known as the "Rogatchover Gaon"—declared, "Heaven forbid that we should throw off the yoke of exile from upon our necks through violence, hard work, entreaties or plans...if we conquer the Land before the coming of the king of peace [the messiah], grievous wars will follow....One Jewish life is worth more than the Land."[69] If life is endangered in pursuit of a cause that is not meritorious, not a mitzvah, then loss of life in such a pursuit is a tragedy. Since, as the Rogachover Gaon correctly anticipated, many lives would be lost pursuing Jewish conquest of the land, Zionism itself is a tragedy. Add to this the fact that Zionists have given up faith in the coming of the messiah—nay, that most have given up faith altogether—and you have a movement that, from the traditional perspective, can only be condemned.

Rabbi Avigdor Miller, an American *haredi* rabbi whose opinion closely mirrors that of Potok's fictional "Reb Saunders," takes on the "land-centrism" of Zionism more directly:

MODERN JEWS ON DIASPORA    201

> Some people make a very great error. They think that what happened to us was a big misfortune. We're supposed to be in our land all the time. A landless people is not a people. And all the history of the Jewish people since leaving their land is just an unfortunate appendage added to the real Jewish history....This approach is fundamentally wrong and based on atheism: on a lack of understanding that Hashem is King, and that whatever happens in this world is only His plan.[70]

Modern Jewish nationalists, who equate the "normal" human condition with residing in one's own land, are, Miller suggests, fundamentally mistaken. Human dignity is not reliant on land. Humans living outside of "their" land are not, as some Zionists argued, outside of history. On the contrary, dignity is realized through following God's commands, and God's will has been, for the last many centuries, that Jews reside in exile. To the religious Jew who retains his faith in traditional Jewish opinions, exile is where Jews are now meant to be. Exile is part of the divine plan, and humans should not, therefore, seek to undermine or short-cut it.

Perhaps the most influential of the anti-Zionist modern rabbis is Rabbi Joel Teitelbaum, the Satmar Rebbe. Teitelbaum was born in the Austro-Hungarian empire in 1887, the scion of a distinguished Hasidic family. He was steeped in the traditional Jewish world of eastern Europe and vigorously rejected the ideological developments of modernity. Teitelbaum expressed his opposition to Zionism throughout his life, and he communicated this opposition to his many followers. He has been blamed for discouraging his followers from fleeing to Palestine at a time when they were threatened by the advancing armies of the Nazis.

A representative range of Teitelbaum's opinions on Israel and exile was gathered into a single volume, *Gahalei Eish* (*Burning Coals*), in 1984. To begin with, Teitelbaum states simply that exile, with the exiles of Israel scattered to all "seventy nations," is a divine decree, one that will be reversed only when God decrees the end of exile with the coming of the messiah. But his defense of exile goes further. First, he reiterates the recognition, which we have seen elsewhere, that "On account of the fact that Israel are exiled to all four directions of the earth, they are saved from destruction (God forbid), because all of the nations [at once] will not kill them (God forbid)."[71] The benefit of exile is even more considerable, though. In fact, he argues, the presence of Israel in exile also protects Jews who reside in the Holy Land:

202    EMBRACING EXILE

Since the majority of Israel is in exile, and the enemy is silenced from [doing] destruction, there is also a guarantee for those in the Land of Israel…consequently, since Israel is in exile, this is salvation for those in the Land of Israel, since on account of the guarantee for the former there is also a guarantee for the latter, that they not be destroyed.[72]

God's promise that there would be no destruction [of Israel], God forbid, applies only when we are in the lands of our enemies and not in the Land of Israel…and if most of Israel is in the lands of their enemies, and suffer the decree of exile, then God's promise to protect Israel from destruction, even those living in the Land of Israel, is in force.[73]

Reversing the Zionist argument, Teitelbaum argues (based upon kabbalistic and other sources) that exile protects Jews from destruction, even those in the Land of Israel. Finding divine protection by living according to divine decree, exilic Jews assure divine protection for Jews the world over.

Elsewhere, Teitelbaum argues from the realities of Jewish history, or, we might say, from the model of Jewish sages throughout history. In his words:

All of the sages of the Babylonian Talmud, and all of the Geonim and the early medieval sages, and Alfasi, and Maimonides, and the Ba'al Shem Tov and his disciples, and the Vilna Gaon, and so forth, all lived outside of the Land…and they didn't say we all have to go up to the Land of Israel…and the Sacred Ari [Rabbi Isaac Luria, sixteenth century] says that every person in Israel must live in the place that is fit for him, according to the source of his soul.[74]

There are actually three arguments for diaspora in this brief section. First, most of the great sages of Israel have, since the Temple's destruction, lived in exile. Their model alone tells us where a Jew ought to live (until the arrival of the messiah): in exile. Moreover, their silence regarding an obligation to go to the Land is as eloquent as the model of their life-choices; had they believed that a Jew should go to the Holy Land, they would have said so. Finally, the Ari said that each Jew has a place in the world that is fitting (a "soul-fit") for him or her; for only a few Jews, that place is the Land of Israel.

Pursuing his argument for the legitimacy—nay, the superiority—of Jewish life in diaspora, Teitelbaum must account for the Talmudic teaching that declares Jews living outside the Land to be Godless. His appropriation of this teaching to support his own end is simple: the God-Godless dichotomy of the Land of Israel versus outside the Land applies only when God is actually in the Land, that is to say, when the Temple is standing. Without the Temple, though, God is not in the Land, and at such a time, "there is no difference between the Land and outside the Land."[75]

Finally, Teitelbaum picks up on a trope from earlier Hasidic teachers—the notion that one can be in the Land of Israel in exile—and literalizes it. For earlier Hasidic masters, the one who prayed with proper intent could effectively transport himself (and yes, they certainly had in mind a "him") to the Holy of Holies, or the scholar of Torah could partake of the atmosphere of the Land of Israel, which makes one smart. But Teitelbaum goes a step further:

> If a person merits great holiness outside of the Land, it is possible that the soil of the foreign land will be uprooted and the soil of the Land of Israel will come to the place where he is standing.[76]

If we take him at his word, this means that the actual land of the Land can be manifest anywhere. The holiness of the person can actually drive away the earth of the foreign land and cause the earth of the Land to take its place. If this is true, then there is no advantage in going to the Land. In a manner totally consistent with the rest of his anti-Zionist system, in our time—as in all times before the coming of the messiah—there is no difference between the Land and any other land. With no advantage to living in the Land, and with every reason—that is, divine decree—to remain in exile, the Jew should eschew the dream of mundane return and preserve the dream of messianic return, of ultimate redemption.

In the history of Jewish justifications and affirmations of diaspora, exile has been justified as the place where sin is purged through suffering. It has been affirmed as a place for new Jewish life. Diaspora has been cast as a place where Jews might attract converts to the path of the one true God, and the place where Jews—as the one "world-people"—naturally belong. The boundaries between Promised Land and exile have been erased, leaving the notion of exile essentially meaningless, at least until the messianic future. Diaspora has been praised as the place of Torah and the place where God follows the beloved people in their wanderings. The Holy Land has been drawn into the diaspora, whether in Galicia or Ukraine or the Upper West Side of Manhattan. From the beginning to the present, Jews, experienced travelers that they have been, have justified their wanderings and affirmed the homes to which they have wandered.

This affirmation has not meant negating the past. As this experienced diaspora people made the best of their new homes, they rarely forgot their old ones (plural)—not just the Promised Land of Israel but also Spain, Portugal, Poland, Lithuania, Russia, Syria, Egypt, Turkey, and others. They remembered an old homeland even while building a new one, and the Jews' dual diaspora orientation became an orientation defined by multiple poles. As a consequence, Jewish diaspora tradition grew as do all vibrant traditions, layering the past with the present and accumulating teachings, experiences, and strategies without number. It was this ever-growing tradition, oriented around ever-multiplying homes, that made Jewish diaspora livable despite the hard times, and so rich and creative in times that were not so hard.

Jews have learned a lot from their diaspora experience, and that experience has much to teach others. What does it mean to live life as a guest, as George Steiner emphasized? What does it mean to live life as a refugee? It is not just Jewish history that has lessons to teach in response to these questions, but, as we have seen, Jewish thought as well. Jews have a history of grappling with the experiences of fleeing, immigrating, and building new homes, and their experiences have taught them to make sense of this common human fate.

# 11

# Exiles and Their Diasporas

## The Lessons of the Jews

From the very beginning, Jews have recognized that to be human means to be a refugee. To be born means to be expelled from your first home. Human history begins with exile from the Garden, and the history of humans cast from their homes to seek refuge will never end; today, millions of Ukrainians have been rendered refugees, seeking safe new homes as they flee Russian forces. "Leave your homeland, your birthplace, your father's house" was not just God's commandment to Abraham; it was a condition for surviving as a human across history.

All peoples have, at one point or another, been refugees. Conquest has required them to leave their current homes and find others. Violence and destruction have required them to flee for their lives. Famine and drought have left them no choice but to depart for other territories, seeking new wells and streams, new hunting grounds, new fields. Subject your DNA to genetic testing and you will find that you derive, in different percentages, from stock that originated in a wide variety of locations. We are all what we are only because our ancestors left their homes and mixed with others.

But communities of refugees do not necessarily become diasporas. In fact, most refugees do not coalesce and survive to become diasporas. Over the course of time, most simply disappear, mixing with a new population to create something different but indistinct. A diaspora, by contrast, retains its identity, retains its sense of being distinct, and of being from somewhere else.[1]

A community of refugees may become a diaspora for various reasons, on account of forces of both push and pull. Refugees may retain a common belief or set of practices, longing to return to their homeland. Their practices may create boundaries—higher or lower, more or less permeable—that allow them to remain somewhat apart, strengthening their sense of distinctiveness and reinforcing their identity. Or the prior residents of their new home may push them away, push them down, insist on their separation and

## 206    EMBRACING EXILE

dwelling apart. Their neighbors may consider them "impure" and thus avoid contact. They may consider their neighbors "impure." In these ways and more, recent refugee communities may become diasporas, and those diasporas may survive for a very long time.

Unlike refugee status, diaspora is not a natural thing; it requires work. The boundaries of a diaspora must be regularly reinforced, whether from the inside or from the outside. But such reinforcement is complex, and it will often be contested. Some members of a diaspora will want to build high, thick walls, walls that refuse the mixing of those inside with those on the outside. Other members of the same diaspora may recognize the value of relations with those beyond the wall, even appreciating what they offer and the ways the diaspora culture may be enriched by such contact. At the same time, some beyond the wall may wish to keep members of the diaspora community as distant as possible, insisting that apart truly be apart, that the gate to the ghetto be closed at night, and perhaps even during the day. Others may wish to create ties with members of the diaspora, even to the point of accepting them so completely that they run the risk of disappearing as a diaspora.

The African diaspora in the United States knows many of these dynamics and forces, though they have been heavily skewed in a particular direction. The Blackness of African skin has, through much of American history, allowed for relatively easy identification of this forced diaspora. The "racial science" of the late nineteenth and early twentieth centuries "proved" the rightness of earlier color prejudice. And though sexual relations between Black Africans and white Europeans—sometimes consensual, more often forced upon enslaved Africans by white masters—often made a person's "race" less than obvious, racism assured that even a small amount of "impure" Black blood would render someone impure, and thus to be avoided.

Black persons were (and often still are), despite generations on American soil, housed apart. They were forced into separate neighborhoods, forced to travel on different buses and to drink from different water fountains. Even after many such separations became illegal, separation was nevertheless enforced through more "subtle" means. A group set apart, whose home-lands were worn in their skin, could hardly not become a diaspora.

In early generations of African residence on American shores, the stories and traditions of Africa were still alive. But white, European Americans sought to "civilize" the captured, enslaved peoples, and this meant they were Christianized, their African cultures actively suppressed. This did not mean that African traditions disappeared entirely, but they became muddled, hard to identify as contributory DNA in the lived practices of now Christian former Africans. They did not, by and large, constitute a homing beacon for the lands from which they emerged.

But with the ongoing failure of America to offer a home to people of African origins, people who saw those origins in their skin sought to reactivate the memory and traditions of home. At various times, but particularly in the latter half of the twentieth century, this aspiration gained renewed force, as various Black leaders offered ideologies that reclaimed Africa—seizing on symbols and arts and rituals that expressed their connections to their origins, with some even urging a return to Africa. The African diaspora survived largely thanks to enforced separation. It finally gained an identity as a diaspora when it claimed ownership over its own, distinct culture and fate.

Jews, in their many diaspora homes, have experienced all these dynamics. In various times and places, Christian and Muslim authorities (more the former than the latter) have forced Jews to dwell apart. They have forbidden marriage with Jews (as Jewish authorities did with them) and often marked them as inferior. In "civilized" modern Europe, they were often seen as "primitive" or at least uncouth. They were said to be dishonest, manipulative, and so forth, and thus to be avoided. When Europe became racist in the proper sense of the term, they were said to be racially inferior, the source of pollution and disease. Under the worst regime of European racism, they were murdered to protect the purity of white Europeans.

On their side, from early times, Jews marked gentiles and their foods as "impure"—particularly gentile wine. Over time, they made their eating laws more and more stringent, strengthening the barrier that should have separated them from their neighbors. After all, if you cannot eat together, it is difficult to develop warm relations; if you cannot drink together, your caution will never be lowered. In central and eastern Europe during earlier centuries of modernity Jews spoke their own language, often understanding little if anything of the languages of their neighbors. If you cannot converse, how can you develop relations? And these Jews, unlike most Jews who came before them, wore clothes that identified them and set them apart, allowing their neighbors to avoid them or ridicule them, both reinforcing separation.

Yet unlike Africans in America, Jews in Europe and north Africa were not set apart by something as obvious as their skin color, and there were, as a consequence, many times and places where Jews themselves diminished

208 EMBRACING EXILE

their separation. For example, in the ancient Roman east, Jews dressed in all obvious ways like their neighbors. The same was true in medieval Cairo and renaissance Italy. In none of these settings would one necessarily have been able to identify a Jew by his or her appearance. In most settings, Jews spoke the languages of their neighbors—Aramaic, Arabic, or Italian in Babylonia, Egypt, and Italy, Spanish or French or Persian in other diaspora homes. The Sephardic diaspora in seventeenth-century Amsterdam translated its prayers into Portuguese and Spanish, but they spoke common Dutch and dressed as common Dutch folk on the street. In Italy, Jews loosened inherited wine restrictions, even drinking "gentile wines," even with their gentile neighbors. And rabbinic authorities in "golden age" Poland complained that Jews ate food served in gentile inns.

So Jews survived their diasporas, forging powerful diaspora identities, in various and highly adaptive ways. They acculturated but preserved their identities as Jews; they prayed to return "home" while making homes in their diasporas. In all these settings, over many centuries, Jews had more experience with diaspora than any other people. Their experiences in diaspora and their models of adaptation can offer a model for other refugee communities, which may or may not become diasporas.

Before seeking lessons in the Jewish experience, though, it is worth asking about the value of a diaspora. What is to be gained by a diaspora people and by their neighbors when refugees insist on maintaining their customs, their language (at least for certain purposes), their sense of commonality among themselves and difference from others, and their connection to their origins, rather than assimilating into their new host culture and disappearing as an identifiable group?

In pre-modern settings, small, local groups often preserved their distinctive identities over the course of generations. There was less pressure to give up difference because there were many groups with many differences. Residents of a village or region on one side of a river might have had a clear sense of distinctiveness from those residing on the other side, even considering them "foreign." This was the way the world was.

In modernity—in the world dominated by the nation-state—there is more pressure to conform, to join the majority and abandon the qualities that sets one and one's community apart. This is true, first, because modern technologies have erased local boundaries, yielding more homogenized regional or national communities. Printing presses, issuing books in the language of a land's largest city or cities, eliminated far-flung dialects. More recently, radios and then televisions and then the internet broadcast the tastes and conventions of powerful urban centers, diminishing the differences between regional and local cultures. But it is also true because of the nature and ideology of the nation-state itself. Nation-states privilege as citizens and rights-holders members of the "nation," whether French or British or even American (ironically, a nation that, even more than others, must be historically constructed, leading to discrimination against those who are "un-American," whether people of color or non-Christians). This means that those who do not belong to the nation are relegated to the role of minorities, with accompanying disadvantages.

As a result of these differences between the modern and earlier worlds, modern diasporas face a greater challenge, with more at stake in preserving their distinctiveness or erasing it. When there is no national majority, when many occupy the "minority" position, a diaspora is, to a great extent, just like other local groups, though one should not overstate the point. In their premodern diasporas, Jews were like other local communities despite their difference. But they were also different in their refusal to submit to the faith of the king—a faith that held many other communities together. In modernity, though, diasporas can be seen as stubborn minorities, refusing the identity of the nation to maintain its own difference. In such a setting, assimilation is a virtue, and the community that refuses to assimilate is suspect.

It is precisely within the modern state, therefore, that diasporas have such immense value. As much as anything else, a diaspora demonstrates the value of difference, what we more commonly call diversity. A persistent diaspora contributes to the fabric of a nation, adding the spice that enriches the whole. By preserving and continuing the legacy it has inherited, a diaspora broadens the inputs from which a culture may grow. The interchange between diaspora, what we might call "new locals," and "old locals" yields a richer version of both, a formula for multiple new national cultures. At the same time, by maintaining historical, emotional, and even spiritual ties to its old home, while planting roots in its new one, the diaspora teaches that no home is actually natural, whatever the cherished myth wants to insist. In truth, you are not natural on this soil and I a foreign implant. Nor am I still natural on the land I have left behind and unnatural in my present home. If all home is accidental, then you and I can co-inhabit, peacefully and productively, anywhere.

If, ideally realized, this is the promise of diaspora, then what does it take for a community of migrants or refugees to become a flourishing diaspora?

Jewish experience offers an abundance of lessons in response to this question. First and foremost, a community of refugees—soon to be a diaspora—does not have to give up on the hope of returning home someday. They may retain their memory and their hope, assuming the latter is pushed off to an idealized, "redeemed" future. But while they long for "home," they must also make a home. They must—as Jeremiah advises the first Jewish refugees who survived, those exiled to Babylon—"build a home and plant a garden," have children and grandchildren, for without planting the seeds, the newly at home diaspora will never come to be.

The great historian Yosef Hayim Yerushalmi described this balance as "Exile and Domicile."[2] He wrote, "It is simultaneously possible to be ideologically in exile and existentially at home."[3] In the Jewish example, Jews were taught, in their liturgies and rituals, that they were in exile, away from a former home that was also their promised future home. Jews accepted this lesson, affirmed it, and knew to repeat it. But many—and perhaps most— Jews through the ages did not feel they were in exile. They experienced their homes in diaspora as genuine homes and built lives accordingly. The balance between these two poles—when the balancing succeeded—was subtle, and not always easy. But most Jews really were "at home abroad," and this contributed both to their success in diaspora and to the success of the people among whom they made their homes. It is worth repeating: this balance is not easy. But there is no reason why other communities of refugees-cum-diasporas cannot achieve the same.

To build and maintain a distinctive diaspora requires that its members maintain a sense of community, with a distinct identity. But it does not demand that they remain separate from their neighbors in order to preserve those identities. The lesson of Jewish history shows that community survival does not require high boundaries. In fact, Jews have mostly *not* completely separated themselves from their neighbors in their diverse diaspora homes. Instead, they have made themselves at home, often to a surprising degree. They have adopted languages, modes of thought, and styles of dress and music and art, all originating with their neighbors, modifying them slightly or not at all. What was once judged "foreign" was "Judaized," becoming part of Jewish culture and practice. All of this has greatly enriched Jewish life and tradition, contributing to the diversity and depth of what it has meant to be Jewish in different places, in different diasporas.

Jewish refugee experience would also suggest that refugees need not be the same as their neighbors, assimilating their mores and accepting their values carte blanche. On the one hand, communities of refugees-cum-diasporas may adapt at least some of the ways of their neighbors without fear of assimilation. On the other, refugees may live their identities wherever they are with conviction, even if this offers a kind of resistance to the dominant local culture. The receiving population may resist the difference, demanding assimilation or threatening rejection. In such a setting, refugees will have a higher hill to climb. But Jewish experience shows that when refugees choose to be at home in their new home, even while retaining important elements of their inherited legacy, loyal difference is generally ultimately accepted, at least for a time.

It is not only receiving populations that may offer resistance, but the community of migrants/refugees as well. Many Jews have, through the ages and still today, resisted becoming "like them," fearing that this move will require them to give up too much (ironically, it is precisely where Jews have lived most comfortably, in the greatest numbers—places like Poland in the seventeenth to early twentieth centuries, or ultra-Orthodox neighborhoods in Brooklyn today—that such resistance to outside influence has been most successful). Arguments will rarely change the minds of people with these opinions. But the lessons of living as a diaspora will exert their influence, impacting the futures of even the diaspora's "resisters," even without their awareness. For example, living in careful and sometimes precarious balance between their own culture and that of their neighbors, Jews have both absorbed the creativity of others and made their own contributions in return. Christian symbols, such as the canopy, have become the universally recognized signs of a Jewish wedding[4]—a sign that has been borrowed back to Christian and other celebrations. As residents abroad, Jews have learned and adapted the philosophy, poetry, and art of their hosts, again, even without full awareness. This influence has not flowed only in one direction (even though the dominant culture exerts its influence more powerfully). So Jews, as "People of the Book," have shared their sacred books with others, having considerable impact on their religious formations and expressions. Similarly, the works of Jewish philosophers, poets, lawyers, and commentators have not been unknown to their neighbors, and these works enriched the creations of Christians and Muslims more than is commonly recognized. This adaptability, this (partially) welcomed symbiosis, has enabled Jews to survive and even to flourish in their many and various homes, confidently claiming their places across the vast map of humanity.

It is not difficult to think of contemporary parallels to the Jewish diaspora experience. Whether in London or New York or Berlin, one may easily

212   EMBRACING EXILE

discover communities of former refugees who have become "locals" while preserving powerful ties to their home cultures. In the United States the pressure of the "melting pot" ideology has receded in favor of a more complex, multicultural perspective, and even if there has been resistance on the part of older Americans, immigrants today are more confident in asserting their unique identities. Will this continue? Not uniformly, and not without back-peddling—just as intolerance has raised its head again and again in Jewish history, so will it again here. But Jews often stayed in their diaspora homes, and even returned to them after experiencing extreme intolerance. Others may do the same as well.

Some of this description may sound like cultural appropriation, and in a world where there is appropriate sensitivity to such appropriation, it is essential to say something about this. "Appropriation" refers to the adoption by a dominant, even colonial power of the cultural expressions of dominated, even oppressed groups. Such appropriation is often done without sensitivity or respect, committing injury by "borrowing" the ways of the subject culture and claiming them as one's own. This is very different from cultural influence and adaptation, which is often, though not always, unconscious, and is in any case inevitable. There is no such thing as different cultures living together without influencing one another. Some cultural creators may perceive the brilliance of the neighboring culture and adopt its lessons consciously. More often, the influences will be subtle and unconscious, but no less real. This is the cultural borrowing from which Jews (almost always a subject culture) and their neighbors have both benefitted.

A discussion of refugees and their fate is particularly important at this point in human history, owing to anticipated consequences of climate change. If current projections are correct (and, if anything, projections regarding climate change have almost all been too optimistic, even the most pessimistic of them), over the course of the next several decades, the rise in ocean levels and other climate events will force the evacuation of as many as 200 million people from their current homes.[5] Many of these climate-refugees will remain within their home countries, but perhaps a quarter—that is, 50 million people—will seek homes beyond foreign borders, creating an unprecedented refugee challenge. I use the term "challenge" advisedly here because the history of refugees and their acceptance ("absorption," a term commonly used in this context, has objectionable implications) suggests that "crisis" may be a more accurate term. Refugees have often not fared well in the lands of their hoped-for asylum. But some Jewish experiences, at least, show that crisis is not the necessary outcome. Difficulties can be overcome and communities of refugees can become viable, even vibrant, diasporas.

The assertion that diaspora must be central to our vision at this time does not require that we identify an immediate, precipitating cause such as the climate crisis and consequent refugee crisis. The truth is that exile/ diaspora is arguably *the* human condition at any time or place. Consider the observation of the ancient rabbis, as explained by the Maharal of Prague. In the ancient teaching, Israel was made to swear that she would not rebel against the nations, that she would remain in exile. That oath, like any, had to be in the name of something ("I swear by…"), a something that would affirm and validate the oath. According to one view, she swore by heaven and earth, according to another she swore by the forefathers—both eternal, steady externalities that would serve as a permanent hook on which the oath could be hung. But then another, very different sort of suggestion is raised: she swore by the generation of persecution. Why? "Because," the Maharal writes, "they would comb their flesh with combs of iron."[6] Despite this, he adds, that generation remained in exile, recognizing their presence there as a fulfillment of divine command, as an expression of the divinely ordained order of the world.

By virtue of its function in connection with the oath, "the generation of persecution" cannot be just a single, fleeting generation. It must—like heaven and earth, like the merit of the forefathers—be constant and eternal. Somehow, all generations must be generations of persecution, in danger of experiencing the worst pains of the flesh. Indeed, how could we imagine otherwise? Has there ever been a generation that has not been, somewhere in the world, a generation of persecution? No, such a reality has never been. And if "exile" means to be potentially subject to the pains of persecution, then there has never been a generation that is not in exile.

Hana Yanagihara offers a profoundly insightful comment in her novel *In Paradise*, in the voice of one of its main protagonists, Charles, who survives after multiple pandemic plagues, in New York City, 2079. "You forget," Charles writes, "how much you need to be touched."[7] The intimacy and comfort of fleshly contact is, Charles claims, what we need to survive as much as anything else, perhaps more so. The infant who has no such contact will languish. The adult who has no one to hug will wither. Without the comfort and pleasure of flesh to flesh, we will not survive.

But the same flesh that nourishes us can also be the site of our greatest anguish. Illness will hurt our flesh, accident will bruise it, cruelty will torture it. None of us will escape entirely "the combing of the iron combs." Our flesh is our exile and our salvation. We—humans—cannot escape this reality, however, at times, we may wish to.

Eve and Adam were cast out of the Garden, so exile is the human condition. All of us must leave our homeland, our parents' home, so exile is the human condition. We are all in exile, and here we must stay. We can lament it as "exile," or we can embrace our exiles as our common home, in our multiple and diverse diasporas.

# Notes

## Chapter 1

1. As Kevin Kenny comments, "In the absence of a Jewish state for nearly two millennia, nearly all Jewish people lived without a single homeland. For this very reason, their sense of diaspora cannot have been unremittingly negative." See *Diaspora, A Very Short Introduction* (New York: Oxford University Press, 2013), p. 52.
2. Erich Gruen develops this thesis in connection with the diaspora communities of antiquity, together with the literatures they produced. See *Diaspora: Jews amidst Greeks and Romans* (Cambridge, MA: Harvard University Press, 2002), p. 234. This book develops what is fundamentally the same thesis for Jewish history as a whole.
3. Daniel Bell, *The End of Ideology: On the Exhaustion of Political Ideas in the Fifties* (Cambridge, MA, and London: Harvard University Press, 2000), p. 399.
4. Bell, p. 398.
5. Bell, p. 397.
6. London and New York: Routledge, 2023.
7. Cohen, p. 3.
8. P. 10.
9. P. 8.
10. P. 185.
11. As Kenny comments, "Settling abroad…did not mean forgetting the lands from which migrants came and to which they dreamed they might one day return." See *Diaspora, A Very Short Introduction*, p. 40.
12. Yes, this is intended as an echo of the title of Arthur Hertzberg's influential *The Zionist Idea*.
13. An excellent new summative work is *The Oxford Handbook of the Jewish Diaspora*, by Hasia Diner (New York: Oxford University Press, 2021). Important new historiography on Jewish diasporas may also be found in *Cultures of the Jews: A New History*, ed. by David Biale (New York: Schocken Books, 2002).
14. In the sixteenth century, the Maharal of Prague regularly used the term "*pizur*" ("dispersion"), picking up on the occasional biblical (see Jer. 50:17 and Joel 4:2) and rabbinic (see b. Pes. 87b) usages of this verb to describe the scattering of Israel. The vast majority of those writing in Hebrew through the ages used the term "*galut*."
15. This is the version of the text at the beginning of par. 5, recorded in the critical edition of Mordecai Margulies (New York and Jerusalem: Jewish Theological Seminary, 1993), p. 532, l. 3.
16. In Robert Chazan's words, "Traditional Jewish thinking posits three exiles from the Promised Land…the third as the result of…Roman imperial reaction to the failed Jewish revolt of 66. In fact, however, there was no such Roman edict"; see *Refugees or Migrants: Pre-Modern Jewish Population Movement* (New Haven and London: Yale University Press, 2018), pp. 83–84. The frequency with which this misconception—that the Romans initiated a new exile—is repeated, without correction, is stunning. Consider, for example, this statement by Samuel Gringauz in a symposium on Galut in *Midstream*, March 1963: "The uniqueness of the phenomenon [= Galut] is that it is a specifically Jewish experience. It is derived, historically, from the compulsory banishment of the Jews from their homeland by the Romans" (p. 18). Now, *Midstream* was published by the Theodor Herzl Foundation, and it is explicitly identified as a Zionist publication. But this doesn't excuse the lack of editorial oversite and fact-checking. Jews were not "banished from their homeland by the Romans." This is pure fiction. In fact, Jewish life and productivity continued in Palestine for centuries after the Roman victories in their wars against the Jews.
17. Quoted in Yoram Erder, *The Karaite Mourners of Zion and the Qumran Scrolls* (Turnhout, Belgium: Brepols, 2017), p. 98.

216  NOTES TO PAGES 16–49

18. Jewish Prayer Book, Musaf service for festivals.
19. I use the terms "Zionist" and "Zionism" in this book as a descriptive term or designation, without any suggestion of evaluation, for good or for bad. "Zionism" is Jewish nationalism (and a "Zionist" a Jewish nationalist) that aspires to a Jewish nation-state in "Zion" = Palestine. Zionism is a modern, secular phenomenon (at least at its origins) that emerged in the late nineteenth century under the influence of other European nationalisms. From the perspective of traditional Judaism, Zionism was a radical movement, insisting on a return to Zion "now," while traditional Judaisms of the Middle Ages and earlier modernity insisted that the return to Zion would only come in response to God's beckoning, at the time of the messiah.
20. Arthur Hertzberg, The Zionist Idea: A Historical Analysis and Reader (New York: Harper & Row, 1966), p. 539.

## Chapter 2

1. A worthwhile review of the controversies concerning the early monarchy may be found in Iain Provan, V. Philips Long, and Tremper Longman III, A Biblical History of Israel (Louisville, KY: Westminster John Knox Press, 2003), pp. 193–238.
2. A useful account of critical views concerning the origin of the biblical books is Richard Elliot Friedman's Who Wrote the Bible? (Englewood Cliffs, NJ: Prentice Hall, 1987; new edition. New York: Simon and Schuster, 2019).
3. Adele Berlin, "Interpreting Torah Traditions in Psalm 105," in Jewish Biblical Interpretation and Cultural Exchange, ed. by Natalie B. Dohrmann and David Stern (Philadelphia: University of Pennsylvania Press, 2008), pp. 26–29.

## Chapter 3

1. I use the term "Jew," here and elsewhere, despite controversy concerning its meaning and possible misunderstanding, depending upon the context. Those who had been exiled from Judea were certainly "Judeans," but they weren't "Jews" in the sense with which we commonly use that term. Nevertheless, "Jew" is a reasonable substitute for "Judean," and to avoid awkwardness of expression, I will prefer "Jew" or "Israel" throughout my discussion of biblical texts. For the controversy to which I refer, see Daniel Boyarin, The Genealogy of a Modern Notion (New Brunswick, NJ: Rutgers University Press, 2019).
2. Yosef Hayim Yerushalmi comments, with respect to exile, that "all genres of Jewish literature are saturated with it," including the Hebrew Bible itself. Yerushalmi already draws attention to some of the texts I discuss following. See Yerushalmi, "Exile and Expulsion in Jewish History," in Crisis and Creativity in the Sephardic World..., ed. by Benjamin Gampel (New York: Columbia University Press, 1997), pp. 4–5.
3. The Religion of Israel: From Its Beginnings to the Babylonian Exile, trans. and abridged by Moshe Greenberg (New York: Schocken Books, 1972), pp. 447–48.
4. As Elias Bickerman comments, "There is no 'Jew problem' in the Scroll of Esther." See Four Strange Books of the Bible (New York: Schocken, 1967), p. 188.
5. See Bickerman, pp. 208–9. But note that Bickerman adds, on p. 206, "As a matter of fact, the author's knowledge of the Persian court is not precise enough." External evidence makes a date later than the second century BCE impossible for the book, and most scholars offer third–second century BCE as the likely time of the book's composition. Noting the fact that Esther contains no Greek words, "as well as the absence of all Greek influences," Carey Moore (Esther [New York: The Anchor Bible, Doubleday, 1971]) suggests that "the first edition probably goes back to the fourth century, or Persian Period, and the final edition appeared in the Hellenistic Period"; see pp. lviii–lix. In any case, this combination of geographical proximity with some chronological distance explains the author's familiarity with the culture he describes, while also accounting for errors in fact.
6. See Moore, p. 30.
7. As Erich Gruen comments, "Nothing in the text implies that Jews in the Persian domains lived in dread of disaster. The contest was one between Haman and Mordechai, a personal rivalry for influence in the court, not a clash of ethnicities in the empire." See Diaspora, p. 147, and see my comments following.
8. P. 36.
9. I am grateful to my student Benjamin Pagovich for this insight concerning the relative chronology of the return from exile and the events described in this book.

NOTES TO PAGES 49–70   217

10. Bickerman remarks, "The royal government remained neutral"; p. 194.

11. In a related vein, Bickerman describes the book's diaspora message, at least as understood by its readers, in this way: "The promise given to the Chosen People in the Holy Land (Exod. 23:27) was also fulfilled in the Diaspora: if you will obey God's commandments, God will lay fear of you upon the nations (Deut. 11:25)"; p. 205.

12. A useful and reasonable summary of the probable dates of different parts of the book may be found in Louis F. Hartman and Alexander A. Di Lella, *The Book of Daniel*, The Anchor Bible 23 (Garden City, NY: Doubleday and Co., 1977), pp. 13–14.

13. For a detailed analysis of the prophecy and "translation" of the apocalyptic visions into the historical events they embed, see Hartman and Di Lella, pp. 286–305.

14. Fragments of Tobit in Hebrew and Aramaic were found at Qumran, thus demanding a dating before the Roman war of the first century. Nothing in the book suggests awareness of the renewed independence of Jews in the Land under the Hasmoneans, thus making an early second-century BCE dating most likely.

15. The reading I offer here differs in significant ways from that of Amy-Jill Levine, "Diaspora as Metaphor: Bodies and Boundaries in the Book of Tobit," in *Diaspora Jews and Judaism: Essays in Honor of, and in Dialogue with, A. Thomas Kraabel*, ed. by J. Andrew Overman and Robert S. MacLennan (Atlanta: Scholars Press, 1992), pp. 105–17. Several of the experiences she attributes to "the acute conditions of exile" (p. 109) are not unique to exile at all: contact with the deceased was an unavoidable human experience in antiquity and beyond, and Jews in the Holy Land—whether of the fictional biblical period assumed in the book or in the Hellenistic period during which it was written—would have lived side by side with the non-Jewish "other," thus necessitating an emphasis on endogamy (consider Deut. 7:1–4). Life in the Land was hardly secure, as it was the conquering armies of empire that led Jews to exile in the first place.

16. In her analysis of the book, Levine emphasizes that, in Tobit, "a genealogical focus replaces a geographical one" (p. 107), adding that "on the symbolic level, she [Sarah] reveals that exiled Israel is only redeemed through the restoration of genealogical continuity" (pp. 112–13). What she fails to notice is that endogamy ("genealogy") thus offers a portable "home," a place of potential stability and even of redemptive promise—perfect affirmations of the possibility of Jewish life in exile. Moreover, the Talmud—based upon a clear biblical source—later insists that Jews in the Babylonian exile maintained a higher degree of endogamy than those in Palestine (contrary to modern assumptions). This may be a subtle affirmation by the author of Tobit of the legitimacy of diaspora, even while praying for eventual redemptive return.

## Chapter 4

1. For a fuller description of the events of this period and their consequences, see David Kraemer, *A History of the Talmud* (Cambridge and New York: Cambridge University Press, 2019), pp. 36–46.

2. For more detail on Jewish life in Babylonia during this period, see Kraemer, *A History of the Talmud*, pp. 126–34.

3. For an extended exposition of the Talmud's "Persian-ness," see Shai Secunda, *The Iranian Talmud: Reading the Bavli in Its Sasanian Context* (Philadelphia: University of Pennsylvania Press, 2014).

4. A detailed analysis of this same text, with different emphasis, may be found in Jeffrey Rubinstein, "Addressing the Attributes of the Land of Israel: An Analysis of Bavli Ketubot 110b–112a" (in Hebrew), in *Center and Diaspora: The Land of Israel and the Diaspora in the Second Temple, Mishna, and Talmud Periods*, ed. by Isaiah M. Gafni (Jerusalem: The Zalman Shazar Center for Jewish History, 2004), pp. 159–88.

5. In *Reconstructing the Talmud, An Introduction to the Academic Study of Rabbinic Literature* (New York: Mechon Hadar, 2014, pp. 261–62), Joshua Kulp and Jason Rogoff suggest that the first part of this text is Palestinian but the latter part, beginning with "And is it true that anyone who does not live in the Land of Israel has no God?," is actually "stammaitic," that is, the later voice of the *gemara*. I disagree with their source criticism, and, in any case, the Talmud here clearly represents this all as a single tannaitic text. For analytical purposes, therefore, that is the assumption we must make.

6. I do not agree with Rubinstein's assessment (p. 179) that, even here, R. Judah grants the superiority of the Land of Israel. He supports this assessment by noting the "as though" in

218   NOTES TO PAGES 70–99

R. Judah's teaching. To begin with, it is imprudent to hang so much on a single word pre-served in the written tradition, the relationship of which to its oral foundations is unknown and irrecoverable. Second, even granting the presence of the term, how we interpret this "as though" (*k'ilu*) depends on how we hear it. "As though [dwells in the Land of Israel]," expressed as a declaration and without a lilt, suggests no conditionality concerning the two sides it wishes to equate. Spoken with a slightly raised voice, as a mocking teenager might, it would diminish the equation. Given the overall thrust of R. Judah's teachings, I doubt it is the teen's voice we should hear here.

7. Manuscripts and other versions include mention of other diasporas here, including Elam and Edom. The briefer printed version is a product of censorship.

8. See Daniel Boyarin's discussion, *A Traveling Homeland: The Babylonian Talmud as Diaspora* (Philadelphia: University of Pennsylvania Press, 2015), pp. 34–36.

9. A similar claim is made in a similarly "geographical" law pertaining to damage done by light cattle; see B.Q. 80a.

10. Various versions of this text are recorded in different witnesses. Whatever their differences, they all agree that the original Talmudic reference is to Rome.

11. For a detailed analysis of this prayer, see "Rabbinic Popular Prayer: An Interpretation of the Amidah in Light of the Social-Material Realities of Late Antiquity," in *Meḥevah le-Menaḥem: Studies in Honor of Menaḥem Hayyim Schmelzer*, ed. by Shmuel Glick, Evelyn M. Cohen, and Angelo M. Piattelli (Jerusalem: Jewish Theological Seminary and the Schocken Institute, 2019), pp. 63*–79*.

## Chapter 5

1. For all of this, see Bernard Lewis, *The Jews of Islam* (Princeton, NJ: Princeton University Press, 1984), pp. 10–14.

2. See Raymond Scheindlin, "Merchants and Intellectuals, Rabbis and Poets," in *Cultures of the Jews: A New History*, ed. by David Biale (New York: Schocken Books, 2002), pp. 317–18.

3. See Scheindlin, "Merchants and Intellectuals," pp. 37–38.

4. *The Itinerary of Benjamin of Tudela*, trans. by Marcus Nathan Adler (New York: Philipp Feldheim, Inc., 1908), pp. 55–64.

5. On which, see Justin Marozzi, *Baghdad: City of Peace, City of Blood* (Philadelphia: Da Capo Press, 2014), pp. 27–125.

6. For discussion of these developments, see Kraemer, *A History of the Talmud*, pp. 180–88.

7. Quoted in Robert Brody, *The Geonim of Babylonia and the Shaping of Medieval Jewish Culture* (New Haven and London: Yale University Press, 1998), p. 114.

8. See Kraemer, *A History of the Talmud*, pp. 189–90, and the literature cited there.

9. See Gerson D. Cohen, *A Critical Edition with a Translation and Notes of the Book of Tradition (Sefer ha-Qabbalah) by Abraham Ibn Daud*, Judaica Texts and Translations 3 (Philadelphia: Jewish Publication Society of America, 1967), pp. 63–67.

10. Cited in Maria Rosa Menocal, *The Ornament of the World* (Boston: Little, Brown & Co., 2002), p. 84. For greater detail on Cordoba in this period, see there, pp. 79–90.

11. My analysis here relies, in many of its points, on Daniel Boyarin's insightful reading of this story. See *A Traveling Homeland*, pp. 9–25.

12. Naturally, there have been naysayers to this "golden age" characterization; an outstanding recent example is Dario Fernandez-Morera, *The Myth of the Andalusian Paradise* (Wilmington, DE: ISI Books, 2016). In my reading, there are a variety of problems with his sources and conclusions—for example, he often cites restrictive Islamic laws without noting that there were numerous times and places when they were not enforced—and I am more inclined, therefore, to follow Scheindlin, cited earlier.

13. Raymond P. Scheindlin, *Wine, Women, and Death: Medieval Hebrew Poems on the Good Life* (New York and Oxford: Oxford University Press, 1986), pp. 41–42.

14. *Wine, Women, and Death*, p. 44.

15. Scheindlin accepts 1085. For his brief account of the facts of Halevi's life, see *The Song of the Distant Dove* (New York: Oxford University Press, 2008), pp. 15–16.

16. See Menocal, p. 145.

17. Par. 14.

18. Par. 30.

NOTES TO PAGES 99–120    219

19. Par. 34.
20. Pars. 34–38.
21. Par. 44.
22. *Song of the Distant Dove*, pp. 199–201, with modifications by this author.
23. The most complete description of life in Jewish Fostat, based upon the evidence of the Genizah, is found in S. D. Goitein, *A Mediterranean Society*, 5 vols. (Berkeley, Los Angeles, and London: University of California Press, 1967–88).
24. *Song*, p. 202.
25. In addressing this point, Ivan Marcus comments: "Although many writers have emphasized the violence and insecurity that beset the Jews of Ashkenaz, Jews would not have survived there, let alone created what they left us, had that been the main story. Christian persecution was usually the exception rather than the rule, and it characterized some times, not others." See Marcus, "A Jewish-Christian Symbiosis: The Culture of Early Ashkenaz," in *Cultures of the Jews*, ed. by David Biale, p. 450.
26. Robert Chazan's work has shown that claims of Crusader destruction have been exaggerated. Describing his own conclusions, he writes, "The tangible impact of crusader violence on European Jewry was quite limited. While the violence was aimed at and resulting in the destruction of three of its leading communities, the bulk of early Ashkenazic Jewry emerged from the crisis unscathed and in fact its rapid development continued with little impediment." See *European Jewry and the First Crusade* (Berkeley, Los Angeles, and London: University of California Press, 1996), p. 8.
27. Chazan, pp. 138–39.
28. As Ivan Marcus comments, "Member of each culture were sometimes attracted to the other one." He later adds, "Sources also suggest close social relations between Jews and Christians in Ashkenaz." See Marcus, pp. 461 and 485.
29. On the images in this manuscript, along with the wedding poem, see Kirsten A. Fudeman, *Vernacular Voices: Language and Identity in Medieval French Jewish Communities* (Philadelphia: University of Pennsylvania Press, 2010), pp. 125–35.

## Chapter 6

1. For an excellent brief account of the transitions in al-Andalus during this period, see Joel L. Kraemer, *Maimonides: The Life and World of One of Civilization's Greatest Minds* (New York: Doubleday, 2008), pp. 23–41.
2. For a detailed history of these events, see Benjamin Gampel, *Anti-Jewish Riots in the Crown of Aragon and the Royal Response, 1391–1392* (New York and Cambridge: Cambridge University Press, 2016).
3. See Daniel Abrams, *Kabbalistic Manuscripts and Textual Theory* (Jerusalem and Los Angeles: The Magnes Press and Cherub Press, 2010).
4. As Eitan Fishbane describes it, "a past that never was—the veiled futurity of redemption dressed in the garb of an imagined olden time." See *The Art of Mystical Narrative: A Poetics of the Zohar* (New York: Oxford University Press, 2018), p. 28.
5. In Fishbane's words, the creators of the Zohar "saw themselves as recreating the (imagined) existential state of R. Shimon and his disciples in the Holy Land in thirteenth- and fourteenth-century Castile." See p. 32, n. 81.
6. This was first and most influentially expressed by Gershom Scholem in *Major Trends in Jewish Mysticism* in 1941; see *Major Trends* (New York: Schocken Books, 1961), pp. 244–86 (Seventh Lecture: Isaac Luria and his School). Moshe Idel has critiqued Scholem on his claims for Lurianic Kabbalah as a popularizing movement, but he supports Scholem's interpretation of Luria's Kabbalah as a response to the expulsion. See *Kabbalah: New Perspectives* (New Haven and London: Yale University Press, 1988), pp. 256–60.
7. It was during this period that the Venice Ghetto was established, and while its founding is evidence of the "precarious stability" of Jews in Venice at this time, we should not let the term "ghetto"—later used to describe a very different institution created by the Nazis—confuse us. The residence of Jews in Venice was affirmed by law, and their situation "was a good one compared to that of Jews elsewhere." Jews were confined to the Ghetto only from midnight (or darkness; this regulation changed over time) until morning, and the Ghetto was otherwise open to passage in both directions; see Richard Calimani, *The Ghetto of Venice*, trans. by Katherine Silberblatt Wolfthal (Milan: Oscar Mondadori, 1995), pp. 38 and 33. Concerning

220   NOTES TO PAGES 120–47

the openness of the Ghetto, Mark Cohen and Theodore Rabb comment, "Members of the two groups [Jews and Christians] continued to have frequent contact…and people moved in and out freely. Indeed, a venture outside the ghetto…[was] a commonplace"; see *The Autobiography of a Seventeenth-Century Venetian Rabbi*, trans. and ed. by Mark R. Cohen (Princeton, NJ: Princeton University Press, 1988), pp. 5–6. Concerning general conditions of life for Jews in northern Italy at this time, see Elliot Horowitz, "Families and their Fortunes: The Jews of Early Modern Italy," in *The Cultures of the Jews*, ed. by David Biale (New York: Schocken Books, 2002), pp. 573–636.

8. All translations are from *Samuel Usque's Consolation for the Tribulations of Israel*, trans. by Martin A. Cohen (Philadelphia: Jewish Publication Society of America, 1965); the current excerpt is from p. 168.

9. Cohen, *Usque's Consolation*, pp. 211–12.

10. For classical rabbinic precedent of these views, see my discussion in *Responses to Suffering in Classical Rabbinic Literature* (New York and Oxford: Oxford University Press, 1995), pp. 88–89.

11. Cohen, p. 227.

12. Cohen, p. 231.

13. Though the port of Amsterdam was also a hub in the international trade of enslaved African peoples, some of whom were held—contrary to local law—in Amsterdam itself. For a short introduction to the history of slavery and the Netherlands, see Dienke Hondius, Nancy Jouwe, Dineke Stam, and Jennifer Tosch, *The Netherlands: Slavery Heritage Guide* (Dutch and English) (Volendam: LM Publishers, 2019), pp. 9–17.

14. *Theologico-Political Treatise*, preface.

## Chapter 7

1. For details on the Maharal's career, see Alexandr Putik and Daniel Polakovic, "Judah Loew ben Bezalel, Called Maharal—A Study on His Genealogy and Biography," in *Path of Life: Rabbi Judah Loew ben Bezalel*, ed. by Alexandr Putik (Prague: Academia and Jewish Museum in Prague, 2009), pp. 61–78.

2. On the city of Prague and its Jewish community during this period, see Vit Vlnas, "Castle, City, Ghetto: On Prague at the Times of Rudolph II and Maharal," in *Path of Life*, pp. 222–42.

3. *Faith Shattered and Restored* (New Milford, CT, and Jerusalem: Maggid Books, 2017), pp. 181–82.

## Chapter 8

1. Abraham Joshua Heschel, *The Earth is the Lord's* (New York: Harper & Row, 1966), p. 26.

2. Quoted in Antony Polonsky, *The Jews in Poland and Russia*, Vol. I: *1350–1881* (Oxford and Portland, OR: Littman Library of Jewish Civilization, 2010), p. 31.

3. On all of this, see Polonsky, pp. 17–113; on the latter point, see p. 107.

4. See Polonsky, pp. 128–29.

5. Moshe Rosman, as quoted by Polonsky, p. 152.

6. Polonsky, p. 151.

7. Quoted in M. Idel, "Eretz Yisrael hu chiyyut me'ha-bore B"H: al meqoma shel Eretz Yisrael be'Chassidut," in *Eretz Yisrael be'hagut hayehudit be'et hachadasha* (*The Land of Israel in Modern Jewish Thought*), ed. by A. Ravitski (Jerusalem: Yad Izhak Ben-Zvi, 1998), p. 261.

8. Ibid.

9. See Arthur Green, *Tormented Master: A Life of Rabbi Nahman of Bratslav* (Tuscaloosa: University of Alabama Press, 1979), pp. 161–69.

10. See Alon Goshen-Gottstein, "The Land of Israel in the Thought of Rabbi Nahman of Braslav," in *The Land of Israel in Modern Jewish Thought* (Hebrew), ed. by Aviezer Ravitsky (Jerusalem: Yad Izhak Ben-Zvi, 1998), pp. 296–97.

11. Quoted in Goshen-Gottstein, p. 277.

12. Quoted in Goshen-Gottstein, p. 277.

13. Quoted in Goshen-Gottstein, p. 280.

14. P. 278.

## Chapter 9

1. See Amos Elon, *The Pity of it All: A Portrait of the German-Jewish Epoch 1743–1933* (New York: Picador, 2002), pp. 67–68.

NOTES TO PAGES 147–66 **221**

2. Moses Mendelssohn, *Jerusalem and Other Jewish Writings*, trans. and ed. by Alfred Jospe (New York: Schocken Books, 1969), p. 104.
3. https://www.napoleon.org/histoire-des-2-empires/articles/lettre-du-22-juillet-1806-a-champagny-ministre-de-linterieur-les-12-questions-a-faire-a-lassemblee-des-juifs/; the translation is mine.
4. *Transactions of the Parisian Sanhedrim: or, Acts of the Assembly of Israelitish deputies of France and Italy, convoked at Paris by an imperial and royal decree, dated May 30, 1806*, translated from the original publication of Diogene Tama; with a preface and illustrative notes by F.D. Kirwan (London: Charles Taylor, 1807), p. 181.
5. Ibid.
6. Elon, p. 164.
7. Elon, p. 159.
8. P. 167.
9. Ibid.
10. Heinrich Graetz, "The Diaspora: Suffering and Spirit," in *Modern Jewish Thought*, ed. by Nahum Glatzer (New York: Schocken Books, 1977), p. 20.
11. Ibid.
12. Ibid., p. 21.
13. Ibid.
14. See Jakob J. Petuchowski, *Prayerbook Reform in Europe: The Liturgy of European Liberal and Reform Judaism* (New York: The World Union for Progressive Judaism Ltd. 1968), pp. 292–93.
15. Quoted in Michael A. Meyer, *Response to Modernity: A History of the Reform Movement in Judaism* (New York and Oxford: Oxford University Press, 1988), p. 293.
16. Quoted in *The Zionist Idea: A Historical Analysis and Reader*, ed. and with an introduction by Arthur Hertzberg (New York: Atheneum, 1982), p. 266.
17. Ibid., p. 272.
18. Ibid. p. 267.
19. Ibid., p. 275.
20. Simon Dubnow, *Nationalism and History: Essays on Old and New Judaism*, ed. with an introductory essay by Koppel S. Pinson (Philadelphia: Jewish Publication Society of America, 1958), p. 80.
21. Dubnow, pp. 83–85, emphases added.
22. Ibid., p. 85.
23. Dubnow, pp. 126–27.
24. Dubnow, p. 186.
25. Dubnow, p. 190.
26. *Jews and Diaspora Nationalism: Writings on Jewish Peoplehood in Europe and the United States*, ed. by Simon Rabinovitch (Waltham, MA: Brandeis University Press, 2012), p. 103.
27. Rabinovitch, p. 77.

## Chapter 10

1. According to one estimate, by the mid-30s, 64 percent of New York City's dentists and 55 percent of its doctors were Jewish, while 65 percent of its judges and lawyers were Jewish. See Jacob Lestschinsky, "The Economic and Social Development of the Jewish People," in *The Jewish People, Past and Present*, vol. 1 (New York: Jewish Encyclopedic Handbooks Inc., and Central Yiddish Culture Organization, 1946), p. 401. Jonathan Sarna has expressed doubts about the statistics to me in private correspondence, but even if the numbers are exaggerated, the trends they represent are true.
2. Nahum Glatzer, *Franz Rosenzweig: His Life and Thought* (New York: Schocken Books, 1961), p. 294.
3. Glatzer, pp. 294–95.
4. Ibid., p. 295.
5. Ibid., p. 293.
6. "On the Fate and Survival of the Jews," in *Modern Jewish Thought: A Source Reader*, ed. by Nahum N. Glatzer (New York: Schocken Books, 1977), p. 103.
7. Ibid. 104.
8. Ibid., p. 106.
9. Ibid., p. 102.

222 NOTES TO PAGES 167–88

10. *The Jewish Writings*, ed. by Jerome Kohn and Ron H. Feldman (New York: Schocken Books, 2007), p. 303.
11. P. 224.
12. P. 366.
13. P. 361.
14. *Midstream: A Monthly Jewish Review*, v. IX, n. 1: 6.
15. P. 28.
16. Pp. 28–29.
17. G. Cohen, *Jewish History and Jewish Destiny* (New York: JTSA Press, 2011), pp. 151–52.
18. P. 156.
19. *Emet ve-Emunah: Statement of Principles of Conservative Judaism* (New York: Jewish Theological Seminary of America, The Rabbinical Assembly, and United Synagogue of America, 1988).
20. P. 35.
21. *Emet ve-Emunah*, p. 38.
22. Pp. 39–40.
23. See "Reform Judaism and Zionism: A Centenary Platform" ("The Miami Platform"), accepted by the Central Conference of American Rabbis, June 24, 1997 (https://www.ccarnet.org/rabbinic-voice/platforms/article-reform-judaism-zionism-centenary-platform/).
24. See Brett Ashley Kaplan, *Jewish Anxiety and the Novels of Philip Roth* (New York and London: Bloomsbury, 2015) for a fine analysis of Jewish themes across Roth's oeuvre.
25. Philip Roth, *Operation Shylock* (New York: Vintage International, 1994), p. 32.
26. P. 41.
27. P. 42.
28. P. 122.
29. P. 122.
30. Alan Mintz, *Ancestral Tales* (Stanford: Stanford University Press, 2017), pp. 59–60.
31. S. Y. Agnon, *A City in Its Fullness*, ed. by Alan Mintz and Jeffrey Saks (New Milford, CT, and London: Toby Press, 2016), p. 31.
32. *A City in Its Fullness*, pp. 31–37. Agnon's story does not stand alone in representing a town in Poland as the fulfillment of a journey to the "promised land." As Haya Bar-Itzhak comments, in a various legends concerning the founding of Jewish life in Poland, "providence does not forsake the wanderers and directs them to Poland, the sanctuary where they can find repose." See her discussion in "Poland," in *Jewish Topographies: Visions of Space, Traditions of Place*, ed. by Julia Brauch, Anna Lipphardt, and Alexandra Nocke (Aldershot: Ashgate Publishing Ltd., 2008), pp. 169–72 (the present quote is on p. 169).
33. *A City in Its Fullness*, pp. 40–43.
34. P. 48.
35. P. 55.
36. P. 560.
37. Cited in Bar-Itzhak, pp. 171–72.
38. Bar-Itzhak, p. 170.
39. Hebrew original: Israel: Or Yehuda, 2013; English translation: New York, Harper, 2017.
40. See Sandee Brawarsky, "In Dreams Begin Responsibilities," Jewish Telegraphic Agency, November 15, 2017; https://www.jta.org/2017/11/15/ny/in-dreams-begin-responsibilities.
41. *The Ruined House*, p. 109.
42. Pp. 421–22.
43. P. 3.
44. P. 497.
45. According to Akao Mitsuharu ("Hasidic Pilgrimage to Uman, Past and Present: The Ambiguous Centrality of a Jewish Sacred Place in Ukraine," *Jews and Slavs* 11 (2003): 121), over 7,000 pilgrims make their way to Uman annually, the vast majority of whom are Israeli.
46. Zvi Mark, *The Revealed and Hidden Writings of Rabbi Nachman of Bratslav: His Worlds of Revelation and Rectification* (Berlin: de Gruyter, 2015), p. 329.
47. See Akao Mitsuharu (2003), "Hasidic Pilgrimage to Uman, Past and Present: The Ambiguous Centrality of a Jewish Sacred Place in Ukraine." In Wolf Moskovich, Shmuel Shvarzband, and

Anatoly Alekseev, eds., *Jews and Slavs* (Jerusalem: Hebrew University of Jerusalem, and St. Petersburg: NAUKA Publishers, 1993–), 11:138.

48. Alla Marchenko, "In the Eyes of Uman Pilgrims: A Vision of Place and Its Inhabitants," *Contemporary Jewry* 38.2 (2018): 238. DOI:10.1007/s12397-017-9247-0.

49. See Zvi Mark, "The Zaddik in the Throat of the Sitra Achra: The Holy Person and the Impure Place—Concerning Pilgrimage to the Tomb of R. Nachman of Bratzlav on Rosh Hashana" (Hebrew). *Reshit*, vol. 2, January 1, 2010, https://heb.hartman.org.il/on-the-pilgrimage-to-rabbi-nachman-of-breslov/, n.p.

50. Ibid.

51. Quoted in Haim Yacobi, "From State-Imposed Urban Planning to Israeli Diasporic Place," in *Jewish Topographies*, p. 73. See there, pp. 72–75, for the general details discussed here.

52. See Andre Levy, quoted in Yacobi, p. 75.

53. https://forward.com/culture/367139/you-really-need-to-read-this-terrific-interview-with-george-steiner/.

54. Yuri Slezkine, *The Jewish Century* (Princeton, NJ: Princeton University Press, 2004), p. 7.

55. P. 24.

56. P. 40.

57. Pp. 40–41.

58. P. 102.

59. P. 208.

60. Shimon Gershon Rosenberg (Shagar), *Faith Shattered and Restored: Judaism in the Postmodern Age*, trans. by Elie Leshem (New Milford, CT: Maggid Books, 2017), p. 181.

61. Shagar, p. 182.

62. P. 183.

63. P. 185.

64. *Parting Ways: Jewishness and the Critique of Zionism* (New York: Columbia University Press, 2012).

65. *Parting Ways*, p. 15.

66. P. 1.

67. P. 6.

68. Chaim Potok, *The Chosen* (New York: Fawcett Crest, 1967), p. 188.

69. R. Avigdor Miller, *In the Footsteps of the Flock: The Views of Gedolei HaTorah on Exile, Redemption and Eretz Yisroel, Arranged According to the Weekly Torah Readings*, ed. by Yirmiyahu Cohen (Brooklyn: Natruna, 2007), pp. 51–52.

70. Miller, p. 5.

71. Joel Teitelbaum, *Sefer Gahalei Esh*, compiled by Alter Moshe Goldberger Alter (Monroe, NY: Kiryas Yoel, 1984), p. 39.

72. Teitelbaum, p. 40.

73. P. 295.

74. P. 296.

75. P. 294.

76. P. 300.

## Chapter 11

1. Cohen, *Global Diasporas*, pp. 1–9.

2. P. 6.

3. P. 11.

4. See J. Gutmann, "Jewish Medieval Marriage Customs in Art: Creativity and Adaptation," in *The Jewish Family: Metaphor and Memory*, ed. by D. Kraemer (New York and Oxford: Oxford University Press, 1989), pp. 48–50.

5. Viviane Clement, Kanta Kumari Rigaud, Alex de Sherbinin, Bryan Jones, Susana Adamo, Jacob Schewe, Nian Sadiq, and Elham Shabahat, 2021. *Groundswell Part 2: Acting on Internal Climate Migration* (Washington, DC: World Bank, 2021). https://openknowledge.worldbank.org/handle/10986/36248. License: CC BY 3.0 IGO.

6. *Netzah Yisrael*, chapter 24; Jerusalem: *Makhon Yerushalayim*, 1997, vol. 1, p. 519.

7. (New York: Doubleday, 2022), p. 639.

# Bibliography

Abrams, Daniel. *Kabbalistic Manuscripts and Textual Theory*. Jerusalem and Los Angeles: Magnes Press and Cherub Press, 2010.

Adler, Nathan. *The Itinerary of Benjamin of Tudela*. New York: Philipp Feldheim, 1908.

Agnon, S. Y. *A City in Its Fullness*. Ed. Alan Mintz and Jeffrey Saks. New Milford, CT, and London: Toby Press, 2016.

Arendt, Hannah. *The Jewish Writings*. Ed. Jerome Kohn and Ron H. Feldman. New York: Schocken Books, 2007.

Bar-Itzhak, Haya. "Poland." In *Jewish Topographies: Visions of Space, Traditions of Place*. Edited by Julia Brauch, Anna Lipphardt, and Alexandra Nocke. Aldershot: Ashgate, 2008, pp. 161–79.

Bell, Daniel. *The End of Ideology: On the Exhaustion of Political Ideas in the Fifties*. Cambridge, MA: Harvard University Press, 2000.

Berlin, Adele. "Interpreting Torah Traditions in Psalm 105." In *Jewish Biblical Interpretation and Cultural Exchange*. Edited by Natalie B. Dohrmann and David Stern. Philadelphia: University of Pennsylvania Press, 2008, pp. 239–43.

Bickerman, Elias. *Four Strange Books of the Bible*. New York: Schocken Books, 1967.

Boyarin, Daniel. *A Traveling Homeland: The Babylonian Talmud as Diaspora*. Philadelphia: University of Pennsylvania Press, 2015.

Boyarin, Daniel. *Judaism: The Genealogy of a Modern Notion*. New Brunswick, NJ: Rutgers University Press, 2019.

Brawarsky, Sandee. "In Dreams Begin Responsibilities." Jewish Telegraphic Agency, November 15, 2017; https://www.jta.org/2017/11/15/ny/in-dreams-begin-responsibilities.

Brody, Robert. *The Geonim of Babylonia and the Shaping of Medieval Jewish Culture*. New Haven: Yale University Press, 1998.

Butler, Judith. *Parting Ways: Jewishness and the Critique of Zionism*. New York: Columbia University Press, 2012.

Calimani, Richard. *The Ghetto of Venice*. Translated by Katherine Silberblatt Wolfthal. Milan: Oscar Mondadori, 1995.

Chazen, Robert. *European Jewry and the First Crusade*. Berkeley, Los Angeles, and London: University of California Press, 1996.

Chazen, Robert. *Refugees or Migrants: Pre-Modern Jewish Population Movement*. New Haven: Yale University Press, 2018.

Clement, Viviane, Kanta Kumari Rigaud, Alex de Sherbinin, Bryan Jones, Susana Adamo, Jacob Schewe, Nian Sadiq, and Elham Shabahat. *2021. Groundswell Part 2: Acting on Internal Climate Migration*. Washington, DC: World Bank. https://openknowledge.world-bank.org/handle/10986/36248.

Cohen, Gerson D. *A Critical Edition with a Translation and Notes of the Book of Tradition (Sefer ha-Qabbalah) by Abraham Ibn Daud*. Judaica Texts and Translations 3. Philadelphia: Jewish Publication Society of America, 1967.

Cohen, Gerson D. "The Blessings of Assimilation." In *Jewish History and Jewish Destiny*. Edited by Gerson Cohen. New York: JTSA Press, 2011, pp. 145–56.

Cohen, Mark, ed. and trans. *The Autobiography of a Seventeenth-Century Venetian Rabbi*. Princeton, NJ: Princeton University Press, 1988.

226 BIBLIOGRAPHY

Cohen, Martin A., trans. *Samuel Usque's Consolation for the Tribulations of Israel.* Philadelphia: Jewish Publication Society of America, 1965.

Cohen, Robin. *Global Diasporas: An Introduction, 25th Anniversary Edition.* London and New York: Routledge, 2023.

Diner, Hasia, ed. *The Oxford Handbook of the Jewish Diaspora.* New York: Oxford University Press, 2021.

Elon, Amos. *The Pity of It All: A Portrait of the German-Jewish Epoch 1743–1933.* New York: Picador, 2002.

*Emet ve-Emunah: Statement of Principles of Conservative Judaism.* New York: Jewish Theological Seminary of America, The Rabbinical Assembly, and United Synagogue of America, 1988.

Erder, Yoram. *The Karaite Mourners of Zion and the Qumran Scrolls.* Turnhout: Brepols, 2017.

Fishbane, Eitan. *The Art of Mystical Narrative: A Poetics of the Zohar.* New York: Oxford University Press, 2018.

Friedman, Richard Elliot. *Who Wrote the Bible?* Englewood Cliffs, NJ: Prentice Hall, 1987; new edition. New York: Simon and Schuster, 2019.

Fudeman, Kirsten A. *Vernacular Voices: Language and Identity in Medieval French Jewish Communities.* Philadelphia: University of Pennsylvania Press, 2010.

Gampel, Benjamin. *Anti-Jewish Riots in the Crown of Aragon and the Royal Response, 1391–1392.* New York and Cambridge: Cambridge University Press, 2016.

Glatzer, Nahum. *Franz Rosenzweig: His Life and Thought.* New York: Schocken Books, 1961.

Glatzer, Nahum, ed. *Modern Jewish Thought: A Source Reader.* New York: Schocken Books, 1977.

Goitein, S. D. *A Mediterranean Society.* 5 vols. Berkeley: University of California Press, 1967–88.

Goshen-Gottstein, Alon. "The Land of Israel in the Thought of Rabbi Nahman of Braslav." In *The Land of Israel in Modern Jewish Thought* (Hebrew). Edited by Aviezer Ravitsky. Jerusalem: Yad Izhak Ben-Zvi, 1998, pp. 276–300.

Green, Arthur. *Tormented Master: A Life of Rabbi Nahman of Bratslav.* Tuscaloosa: University of Alabama Press, 1979.

Gringauz, Samuel. "The Meaning of Galut in America Today" (symposium), *Midstream: A Jewish Quarterly Review.* Vol. IX, n. 1 (1963): 18.

Gruen, Erich. *Diaspora: Jews amidst Greeks and Romans.* Cambridge, MA: Harvard University Press, 2002.

Gutmann, Joseph. "Jewish Medieval Marriage Customs in Art: Creativity and Adaptation." In *The Jewish Family: Metaphor and Memory.* Edited by D. Kraemer. New York and Oxford: Oxford University Press, 1989, pp. 47–62.

Hartman, Louis F. and Alexander A. Di Lella. *The Book of Daniel.* The Anchor Bible 23. Garden City, NY: Doubleday, 1977.

Hertzberg, Arthur, ed. *The Zionist Idea: A Historical Analysis and Reader.* New York: Atheneum, 1982.

Hondius, Dienke, Nancy Jouwe, Dineke Stam, and Jennifer Tosch. *The Netherlands: Slavery Heritage Guide* (Dutch and English). Volendam: LM Publishers, 2019.

Horowitz, Elliot. "Families and Their Fortunes: The Jews of Early Modern Italy." In *The Cultures of the Jews.* Edited by David Biale. New York: Schocken Books, 2002, pp. 573–636.

Idel, Moshe. "*Eretz Yisrael hu chiyyut me'ha-bore B"H: 'al meqoma shel Eretz Yisrael be'Chassidut.*" In *Eretz Yisrael be'hagut hayehudit be'et hachadasha* (*The Land of Israel in Modern Jewish Thought*). Edited by A. Ravitski. Jerusalem: Yad Izhak Ben-Zvi, 1998, pp. 256–75.

Idel, Moshe. *Kabbalah: New Perspectives.* New Haven and London: Yale University Press, 1988.

Kaplan, Mordecai. *Judaism as a Civilization.* New York and London: Thomas Yoseloff, 1934.

BIBLIOGRAPHY    227

Kaufmann, Yehezkel. "On the Fate and Survival of the Jews." In Glatzer (1977), *Modern Jewish Thought*. New York: Schocken Books, 1977, pp. 101–8.

Kaufmann, Yehezkel. *The Religion of Israel: From Its Beginnings to the Babylonian Exile*. Translated and abridged by Greenberg, Moshe. New York: Schocken Books, 1972.

Kenny, Kevin. *Diaspora: A Very Short Introduction*. New York: Oxford University Press, 2013.

Kraemer, David. *A History of the Talmud*. Cambridge and New York: Cambridge University Press, 2019.

Kraemer, David. "Rabbinic Popular Prayer: An Interpretation of the Amidah in Light of the Social-Material Realities of Late Antiquity." In *Meḥevah le-Menaḥem: Studies in Honor of Menaḥem Hayyim Schmelzer*. Edited by Shmuel Glick, Evelyn M. Cohen, and Angelo M. Piattelli. Jerusalem: Jewish Theological Seminary and the Schocken Institute, 2019, pp. 63*–79*.

Kraemer, Joel L. *Maimonides: The Life and World of One of Civilization's Greatest Minds*. New York: Doubleday, 2008.

Kulp, Joshua and Jason Rogoff. *Reconstructing the Talmud, An Introduction to the Academic Study of Rabbinic Literature*. New York: Mechon Hadar, 2014.

Lestschinsky, Jacob. "The Economic and Social Development of the Jewish People." In *The Jewish People, Past and Present*, vol. 1. New York: Jewish Encyclopedic Handbooks Inc., and Central Yiddish Culture Organization, 1946, pp. 391–406.

Levine, Amy-Jill. "Diaspora as Metaphor: Bodies and Boundaries in the Book of Tobit." In *Diaspora Jews and Judaism: Essays in Honor of, and in Dialogue with, A. Thomas Kraabel*. Edited by J. Andrew Overman and Robert S. MacLennan. Atlanta: Scholars Press, 1992, pp. 105–17.

Lewis, Bernard. *The Jews of Islam*. Princeton, NJ: Princeton University Press, 1984.

Marchenko, Alla. "In the Eyes of Uman Pilgrims: A Vision of Place and Its Inhabitants." *Contemporary Jewry* 38.2 (2018): 227–47.

Marcus, Ivan. "A Jewish-Christian Symbiosis: The Culture of Early Ashkenaz." In David Biale, ed. *Cultures of the Jews*. New York: Schocken Books, 2002, pp. 449–516.

Mark, Zvi. *Revelation and Rectification in the Revealed and Hidden Writings of R. Nahman of Breslav* (Hebrew). Jerusalem: Magnes Press, 2011.

Mark, Zvi. "The Zaddik in the Throat of the Sitra Achra: The Holy Person and the Impure Place—Concerning Pilgrimage to the Tomb of R. Nachman of Bratzlav on Rosh Hashana" (Hebrew). *Reshit* 2.1 (2010), https://heb.hartman.org.il/on-the-pilgrimage-to-rabbi-nachman-of-breslov/.

Marozzi, Justin. *Baghdad: City of Peace, City of Blood*. Philadelphia: Da Capo Press, 2014.

Mendelssohn, Moses. *Jerusalem and Other Jewish Writings*. Translated and edited by Alfred Jospe. New York: Schocken Books, 1969.

Menocal, Maria Rosa. *The Ornament of the World*. Boston: Back Bay Books, 2002.

Meyer, Michael A. *Response to Modernity: A History of the Reform Movement in Judaism*. New York: Oxford University Press, 1988.

Miller, R. Avigdor. *In the Footsteps of the Flock: The Views of Gedolei HaTorah on Exile, Redemption and Eretz Yisroel, Arranged According to the Weekly Torah Readings*. Edited by Yirmiyahu Cohen. Brooklyn: Natruna, 2007.

Mitsuharu, Akao. "Hasidic Pilgrimage to Uman, Past and Present: The Ambiguous Centrality of a Jewish Sacred Place in Ukraine." In *Jews and Slavs*, v. 11. Edited by Wolf Moskovich, Shmuel Shvarzband, and Anatoly Alekseev. Jerusalem: Hebrew University of Jerusalem, and St. Petersburg: NAUKA Publishers, 2003, pp. 121–51.

Moore, Carey. *Esther*. New York: The Anchor Bible, Doubleday, 1971.

Namdar, Ruby. *The Ruined House*. New York: Harper, 2017.

Petuchowski, Jakob J. *Prayerbook Reform in Europe: The Liturgy of European Liberal and Reform Judaism*. New York: World Union for Progressive Judaism Ltd., 1968.

Polonsky, Antony. *The Jews in Poland and Russia*, Vol. I: *1350–1881*. Oxford: Littman Library of Jewish Civilization, 2010.

## 228 BIBLIOGRAPHY

Provan, Iain, V. Philips Long, and Longman III, Tremper. *A Biblical History of Israel*. Louisville, KY: Westminster John Knox Press, 2003.

Putík, Aleksandr, and Daniel Polakovic. "Judah Loew ben Bezalel, Called Maharal—A Study on His Genealogy and Biography." In *Path of Life: Rabbi Judah Loew ben Bezalel*. Edited by Alexandr Putík. Prague: Academia and Jewish Museum in Prague, 2009, pp. 61–78.

Rabinovitch, Simon, ed. *Jews and Diaspora Nationalism: Writings on Jewish Peoplehood in Europe and the United States*. Waltham, MA: Brandeis University Press, 2012.

"Reform Judaism and Zionism: A Centenary Platform" ("The Miami Platform"). The Central Conference of American Rabbis, June 24, 1997. https://www.ccarnet.org/rabbinic-voice/platforms/article-reform-judaism-zionism-centenary-platform/.

Rosenberg, Shimon Gershon (Shagar). *Faith Shattered and Restored: Judaism in the Postmodern Age*. Translated by Elie Leshem. New Milford, CT: Maggid Books, 2017.

Rosenzweig, Franz. *Franz Rosenzweig: His Life and Thought*. Presented by Nahum Glatzer. New York: Schocken Books, 1961.

Roth, Philip. *Operation Shylock*. New York: Vintage International, 1994.

Rubinstein, Jeffrey. "Addressing the Attributes of the Land of Israel: An Analysis of Bavli Ketubot 110b–112a" (Hebrew). In *Center and Diaspora: The Land of Israel and the Diaspora in the Second Temple, Mishna, and Talmud Periods*. Edited by Isaiah M. Gafni. Jerusalem: The Zalman Shazar Center for Jewish History, 2004, pp. 159–88.

Scheindlin, Raymond. "Merchants and Intellectuals, Rabbis and Poets." In *Cultures of the Jews: A New History*. Edited by David Biale. New York: Schocken Books, 2002, pp. 317–18.

Scheindlin, Raymond. *The Song of the Distant Dove*. New York: Oxford University Press, 2008.

Scheindlin, Raymond. *Wine, Women, and Death: Medieval Hebrew Poems on the Good Life*. New York: Oxford University Press, 1986.

Scholem, Gershom. *Major Trends in Jewish Mysticism*. New York: Schocken Books, 1961.

Secunda, Shai. *The Iranian Talmud: Reading the Bavli in Its Sasanian Context*. Philadelphia: University of Pennsylvania Press, 2014.

Slezkine, Yuri. *The Jewish Century*. Princeton, NJ: Princeton University Press, 2004.

Steiner, George. "Interview with George Steiner." *The Forward*, March 27, 2017; http://forward.com/culture/367139/you-really-need-to-read-this-terrific-interview-with-george-steiner/.

Teitelbaum, Joel. *Sefer Gahalei Esh*. Compiled by Alter Moshe Goldberger. Monroe, NY: Kiryas Yoel, 1984.

Vlnas, Vit. "Castle, City, Ghetto: On Prague at the Times of Rudolph II and Maharal." In *Path of Life*. Prague: Academia and Jewish Museum in Prague, 2009, pp. 222–42.

Weinstock, Moshe. *Uman: The Israeli Journey to the Grave of Rebbe Nachman of Breslov* (Hebrew). Tel Aviv: Yedioth Ahronoth and Chemed Books, 2011.

Yacobi, Haim. "From State-Imposed Urban Planning to Israeli Diasporic Place." In *Jewish Topographies: Visions of Space, Traditions of Place*. Edited by Julia Brauch, Anna Lipphardt, and Alexandra Nocke. Hampshire: Ashgate, 2008.

Yerushalmi, Yosef Hayim. "Exile and Expulsion in Jewish History." In *Crisis and Creativity in the Sephardic World, 1391–1648*. Edited by Benjamin R. Gampel. New York: Columbia University Press, 1997, pp. 3–22.

# Index

For the benefit of digital users, indexed terms that span two pages (e.g., 52–53) may, on occasion, appear on only one of those pages.

Abarbanel, Don Isaac  117–18
Abraham and Sarah  20–1, 29, 31–4, 205
Abraham ibn Daud  93–6
Abuhatzeira, Rabbi Yisrael, *see* Baba Sali
Adam and Eve  20–1, 32, 214
Adler, Laure  191
Agnon, S.Y.  180–4
Agus, Jacob  170
Ahad Ha-Am  156–8, 163–4, 174
Alexander ("the Great")  55–6
Aliyah, traditional prohibition of  68–9
Almohads  109
Almoravids  109
America, Jews in  162–3, 169–70
Amidah (rabbinic silent prayer)  83–4
Amos  22
Amsterdam  116, 125–6
    slavery in  220n.13
Antiochus Epiphanes  53, 55–6
antisemitism  17, 47–8, 154–5, 163
appropriation, cultural  212
Aragon, anti-Jewish riots in  109
Arch of Titus  9
Arendt, Hannah  167–9
Asch, Sholem  184–5
Ashkenaz  11–13, 104–5
assimilation  166, 171, 210–11
Association for Jewish Studies  172–3
Assyrians  21
Auerbach, Berthold  150–1

Ba'al Shem Tov (Rabbi Israel)  136–7
Baba Sali  190
Baba Qamma (Talmud Bavli) 84a–b  75–7
Babylonia  8–10, 21, 26
    academies in  88–90; *see also* yeshiva
    as homeland  33, 40
    exile to  10, 21–2, 25, 31, 37–8, 40
    God in  39–40
    holiness of  69–70, 102
    Jews in  30, 37, 92
    rabbinic authority in  75–9

study halls in  72–3
    superiority in genealogical purity  69
    superiority in Torah  73–4
    synagogues in  71–3
Baghdad  10–11, 87
    Jews in  88–91
    synagogues in  90
    yeshivas in  92
Bar Kokhba  62–6, 83
Baron, Salo  16
Bava Batra (Talmudic tractate) 158b  142
Bavli, *see* Talmud, Babylonian
Bell, Daniel  3–4
Benjamin of Tudela  88–90
Berakhot (Talmudic tractate)  138–9
Berlin  14–15, 146–7
Berlin, Adele  29
Besht, *see* Ba'al Shem Tov
Bible, history of  21–2
biblical history  21
Buczacz  180–4
Butler, Judith  199–200
Byzantium  87

Cairo  103
canonical writings  4–5
Castile  115, 117
Chabad  189–90
*Chabad Journal*  145
Chazan, Robert  215n.16
Christendom
    Jews under  1–2, 105–6, 109, 219n.25
Christians, New, *see* New Christians
I Chronicles 16  84–5
climate change  212–13
Cohen, Gerson D.  171–2
Cohen, Hermann  167
Cohen, Mark  219n.7
Cohen, Robin  5–6
Conservative movement (Jewish)  173–6
*Consolation for the Tribulations of Israel*,
        *see* Usque, Samuel

## 230 INDEX

converts, *see* exile, to attract converts
Cooper, Alan 117
Cordoba 93–5
Corfu 117–18
Council of the Four/Five Lands 135–6
court-Jew 44–5, 52
covenant 101–2
  biblical 20–5, 27–8
  of law 100
Crusader Kingdom 97–8
Crusades 1, 11, 104–5
Cyrus 8–9, 27, 40, 48–9, 53–4

Daniel, book of 15, 53–7
  Greek version 57–8
  in the lion's den 54–5
Darius 53–5
David (King) 21, 24–5
Deuteronomic history 20, 24–5
Deuteronomy 22
  26 33–4
  28 24
  32 117–18
diaspora 203–6; *see also*, exile
  African 206–7
  as blessing 30, 172
  as the human condition 191–2, 213–14
  attracting Gentiles in 60
  benefits of 152, 176
  definition of 5–6
  dual orientation of 6, 85–6, 204, 210
  history of 8–9
  in Israel 189–90
  Israel in 188–9
  Israeli 196–7
  Jewish lessons for 210–13
  negation of 156–7, 166–7
  pilgrimage to 188–9
  Sephardic 116–17, 125, 207–8
  superiority of 152, 159, 202–3
  value of 208–9
diasporism 177–80, 198–9
dispersion, *see* diaspora *and* exile
divine presence, *see* Shekhinah
divorce, see *Get and* Gittin
Dreyfus, Alfred 155
dress, Jewish 13, 171–2, 207–8
Dubnow, Simon 158–60
Dunash ben Labrat 96–7

Egypt 102–4
  Israel in 33–4, 45
  Jews in 103

Elimelekh of Lizhensk 138–40
Elon, Amos 150–1
emancipation 14–15
*Emet ve-Emunah, see* Conservative
  movement
England 120–1
Enlightenment, European 146–7
Ephraim and Menashe 43
Esther, book of 1, 15, 30, 45–53, 118
  3 48
  8 51
  dating of 216n.5
Europe
  Christian 104
  as Jewish homeland 177–8
Eve, *see* Adam and Eve
Exilarch (Babylonian) 77–9; *see also* "Head of
  the Captivity"
  as king 78–9
exile 8–9, 203–4; *see also*, diaspora
  as blessing 115
  as divine mercy 81–2, 122–3
  as God's will 140, 201
  as home 38, 43
  as Israel's "natural" place 129–33, 198
  as place of suffering 24
  as punishment for sin 2–3, 7, 16–17, 20–1,
    24–7, 31, 117
  Babylonian, *see* Babylonia, exile to
  God in 33
  ingathering of 156, 198
  leaving exile in 133–4
  paradise in 97
  sacredness of Land of Israel in 139–45, 203
  Sephardic 125
  Shekhinah in, *see* Shekhinah, exiled
    with Israel
  to attract converts 82, 106–7
  to protect Jews 117–18, 122–3,
    201–2
  to spread God's word 85, 153, 166
Exodus (from Egypt) 20–1
Ezekiel 31, 38–40, 71–3
Ezra 73, 149

Ferrara 119–20
Fostat 93, 103
France 11–12, 120–1, 155
  revolution in 148–50

Galilee, imagined in Zohar 115
*galut* 7; *see also* exile
Garden of Eden 32, 205, 214

# INDEX 231

Genesis
  12  32–3, 205
  47  44
Genesis Rabbah (Midrash)11  74
Geniza, Cairo  103
Gentiles and Jews  101, 105
Germany  17
  Jews in  150–2
*Get* (bill of divorce)  79
ghettos  12–13, 156–7
  of Venice  12–13, 219n.7
Ginsberg, Asher, *see* Ahad Ha-Am
Gittin (Talmud Bavli)  79–80
*Golah ve-Nekhar* (book by Y. Kaufmann)  165–6
"golden age"  11, 13–14, 96, 109–10, 125
Golem  127
Goshen-Gottstein, Elon  144–5
Graetz, Heinrich  151–2
Great War (WWI)  160–1, 163–4, 184
Greeks  8–9
guests, humans as  191–3

Halevi, Judah, *see* Judah Halevi
Haman, *see* Esther, book of
Hannukah  186–7
Hasdai ibn Shaprut  95
Hasidic Masters  3–5
Hasidism  14
  emergence of  136–7
Hasmoneans  8–9
Havurah movement  172–3
"Head of the Captivity" (*reish galuta*)  89–90
Heidegger, Martin  191
Heine, Heinrich  150
Hellenistic kingdoms  55–6
Herzl, Theodor  155
Heschel, Abraham Joshua  135, 137
Hibbat Zion  156
Hidden Jews  119–20
Hillel  73
history, end of  55–6
Holocaust  1, 163, 166–7, 169, 177–8
Hoshea  22

Idel, Moshe  141
ideology
  definition of  3–5
Inquisition  1, 115–16, 119–20, 126
Intifada  177
Iraq  10–11; *see also* Babylonia
Isaac  29
Isaac b. Moses (Rabbi)  12
Isaiah  31

Islam
  Jews under  1–2, 87–8, 109
Islamic conquest  87
Israel, Kingdom of  21, 24–5
Israel, State of  17, 166–7, 169, 180–1, 198–9
  and diaspora  173–80
Italy  13

Jeremiah  31, 37–9, 149, 210
  29  37–8, 149
Jerusalem
  rebuilding of  60
*Jerusalem* (book by Moses Mendelssohn)  147
Jew, definition of  216n.1
*Jewish Catalog*  172–3
Jewish Theological Seminary  176–7, 185–6
Jews
  as a people of exile/diaspora  164–5, 196, 199
  as citizens of the world  170–1
  as Europeans  168
  wandering  34, 193
Josiah (King)  22
Joseph, story of  3–4, 33–4, 40–6, 54
  and his brothers  43–4
  as court-Jew  44
Judah (Kingdom)  21, 24–5
Judah (Rabbi)  68–70
Judah Halevi  11, 97–104
  longing for Zion  98, 101–2
*Judenstaat, Der*  155
Julian (emperor)  83

Kabbalah
  Spanish  110–15
  Lurianic  118–19, 167
Kaplan, Mordecai  17–18
Karaites  93
Kaufmann, Yehezkel  36–7, 165–6
Kazin, Alfred  170–1
*Kedushah* (prayer)  85
Kenny, Kevin  215n.1, 215n.11
Ketubbot (Bavli, 110b–111a)  66–8, 138
Ketubbot (Mishnah, 13:11)  65–6
Khmelnitski uprising  183–4
Kings (book of)  20–1
  II Kings  25
Kuzari  98–102

Lamentations (book of)  21–2, 25–6
languages spoken by Jews  88, 105–6, 110–11,
  116, 120, 125, 135, 147, 152–3,
  171–2, 207–8
Levine, Amy-Jill  217n.15, 217n.16

232   INDEX

Leviticus
  26  23, 28
Leviticus Rabbah (Midrash)
  23  7–8
Lithuania, Jews in  135–6
liturgy, Jewish  16–17
Loew, Judah, *see* Maharal of Prague
Luria, Isaac, *see* Kabbalah, Lurianic

Maccabees  53, 55–6; *see also* Hasmoneans
Maharal of Prague  3–4, 170–1, 184, 197–8,
      213, 215n.14
  life of  127–8
  thought of  127
Maimonides  11, 78–9, 103, 109, 147, 194
manuscripts, Hebrew  105–6, 171–2, 194
  Italian  13, 120
  Spanish  110
Marchenko, Alla  188–9
Marcus, Ivan  219n.25
Mark, Zvi  188–9
Megillah (Bavli, 29a)  70–3
Menachem Nachum of Chernobyl  138, 140–1
Mendelssohn, Moses  146–7
Messiah  150, 155–6, 167, 184, 200–1, 203
  prayer for  83
  waiting for  3, 155–6, 200, 216n.19
Midian  34
Midrash  9
*Midstream* (magazine)  170
Miller, Rabbi Avigdor  200–1
Mintz, Alan  181
Mishnah  9, 186
modernity, early  9–10
modernization of Jews  150, 162–3
Moore, Carey  48
Morocco  190
Mordechai  54; *see also* Esther, book of
  as king of Persia  51
Moses  21, 34–7, 124
Musaf prayer  27
Muslim conquest  10

Nachman of Bratzlav  138, 141–5, 148–9, 188
Nachmanides  35–6
Namdar, Ruby  185–7
Naples  120–1
Napoleon  148–50
nation-states  14–15, 17, 154, 208–9
nationalism, Jewish  154, 157–8
  diaspora  154, 158–60
Nebuchadnezzar  53–4
Nehemiah (book of)  20–1
Netivot, *see* Baba Sali

Neturei Karta  132–3
*Netzah Yisrael* (work by Maharal)  128–34
New Christians  115–16
New York  14–15, 160–2, 169, 186–7, 211
  Lubavitcher Rebbe's tomb in  189–90
*Noam Elimelekh, see* Elimelekh of Lizhansk
Nobel Prize  162–3, 193
Numbers (book of) 32  34–6

*Operation Shylock*  177–80
*Or Zaru'a* (rabbinic work)  12
Ottoman empire  116, 119–20, 123–5
Ovadiah (biblical prophet)  116–17

Palestinians  173, 176, 178–80, 199–200
Paris  107
Patriarch  9, 77–8
"people of the book"  10, 109, 211
Peretz, Y.L.  160
Persia  1, 8–9
  Jews in, *see* Esther, book of
Pesachim (Talmud Bavli)
  66a  95–6
  87b  81
Philippson, Ludwig  150
philosophy (modern)  146
pilgrimage, *see* diaspora, pilgrimage to
Pilgrimage Festivals  27, 189
Pirqoi ben Baboi  91–2
pogroms  154–5, 162
Poland  13–14, 124–5
  as Israel  184–5
  as Promised Land  222n.32
  Jews in  14, 135–7, 184–5, 211
*Portnoy's Complaint*  176–7
Portugal  116–17
Potok, Chaim  200
Prague
  history of  127–8
  Jews in  127–8
prayer books, Reform  152–3
prayers
  as popular rabbinic communication  82–3
  for redemption  3, 83
printing press  136
Psalm 105  28–30, 84–5
Purim  45–6

Qairwan  93

Rabbenu Tam  12
Rabbis  9–11, 14
  emergence of  63
  settling in Babylonia  64

INDEX 233

Rashi 11, 34, 72, 104–5
redemption 7–8, 18; *see also* Zion, return to
  by merit of Babylonian academies 91
  in exile, *see* exile, leaving exile in
  in the future 134
  miraculous 84
Reform 150, 152–4
  opposition to Zionism 153–4
refugees 18–19
  Jews as 18–19
Renaissance 9–10
repentance 26–7
Rhineland 11, 104–5
Romans 1, 8–9, 26, 62, 65–6
  wars with 2, 9–10, 62–3, 135, 215n.16
Rosh Hashana 186–9
Rosen, Rabbi Joseph (the "Rogatchover
    Gaon") 200
Rosenberg, Rabbi Shimon Gershon,
    *see* Shagar
Rosenzweig, Franz 163–5
  opposition to Zionism 163–4
Roth, Philip 176–81, 185–6
Russia 14–15, 17, 162

Safed 118–19
Salonika 116, 121–2, 124–5
Sanhedrin (Talmud Bavli) 77–8
Sanhedrin, French 148–9
Sapir Prize 185–6
Sarah, *see* Abraham and Sarah
Satmar Rebbe, *see* Teitelbaum, Rabbi Joel
Saul (King) 21, 24–5
Scheindlin, Raymond 97, 103–4
Scholem, Gershom 167
*Sefer Hakabbalah* 93
*sefirot* (divine emanations) 111, 114
September 11, 2001 186–7
Shabbetai Tzvi 167
Shagar (Rabbi) 130, 197–9
Shekhinah 70
  exiled with Israel 71–3, 111–14, 140,
    142–3
Sifri (Midrash)
  80 63–4
Sinai 34, 37
Six-Day War 172–3
Slavery in America 206–7
Slezkine, Yuri 195–7
Solomon (King) 21, 24–5
Song of Songs (biblical book)
  2:2 7
Spain 11
  Christian re-conquest of 109

expulsion from 116–17, 123–4
  Jews in 115
Spinoza 116, 125–6
*Star of Redemption* 163–5
state, Jewish 166–7
Steiner, George 190–5, 204
Sternhartz, R. Abraham 188–9
"Story of the Four Captives" 93–5
strangers, impurity of 206–7
study-hall, *see* Yeshiva
synagogues 91–2
suffering 16–18, 120–2
  as punishment for sin 121–2
  cleansing quality of 27–8
Susannah (apocryphal book), *see* Daniel, book
  of, Greek version

Tabernacle 113
Talmud 3–4, 136, 186; for individual tractates,
    *see under* tractate name
  Babylonian 10, 14, 64–5, 80, 90–2
    Persian influence in 64–5
  Yerushalmi 9, 80
Talmudic convention (Kallah) 93
Tanakh, *see* Bible
Teitelbaum, Rabbi Joel (the Satmar Rebbe)
    201–3
Tel Aviv 39
Temple, destruction of 1, 24, 26–8, 37–8, 62–3,
    83, 186–7
"Ten Lost Tribes" 21–2
*The Chosen*, *see* Potok, Chaim
*The Jewish Century*, *see* Slezkine, Yuri
*The Ruined House*, *see* Namdar, Ruby
*tikkun* 112, 119
*Tisha be'Av* (ninth of Av) 26, 153, 187
Tobit (apocryphal book) 58–61
  dating of 217n.14
  endogamy in 217n.16
Toledo 117
Torah 21–2
  canonization in Babylon 36–7
  in Rabbinic Judaism 73–4
Tosafot 11–12, 104–7

Uman (Ukraine) 141
  pilgrimage to 145, 188–9
Union of American Hebrew Congregations
    (UAHC) 153–4
Upper West Side (Manhattan) 179, 185–6
Usque, Samuel 119–25

Venice 116–17, 120; *see also* ghettos, of
    Venice

## 234 INDEX

Wagner, Richard 150–1
Warsaw 14–15, 162

Yanagihara, Hana 213
Yerushalmi, Yosef Hayim 210
Yeshiva 91–2
  Babylonian 88
  heads of 88
  in Eastern Europe 136
Yiddish 135, 160, 162–3
Yom Kippur 186
Yoma (Talmud Bavli) 71b 95–6

Zaddik, burial place of 188–9
Zeira (Rabbi) 68–9
Zhitlowsky, Chaim 160

Zion
  in exile 138–40, 142–5
  in Jewish liturgy 153
  return to 3–4, 6, 152–3
Zionism 7, 14–15, 17, 155, 163, 166–7
  as ideology 3, 17
  cultural 156
  definition of 216n.19
  diaspora 181
  on diaspora 154–6, 168–9, 181
  opposition to 153–4, 163–4, 167, 191,
     195–6, 199–203
  religious 197
  view of history 17–18
Zohar 4–5, 110–15
  development of 110